PROXIMITY POLITICS

JERONIMO CORTINA

PROXIMITY POLITICS

How Distance Shapes Public Opinion
and Political Behaviors

Columbia University Press / *New York*

Columbia University Press
Publishers Since 1893
New York   Chichester, West Sussex
cup.columbia.edu

Copyright © 2024 Columbia University Press
All rights reserved

Library of Congress Cataloging-in-Publication Data
Names: Cortina, Jeronimo, author.
Title: Proximity politics : how distance shapes public opinion and political behaviors / Jeronimo Cortina.
Description: New York : Columbia University Press, 2024. | Includes bibliographical references and index.
Identifiers: LCCN 2024008934 | ISBN 9780231205320 (hardback) | ISBN 9780231205337 (trade paperback) | ISBN 9780231555951 (ebook)
Subjects: LCSH: Public opinion—United States. | Public opinion—Political aspects—United States. | Political culture—United States. | Geographical perception—Political aspects—United States.
Classification: LCC HN90.P8 C687 2024 | DDC 303.3/80973—dc23/eng/20240524

Cover design: Noah Arlow
Cover image: Shutterstock

To Paola, Jacinto, Camilo, Maximiliano, Daniela, Katia, and Anna

CONTENTS

Acknowledgments ix

1 The Forest and the Trees 1

2 Outbreaks, Epidemics, and Pandemics: Zika, Ebola, and COVID-19 25

3 Bombs and Guns: Boston, Paris, and El Paso 55

4 Protests: #BlackLivesMatter 77

5 One Size Does Not Fit All: Attitudes Toward Immigration 93

6 From a Distance: Partisanship, Public Attitudes, and Geographic Proximity Toward the U.S.-Mexico Border Wall 114

7 The Perfect Storm 134

8 The Great Drought 150
With Markie McBrayer

9 So What? 163

Appendix 169

Notes 201

Index 235

ACKNOWLEDGMENTS

Writing a book is a solo endeavor, but it is not a lonely journey. This book would not have been possible without the support and contributions of many individuals and institutions. I am immensely grateful to my colleagues at the University of Houston for their friendship, invaluable guidance, patience, time, and encouragement in this captivating research project: Bettina Beech, Francisco Cantu, Jason Casellas, Samantha Chapa, Jeffrey Church, Shana Hardin, Dan O'Connor, Brandon Rottinghaus, and Tommie Trevino, I am indebted to you.

My appreciation extends to Markie McBrayer for allowing me to use a previous draft of our work, to the Inter-University Consortium for Political and Social Research, the Kaiser Family Foundation, the Kinder Institute for Urban Research, and the Pew Research Center for generously sharing their data. Special thanks to Mollyan Brodie from the Kaiser Family Foundation, Stephen L. Klineberg from the Kinder Institute, and Arun Mathur from the Inter-University Consortium for Political and Social Research.

Finally, I wish to express my gratitude to Stephen Wesley, my editor at Columbia University Press, for his professionalism and for making

ACKNOWLEDGMENTS

this process a very enjoyable experience. To the Editorial Board, thank you for your trust. To the three anonymous reviewers, I am thankful for all your insightful comments and suggestions, the manuscript is better because of you. I would be remiss not to thank all the production team at Columbia University Press: the editing, typesetting, graphic design, and marketing teams.

PROXIMITY POLITICS

1

THE FOREST AND THE TREES

We frequently fail to fully grasp the impact distance has on shaping our thoughts and behaviors. Seldom do we contemplate the space that separates us from two locations, from an event, or even from other people. Distance, however, holds remarkable sway over how we think and understand the world, and it molds our attitudes and actions. Even in today's constant news world and persistent social media, distance continues to be a formidable force.[1]

Imagine this: how would your views on crime change if your neighbor's house, right next door, was burglarized compared to a house located twenty miles away? Take a moment to think about it. In the first scenario, you would likely feel very anxious, with crime taking on a sense of immediate urgency. In the second scenario, you may acknowledge the presence of crime in your city, but your personal anxiety would likely be considerably lower. This example vividly illustrates how geographic distance shapes our emotional and cognitive responses, which in turn shapes our attitudes and our behaviors. The proximity of an event, situation, or group of people often magnifies our emotional reactions and heightens our perception of its significance. It highlights the crucial role distance plays as a filter, which influences how we feel and understand a place, an issue, or a group of people.

In this book, I explore the undeniable impact of distance on the formation of public opinion. I look at its intricate relationship with our geographic location and other influential factors, such as party affiliation, race and ethnicity, immigration status, and the flow of information. The central argument I present is that distance carries two primary effects: it acts as a catalyst for direct contact while simultaneously functioning as a filter that shapes our information processing of events, objects, social groups, and policies. Distance shapes our perceptions by altering our framing of these events and by altering our emotions. Culture, of course, also moderates the relationship between distance and information processing.

The distance between ourselves and an event, an object, a group of people, or a situation may or may not significantly influence our understanding, experiences, reactions, and thoughts about them. But the degree of proximity or separation from these elements determines the lens through which we perceive them. Our attitudes, fears, and behaviors are conditioned by the concept of distance, so we view near events differently from far ones.

When we find ourselves distanced or lacking direct contact with something or someone, our immediate reality fails to provide us with a "here and now" perspective. Therefore, our behaviors and attitudes become molded by decontextualized information—that is, information that is not significantly tied to the here and now and where substantial evidence might be replaced by deep-rooted beliefs or instinctive responses—which may lead us off track from a balanced or more "real" understanding of a place, a group of people, or a political event.

As the following chapters show, the impact of distance on our behaviors and on our understanding of specific situations or people is quite important. Surprisingly, however, there is a significant research gap in this field. A few studies have contributed valuable theoretical and empirical insights to the literature,[2] and my intention is to build on these contributions and attempt to go beyond them to break down a series of intricate mechanisms—such as framing, emotion, and culture—through which distance shapes our attitudes and behaviors.

In this interdisciplinary work, I undertake a systematic exploration of the breadth and influence of distance on individuals' attitudes and behaviors. I dive deep into the interplay between distance and other sociopolitical factors. By doing so, I seek to uncover how individuals respond to comparable events, locations, or groups of people based on their proximity to themselves.

Human behavior is messy, unpredictable, and fascinating. In this book, I touch on a rich set of human experiences, examining how individuals perceive the present reality and context, that is, the here and now of a place in which a particular phenomenon happens. To do this, I explore the cognitive divide that exists between individuals and close and distant locations. I offer a nuanced perspective on how our attitudes and behaviors are shaped when confronted with events, places, objects, or social groups that are in proximity or that are far away.

Although the prevalence of the internet in contemporary society may lead some to assume that geographic proximity no longer shapes public attitudes and behaviors significantly, my research challenges this notion. The influence of distance remains a powerful factor. Through the mechanisms I explore in this book, I aim to shed light on how individuals modify their behaviors and how public opinion fluctuates in response to the same event, depending on its proximity.

Given the complexity of our attitudes and behaviors, I orbit across and between a number of scholarly disciplines, weaving together insights from political science, psychology, sociology, geography, and the study of public opinion. My intention is not to provide a comprehensive review of all that has been written but rather to propel the study of public opinion and behavior by integrating diverse theoretical and empirical approaches that probe the profound influence of distance on these phenomena. In doing so, I aim to contribute to the ongoing revival of research in this captivating field.[3]

I offer a fresh perspective that adds a layer of complexity to the existing literature on public opinion. I present a rich landscape in which attitudes are formed through a diverse array of processes when people immersed in the here and now possess what can be considered "true" attitudes or, at the very least, possess sufficient contextual information to make well-informed judgments about a place, object, or group of people and its localized impacts. In contrast, the distant public paints a different picture, and their attitudes are often characterized by a mixture of "nonattitudes" or "manipulated opinions" at best. The implications of this stark contrast between proximate and distant attitudes extend far beyond mere opinion formation. It directly influences the connection between public opinion and policy outcomes.[4]

In the next sections of this chapter, I provide a working definition of place and distance. I then elaborate on how distance affects public opinion through framing, emotions, and culture. Frameworks help us make sense of the world as we interpret the significance of events, social groups, or objects. We tend to think more about events or objects closer to us, which in turn magnifies commonalities we may share, altering our beliefs, attitudes, and behaviors.

Physical closeness amplifies our emotional connection to objects, events, or social groups and thereby intensifies our reactions, similarly altering our behavior.

Culture acts as a moderating force between distance, framing, and emotions. Culture also helps us geographically demarcate space and dictate in-groups and out-groups, altering our frames and emotions. As I demonstrate, these mechanisms often, although not always, occur in tandem and affect public opinion.

DEFINITIONS

THE ALMOST "KITCHEN SINK" DEFINITION OF PLACE

To answer why geographic distance is important for the formation of public attitudes and behaviors we need to establish a working definition of "place." When I refer to place, I'm alluding to specific locations with unique and shared characteristics.[5] These characteristics can be manifested

in physical aspects such as the terrain, climate, or vegetation; or they can be cultural, such as the history, language, or customs of the individuals who reside there. In addition, places can be defined through their real or imagined connections with other locations. For example, two hypothetical bustling cities hundreds of miles away from each other can both be seen as hubs for trade, art, and politics. Despite existing at two different geographic locations, possessing distinct sizes and shapes, and having unique cultural and historical backgrounds, these two cities share defining features as hubs for trade, art, and politics.

With this last example I want to illustrate that my conceptualization of place attempts to be exclusive enough to accommodate the multifaceted individualistic aspects it holds, but it remains inclusive enough to accommodate the common viewpoints and definitions individuals may hold regarding a particular place (i.e., considered as hubs for trade, art, and politics). Allow me to further illustrate this point with a concrete example of two contrasting cities: Houston and Chicago. They share certain similarities: both have large urban centers, similar population sizes, and diverse populations representing various racial and ethnic backgrounds. However, Houston is in Texas and Chicago is in Illinois, and they diverge in critical indicators that undeniably influence our actions. Chicago's extensive public transportation network allows for seamless travel from point A to any other location within the city, whereas public transportation is severely limited in Houston. Houston and Chicago both carry socially constructed nicknames that shape our understanding of these cities. Houston is renowned as the Space City, owing to NASA's Space Center, and it also holds the nickname of the energy capital of the world because major oil and gas corporations maintain offices within its limits. Chicago is affectionately known as the Windy City because it is on the shores of Lake Michigan.

Within my definition of place, which refers to locations with dissimilar characteristics, it is possible to focus on understanding the factors that make Houston and Chicago unique and common at the same time. For example, in Chicago public transportation may foster encounters and potential engagement with individuals from diverse communities, varying socioeconomic backgrounds, distinct cultural heritages, diverse political beliefs, assorted religious affiliations, and a wide array of sexual orientations. In contrast, options for public transportation are severely restricted in Houston when navigating the expansive 599 square miles of the city. The exposure in Chicago to different people may have the potential to broaden our perspectives on diversity or reinforce our existing beliefs, shaping our behaviors.[6]

My unsophisticated and possibly biased juxtaposition of Houston and Chicago brings attention to the three essential characteristics of a location, as defined by Thomas Gieryn.[7]

1. "A place is a unique spot in the universe."[8] This notion of uniqueness speaks to the specific geographic location of a place, enabling us to distinguish between nearby and distant locales. It draws a stark contrast between the *here and now* and the *there and later*, emphasizing the significance of proximity and immediacy in shaping our experiences and perceptions.
2. "Place has physicality . . . place is stuff."[9] Within the immense cosmos, a place emerges as a convergence of various objects and elements intricately woven together. It is the melding of these components that gives birth to a singular point in space, an extraordinary composition that stands apart from all others. This physical presence serves as the foundation upon which the essence of a place is built.
3. A place transcends mere physicality. It is not confined to its material existence; rather, it possesses a profound historical and social construction. A place is not only a tangible entity but also an intangible realm that exists within our collective imagination, emotions, and comprehension. Its meanings are carefully crafted and passed down through generations, ensuring that its significance endures over time. This interplay between the physical and the intangible adds depth and richness to our understanding and connection with a place.[10]

Places are multidimensional entities. They are intricate tapestries of unique and common physical and historical-social constructions. Places also transcend the boundaries of physical locations and social constructions. Places shape our perceptions, experiences, and sense of belonging. Places are also dynamic and multifaceted systems that play a vital role in how individuals assimilate and analyze information. Places revolve around the arrangement of individuals who occupy diverse positions that create more or less conducive conditions for a set of interactions to unfold (i.e., public transportation differences between Houston and Chicago).[11] Places are containers that encapsulate a number of social, political, and economic processes interconnected and influenced by their geographic surroundings and by our attitudes and behaviors. This complex arrangement generates a distinct area, a "space filled up by people, practices, objects, and representations" that creates the social-geographic space that shapes our social cognition and mediates our interactions at both the individual and institutional level.[12]

Every facet of our lives unfolds within the context of a place. Our jobs are situated in particular physical locations, whether it be in our home or in an office building. Our grocery shopping is confined to specific supermarkets, chosen either out of preference or convenience in proximity to where we live. Our social, economic, and political lives are undeniably tangled with a specific place. We cast our votes within geographically defined electoral districts, and our choices for representation are determined by our residential address. How we vote, where we shop, and how we create and re-create our attitudes and perspectives toward social and political phenomena are thus deeply influenced by the physical, intangible cultural norms, identities, and values that define the place we call home.[13] Understanding political, social, and economic behaviors—and, indeed, human behavior as a whole—is a nearly impossible feat "without understanding the arrangements of specific social actors in unique social times and places" despite the ubiquity of social media.[14] The power of place as a hybrid agent becomes clear: it serves as a conduit for individuals to absorb and dissect information that shapes their social behaviors and attitudes.[15]

In this complex dance between individuals and their surroundings, place emerges as a vibrant force that shapes our perceptions, interactions, and societal dynamics. It is through a deep understanding of the complexities of places as entities that share unique physical and sociohistorical characteristics that we can gain insight into the complexities of human behavior and the mosaic of social connections that make up our world.

Now that I have provided a working definition of place, the logical question that follows is "What is the role of distance in shaping our attitudes and behaviors?"

PUTTING DISTANCE IN ITS PLACE

The *Cambridge Dictionary* offers a concise definition of distance: "the amount of space between two places."[16] In the context of this book, distance refers to the amount of space between two multidimensional entities. In other words, the amount of physical and social difference that two places share, which will impact our perception and understanding of the world, consequently influencing both our direct experiences and our abstract interpretations of distant phenomena.

In the domain of social phenomena, distance creates a psychological divide between oneself and distant locations.[17] This perceptual divide takes multiple forms: physical, temporal, and social. It operates through two primary mechanisms. First, proximity or distance enables personal, direct contact that can reduce prejudice through familiarity, likability, and trust under certain circumstances. Second, distance influences how we process information and comprehend the significance of a particular place, object, event, or policy.[18]

Geographic distance molds how we perceive the contrast between the "here" and the imagined "there." It delineates the boundaries of our immediate reality versus our imaginings of far-off social and political phenomena.[19] Distance determines our exposure and access to people, places, and events, which in turn affects our emotional and cognitive responses.[20] Proximity creates a sense of intimacy and empathy, whereas distance can foster detachment and indifference. If you lived in Houston and had never visited Chicago, you could not have experienced Chicago, been exposed to Chicagoans and their daily lives, or experienced the Cloud Gate by Anish Kapoor in Millennium Park. Simply put, you cannot experience the "here."

Distance also plays a crucial role in shaping our cultural and societal norms. Different regions and communities may have varying distances between them, leading to differences or perhaps similarities in beliefs, values, and behaviors. For example, a person from a rural area may hold a different perspective on environmental issues than someone from an urban setting due to the differing distances they experience in relation to their respective environments. Moreover, distance also plays a significant role in shaping our cultural and societal norms. Different regions and communities have varying distances between them, which can lead to differences in beliefs, values, and behaviors. Deep-dish pizza in Houston is not religion in the same way that barbecue is not religion in Chicago. Distance goes beyond miles or kilometers; it is a complex concept that influences our attitudes and behaviors by shaping our perceptions and behaviors from an emotional perspective.

When we are near a specific location, we can fully immerse ourselves in its reality and context. We experience it firsthand, without perceived barriers between ourselves and the surroundings.[21] Conversely, when we are distanced from a place, there is no direct contact,[22] and we rely on abstract and decontextualized details to form our understanding, often leading to the emergence of new, sometimes inaccurate, associations and meanings.[23] These associations and meanings are often influenced by preexisting beliefs, attitudes, and fears, including our political affiliations, which can significantly impact our individual attitudes.[24]

When it comes to forming judgments about policies or political controversies, or even understanding our immediate world in a manner consistent with our preexisting beliefs, we tend to rely on information that aligns with our own biases, including the positions held by our political parties.[25] This phenomenon, known as self-verification, drives us to seek cues from external sources, such as other people, media outlets, or interpretations, that confirm our preconceived notions about ourselves and the world around us.[26]

The perceptual screen created by self-verification is influenced by the distance between us and a place, group of people, policy, or social phenomena.[27] This distance amplifies or diminishes our selectivity in interpreting and perceiving something or someone, all in an effort to maintain consistency in our perceptions.[28] Our exposure to news, political affiliations, and other influential factors interacts with the distance that separates us from an event, place, object, or person, mediating crucial information that enables individuals to align their beliefs and values with their personal beliefs.[29]

In essence, our distance from something or someone becomes a filter through which we process information and selectively attend to cues that reinforce our existing beliefs and values. This dynamic interplay between distance, preconceptions, and external influences shapes our perceptions, informs our attitudes, and molds our behaviors.

Through this filter and dynamic interplay, distance exerts a profound influence on how we perceive and contemplate events, places, objects, and people. Greater distances stimulate abstract thinking, giving rise to high-level constructs, whereas shorter distances foster an acute focus on specific details, resulting in lower-level constructs that are intricate, unstructured, and contingent upon context—attributes made possible only through proximity, whether temporal, spatial, or social.[30] All this means that when confronted with information about distant events, things, or groups of people our tendency is to describe them in abstract terms, which can introduce errors in judgment when we draw inferences based on this limited understanding.[31] This abstract thinking, although useful in some contexts, can lead to oversimplifications and overlook the intricacies that lie within. However, when we encounter situations in close proximity, our attention sharpens, zooming in on intricate details that comprise the whole. This microlevel focus allows for a deeper understanding of context, capturing the nuances and complexities that might elude us from a distance. By immersing ourselves in the immediacy of the here and now, we gain access to a wealth of information that enriches our comprehension.

The mechanisms by which temporal, spatial, and social distances operate and shape our cognitive processes are obvious. The passage of time can foster a sense of detachment, obscuring the intensity of the past and reducing events to abstract notions. Spatial distance between ourselves and places or objects leads to a similar outcome because we rely on fragmented

and decontextualized information to form impressions. In social interactions, the level of proximity influences our understanding of individuals and groups, shaping our perceptions based on limited exposure or abstract categorizations.

Scholars have invested considerable time and resources in unraveling some of these mechanisms following two distinct paths, shedding light on the diverse ways in which distance influences our attitudes and actions. The first path of inquiry focuses on the effects of hazardous facilities and infrastructure projects on public attitudes. From nuclear plants and wind turbines to hospitals and freeways, scholars explore how the proximity of these installations shapes our perceptions and responses.[32] This line of study often employs the widely popularized Not In My Backyard (NIMBY) framework,[33] which predicts that the closer individuals are to a potentially harmful facility the more likely they are to oppose its presence in their community.[34]

The second path focuses on how geographic distance impacts our attitudes and behaviors through networks or ideology.[35] Proximity to an object, threat, political event, or group of people exerts a significant influence on our perspective and actions compared to those who are more distanced. By exploring the multifaceted web of connections formed by geographic proximity, we can learn how our immediate surroundings shape our beliefs, values, and behaviors.

Through these two avenues of research, scholars have uncovered insights into the ways in which distance operates as a catalyst for attitudinal and behavioral shifts, and they offer valuable perspectives on the relationship between distance, attitudes, and behaviors. More important, previous work invites us to plunge into new questions regarding the influence of proximity and its interaction with different human phenomena, offering insights into the mechanisms that mold public attitudes and human behaviors and paving the way for what I hope is a more comprehensive understanding of our responses to the world around us.

Before presenting a roadmap for the book, allow me to offer some of the mechanisms by which place and distance operate.

THE FOREST AND THE TREES

MECHANISMS

DISTANCE AND FRAMES

Over fifty years ago, Waldo R. Tobler revolutionized geography with a profound insight known as Tobler's First Law: "Everything is related to everything else, but near things are more related than distant things."[36] This pivotal principle casts light on the interconnectedness of the world around us and forms the bedrock of the mechanisms in this book. When we say that two things are related, we acknowledge the existence of a connection, a bond that ties them together in some way. It implies a shared thread, a commonality that connects their fates. This connection can take many forms—spatial, conceptual, or even emotional—and recognizing that the material and socially constructed forms of these entities are related is important. Distance plays a crucial role in shaping the nature of this connection. When objects, policies, places, or a group of people are in close proximity, their interactions are intensified and their shared characteristics are magnified. Closeness nurtures a fertile ground for similarities to emerge and flourish. Whether it be through shared experiences, shared resources, or shared cultural influences, the interlinking of near things fosters a deepening of their connection. In contrast, as the distance between places, events, or people grows, the strength of their connection weakens. The ties that bind them become diluted, and their shared traits fade into the background. Distant things may still bear some degree of relation, but they occupy separate realms and traverse distinct paths.

The significance of Tobler's First Law lies in its recognition of this asymmetric connection. Although everything in the world is interconnected, it acknowledges that the degree of connection is not uniform. Nearness fills objects with a heightened degree of connection, exposing the details of their interdependence.

The proximity of our interactions has a profound impact on our understanding, familiarity, and even our capacity for empathy toward objects or individuals. In sociology, this phenomenon is captured by the concept of homophily, which illuminates our tendency to associate and form connections with those who share similar characteristics or traits. It echoes the age-old adage that "birds of a feather flock together." According to the research of Miller McPherson and colleagues, proximity emerges as the primary catalyst for homophily, as individuals are naturally inclined to have more contact with those who are geographically closer rather than those who are distant.[37] When we engage with others in close proximity, whether temporal, spatial, or emotional, a sense of connection and shared experiences often emerges. Closeness nurtures opportunities for interactions, facilitating the exchange of ideas, perspectives, and commonalities. In these encounters, we find comfort and familiarity, which reinforces our tendency to associate with individuals who mirror our own traits and values. The influence of proximity on homophily becomes particularly pronounced when individuals perceive their community as small. In these circumstances, the perceived closeness among community members fosters a sense of shared identity and common ground. This perceived homogeneity contributes to the reinforcement of existing beliefs, values, and norms, which leads to a collective accord.[38]

As we move further away from the familiar, be it an object, a potential threat, a political event, or a particular group of people, our sense of similarity gradually diminishes. The distance that separates us prompts a departure from our self-contained communities, challenging our perceptions and exposing us to new perspectives.[39] The shift from close to distant comes at a cost. The allocation of resources to gather the necessary information often fails and succumbs to the influence of our preexisting beliefs. In our fast-paced lives, time and motivation become precious commodities. We find ourselves lacking the capacity to dive deep into the details of every issue and truly comprehend the world beyond our immediate surroundings.[40] Instead, we navigate through the "swarming confusion of problems" by employing mental constructs or frames, which serve as interpretative lenses that shape our understanding of the world, endorsing specific viewpoints and making the unfamiliar appear more familiar.[41] Frames are indispensable tools that enable us to structure and make meaning of the information we possess. They provide a coherent narrative, provide order within the chaos, and enable us to grasp complex social and political phenomena and infuse them with a sense of understanding. Like a guiding light, frames illuminate our path, guiding us toward a more nuanced and sophisticated comprehension of the world.[42]

Just as a recipe guides us in the kitchen, frames offer us a set of instructions for crafting our views. They provide us with a framework that allows us to navigate the complexities of the issues at hand. By embracing these cognitive frameworks, we gain the ability to deconstruct a reality far away from us and construct a more informed perspective. But it is crucial to recognize the limitations that frames impose. They offer structure and clarity, but they also have the potential to restrict our understanding, leading us to overlook alternative viewpoints and reinforcing our preexisting beliefs. It is through this lens of perception that we construct our interpretations of a given place, event, or circumstance, channeling our attitudes and behaviors in powerful ways.

These perceptions of distance are not solely a result of objective measurement; they are profoundly shaped by the frameworks we employ. The mental constructs we use to make sense of the world—such as cultural, social, or psychological frameworks—inform our interpretations and determine the emotional weight we assign to different places, events, and circumstances. These frameworks act as filters through which we process information, influencing the lenses through which we view the world.

Through these perceptual frameworks we construct narratives that give meaning to our experiences, helping us make sense of the world by providing a structure, a context, and a reference point for our attitudes. They shape our interpretation of the significance of a place, the impact or gravity of an event, or whether we feel close or far away from a group of people. In essence, these frameworks become channels for the expression and manifestation of our beliefs and thus of our attitudes and behaviors.

PLACE, DISTANCE, AND EMOTIONS

Emotions, far beyond simple categorizations of good or bad feelings, encompass a rich concoction of affects that permeate our interactions with people and the world around us.[43] They are not random; instead, emotions emerge as a well-organized series of reactions that are intricately intertwined.[44] As individuals, we play an active role in generating our emotions, combining various elements of our conscious awareness. Our emotions are tied to an object, policy, event, or group of people that produces a set of sensations, which in turn are influenced and moderated by distance.[45] The interplay between distance and emotions shapes our responses, molding our behaviors and attitudes. Consider the example of encountering a lion. Our proximity to the king of the jungle profoundly affects our emotional state and subsequent reactions. If the lion were a mere meter away, fear would grip us, triggering an immediate fight-or-flight response. However, if the same lion were five hundred meters away, our emotional response might differ significantly because distance acts as a moderating force on our emotions and behaviors.

This interaction between distance and emotions extends to our everyday lives as well, influencing how we perceive and respond to events, places, and even people. The closer we are to a situation, the more intense our emotional engagement tends to be. Conversely, as distance increases, our emotional connection often weakens, potentially leading to detachment or indifference. This emotional modulation through distance not only affects our behaviors but also our judgments and decision-making processes. Recognizing the interdependence of distance and emotions sheds light on the complex ways in which we navigate our world. It unveils the role of our emotions as guides, providing valuable cues that shape our attitudes and behaviors.

Throughout history scholars have grappled with the intricate nature of emotions and the profound effect they have on our thoughts, behaviors, and perception of reality. In the Allegory of the Cave, Plato presents a vivid metaphor in which emotions are symbolized as elusive shadows. According to Plato, these shadows are the very reason prisoners, who are confined and shackled within the cave, only perceive a distorted glimpse of reality and are unable to grasp the true essence of objects illuminated by the sun.[46] In Plato's view, emotions are often perceived as a formidable and enigmatic force that can hinder and obstruct our ability to think logically, impeding our capacity for precise and rational assessments.[47] This perspective suggests that only the conscious mind, with its ability for reasoned thinking, can provide a "vertical representation of the world perceived by the senses and exhibited exclusively within conscious awareness," that is, within the "here."[48]

Emotions possess an intrinsic power, however, and cannot be easily dismissed. They play an indispensable role in shaping our attitudes because they can access the sensory stream long before the brain systems responsible for generating conscious awareness can complete their intricate processes.[49] In essence, emotions serve as catalysts, triggering evaluations that then ignite cognitive and behavioral responses. They possess a certain immediacy, influencing our perceptions and guiding our actions even before we have fully engaged in conscious reasoning.[50]

Plato's allegory highlights the potential pitfalls of being driven solely by emotions, but it also recognizes the integral role emotions play in our human experience. Emotions can reveal valuable insights, signaling the significance of a situation or informing us about our personal desires and motivations: that is, emotions provide us with an intuitive, holistic understanding that complements and interacts with our conscious reasoning.[51]

Anxiety and fear, two deeply resonant emotions, hold a significant place in our exploration of human experiences. These sophisticated and nuanced emotions transcend mere descriptions; they possess the remarkable ability not only to articulate our perceptions of the world but also to serve as powerful tools to predict and explain it.[52]

Anxiety, with its gripping sense of unease and apprehension, emerges when we encounter uncertain situations or anticipate potential threats.[53] It casts a shadow over our thoughts and actions, highlighting the vulnerabilities and uncertainties that permeate our lives. In addition, in the face of imminent danger or perceived harm, fear surges within us. It awakens our primal instincts, triggering a fight-or-flight response as we seek to protect ourselves from harm's reach.[54]

Anxiety and fear, deeply rooted in our cognitive evaluations, emerge as emotional responses fueled by the anticipation of negative outcomes or potential threats.[55] These distinct emotions bear unique characteristics, with anxiety preceding a stimulus and fear arising in its aftermath.[56] Let's go back to the face-to-face encounter with a lion example to showcase their interplay. Again, imagine yourself on a photo safari adventure. Before even glimpsing a lion, a sense of unease and anticipation might surround you, reflecting the anxious emotion that arises when being in the wild. This anxiety stems from the cognitive evaluation of the situation, the awareness that the presence of lions is a possibility. It is an emotion that manifests prior to the actual encounter and is shaped by your thoughts and expectations of what lies ahead. Now fast forward to the moment you come face-to-face with a lion in its natural habitat. At this point, fear surges within you, sparked by the direct stimulation of the lion's presence. The experience of fear is instantaneous and intense, arising from the raw reality unfolding before your eyes. This response is triggered by the immediate sensory input of seeing the lion.

The intensity of both anxiety and fear is deeply connected with the perceived proximity of the lion. The cognitive evaluation of how close or distant the lion is influences the magnitude of these emotions. If the lion appears at a considerable distance, your anxiety may be heightened, amplifying the sense of unease as you contemplate the potential risks. Conversely, if the lion stands nearby, your fear intensifies, reflecting the immediate and palpable threat it poses.

The interaction between anxiety and fear reveals the complex nature of our emotional responses. These emotions act as guardians, signaling our vulnerabilities and guiding our instinctual reactions in the face of potential dangers. They provide us with vital information, shaping our behaviors and influencing our perceptions of risk. Our ability to gauge the proximity of a threat plays a fundamental role in determining the intensity and nature of our emotional responses.

Fear and anxiety, two potent emotions, originate from distinct types of threats. Fear is closely associated with clear and tangible dangers, whereas anxiety arises in response to uncertain and ambiguous threats.[57] Understanding the nuances of these emotions sheds light on how they affect our attitudes and behaviors.

Fear emerges when we confront an undeniable threat that we perceive as unavoidable. Robert Miner's analysis of Aristotle's *Rhetoric* captures this concept: fear cannot exist without the prospect of finding a way to evade it. If, however, there is a glimmer of hope, fear lingers because it is rooted in the belief that there might be a means of escape. In contrast, if hope evaporates and the evil becomes all-encompassing and inescapable, fear loses its menacing power.[58] Fear is a primal and innate response triggered by specific types of events that imply immediate danger.[59]

Anxiety, on the other hand, arises when we sense unforeseen harm looming on the horizon. Thomas Aquinas offers an interesting perspective on the impact of unexpected harm. The *improviso*, that is, the sudden intrusion of unforeseen harm, disrupts our composure, leaving us impatient, troubled, and susceptible to irrational thinking because the presence of evil infiltrates our imagination, influencing our established worldview and disrupting our usual patterns.[60] Consequently, we may experience heightened anxiety when a threat is perceived as distant. Aristotle similarly characterizes fear as a type of sorrow,[61] a mental anguish stemming from the anticipation of future harm, but still clinging to the hope that solutions may arise.[62] Saint Augustine observes that the root cause of fear lies in the potential loss of something or someone we cherish, whether it is acquired or hoped for.[63] This uncertain potential loss serves as a catalyst for anxiety because the unknown can be perceived as potentially dangerous, prompting individuals to seek information related to the threat and evaluate the best course of action.[64]

Our fears and anxieties can be ignited by a wide range of stimuli, both significant and superficial.[65] Exposure to media and media frames, in particular, play a pivotal role in shaping our anticipation of harm by projecting images and narratives that extend beyond our immediate experiences.[66] For instance, the use of violent imagery or jarring and dissonant music in political campaign advertisements, the portrayal of stereotypical and threatening immigrant outgroups, the coverage of deadly viral outbreaks, or the depiction of terrorist attacks can all trigger powerful emotional responses within us.[67]

Our emotions are not solely dictated by external stimuli but are also influenced by our preexisting beliefs and ideologies. Metacognitive beliefs, which encompass our awareness and understanding of our own thought processes and the strategies we employ to regulate our thinking, can mediate anxiety and fear.[68] However, the mechanisms through which these beliefs mediate our emotions are multifaceted and can involve various cognitive biases.[69]

In summary, our fears and anxieties are not solely products of external stimuli. They also reflect the interaction between our internal cognitive processes and the information we receive from the media and other sources. Our emotions are influenced by the frames through which we perceive the world, including the narratives and images presented to us. In addition, our preexisting beliefs and metacognitive awareness shape how we interpret and respond to these stimuli, which are shaped by distance.

PLACE, DISTANCE, AND CULTURE

Emotions are intricately linked with the influence of culture and distance. Culture, a dynamic and ever-evolving network, encompasses a geographically bounded space in which concepts, institutions, individuals, and myths interact creatively.[70] From this rich mix, tangible and intangible historical and social constructs emerge, shaping the very fabric of unique places and intertwining with people's cultural identity.[71] Implicit within this definition is the concept of distance, an invisible force that acts, as previously discussed, as a filter or a divider, creating boundaries that confine collections of beliefs to specific locales. It is within these spatial confines that culture, in its purest form, is created. The very nature of spatial boundaries often leads to the simplification of these beliefs, giving rise to the perception that culture is a static and unchanging entity, defined by a set of fixed ideas, institutions, myths, and intrinsic traits that distinguish group members.[72] This perception, in turn, tends to overemphasize similarities within one's own cultural group while magnifying disparities between diverse cultural groups and different places.[73]

The concept of culture embedded in distance has a long-standing history, dating back to the mid-1950s when Gordon Allport unveiled his influential work, *The Nature of Prejudice*. In this groundbreaking book, Allport plunged into the origins of antipathy and prejudice, revealing that they stem from distorted and rigid notions that give rise to negative attitudes toward specific groups. Within the sphere of classic prejudice, distance emerges as a plausible factor contributing to intergroup animosity. Let's consider the scenario of two countries. For meaningful contact to occur, individuals from one country must venture into the territory of the other, allowing for visible encounters with the out-group. Once this contact is established, Allport's four conditions for optimal intergroup interaction can be cultivated: equal group status, shared goals, cooperation, and authority confirmation.[74] It is important to note that these conditions are interconnected and reliant on one another, forming a delicate web of influences that shape our attitudes toward different groups.[75] The process involves learning about the group, adapting our behaviors, forming emotional connections, and reevaluating our own in-group identity, which will determine our attitudes toward a group.[76]

Within culture, emotions, particularly anxiety and fear, play a pivotal role in shaping our attitudes toward out-groups within the interactive four-step process described previously.[77] These attitudes can be shaped by both context and behaviors, which in turn can produce different attitudinal responses.[78] It is here, however, that the interaction between distance and culture could act as a moderating force on our emotions, influencing our attitudes and behaviors. When there is a shared culture or a sense of congruence between "them" and "us" in terms of race, ethnicity, or culture, individuals tend to be more accepting of those from other groups who are closer to us.[79] In this case, the anxiety or fear associated with the "other" and potential losses, as conceived by Saint Augustine, is absent. Fear and anxiety do not arise when there is no perceived threat, indicating a sense of congruence. On the contrary, when there is a lack of congruence between "them" and "us," having the out-group close to us can trigger prejudice and negative attitudes, especially when external shocks highlight the disparity and make the out-group more visible, as if they were at our very doorstep.[80] Anxiety and fear are influenced by the level of congruence and the visibility of the threat. When the threat is invisible, anxiety emerges, whereas when the threat is visible because it is close to us, fear takes hold, often leading to an overestimation of the magnitude of the threat.[81]

THE FOREST AND THE TREES

THE ELEVATOR PITCH

Before I dive into the structure of this book, let me take a moment to provide a concise summary of my core argument. Distance, in all its diverse forms—be it spatial, temporal, or cultural—has a powerful influence on our understanding of the world and thus on our attitudes and behaviors. It serves as both a catalyst and a filter, shaping our connection to events, objects, groups of people, and policies. The degree of proximity or separation we experience from these elements profoundly affects our perspectives, which are inevitably colored by our emotions and culture. When we lack direct contact, our immediate reality falls short of delivering the vivid and unfiltered here and now experience. Consequently, our behaviors and attitudes become molded by fragmented, decontextualized information, leading to distorted understandings that are further distorted by our personal biases. This intricate interplay between distance, framing, emotions, and culture serves as the bedrock of this book.

HOW THIS BOOK IS ORGANIZED

In the following pages, I use several case studies to illustrate how distance shapes our attitudes and behaviors, each anchored in a particular mechanism. The focus of chapter 2, "Outbreaks, Epidemics, and Pandemics: Zika, Ebola, and COVID-19," explores the relationship between outbreaks, epidemics, and pandemics and public opinion. I examine the shifts in public opinion regarding the Zika and Ebola epidemics prior to and following their arrival in the United States, focusing on the impact of temporal distance as well as the role of news media in bringing the issue close to us. Then I explore the impact of COVID-19 on patterns of mobility and explore how county-level mobility changed given the interaction between the proximity to COVID-19–related deaths and its correlation with political beliefs in the form of the 2020 U.S. presidential election results at the county level.

In chapter 3, "Bombs and Guns: Boston, Paris, and El Paso," I investigate how individuals react to terror attacks, both at home and abroad. In this chapter I uncover the profound impact of distance on people's attitudes and behaviors when faced with a threat, analyzing public opinion to both nearby and distant terrorist attacks. In the first section of this chapter, I focus on dissecting the changes in public opinion following terrorist attacks in different parts of the world. I analyze the contrast between how the public reacts to attacks near the United States and those occurring far away. I consider the role of spatial distance, cultural boundaries, and values and explore how these factors influence people's expectations and responses. In the second section, I focus on the relationship between distance and concealed handgun license applications in Texas following the disturbing El Paso mass shooting of 2019. Here I highlight how proximity to a mass shooting triggers an increase in applications for concealed handgun licenses, illustrating the impact of spatial distance on the public response and the desire for personal protection in the aftermath of a mass shooting anchored in Aristotle's and Aquina's conceptualizations of fear and anxiety.

In chapter 4, "Protests: #BlackLivesMatter," I dive into the interaction between emotions and distance to understand people's preferences when confronted with urban unrest. My objective is to examine the relationship between individuals' warm or cold sentiments toward the Black Lives Matter movement and their distance from where protests took place. I analyze people's preferences regarding how to deal with urban unrest either by focusing on tackling the root issues within policing or by advocating for the use of all necessary force.

In chapter 5, "One Size Does Not Fit All: Attitudes Toward Immigration," I explore the relationship between cultural and ethnoracial closeness and the influence of temporal distance. I examine public attitudes toward immigrants from various groups such as Europeans, Latin Americans, Asians, Africans, and Arabs, and I illustrate how distance from the American ethos affects these attitudes and how external shocks that make some of these groups more evident than others exacerbate the division between groups, leading to increasingly negative perceptions in light of the 9/11 terrorist attacks and the 2006 immigrant marches.

In chapter 6, "From a Distance: Partisanship, Public Attitudes, and Geographic Proximity Toward the U.S.-Mexico Border Wall," I explore the connection between geographic proximity, partisanship, and their interaction in shaping attitudes toward the construction of the border wall between the United States and Mexico. I also examine public opinion based on individuals' perceived distance from their place of residence to the border, considering both economic and national security threats. The overarching objective of this chapter, which is based on my previous work, is to show the substantial impact of distance, whether actual or perceived, in shaping individual attitudes as well as the type of threat and partisan inclinations as moderating factors.

In chapter 7, "The Perfect Storm," I explore whether individuals are more inclined to accept the claims of climate change after experiencing severe weather events. Drawing from three specific weather events that occurred in Houston between 2015 and 2017, I construct a model to examine the sensitivity of individuals' attitudes toward climate change based on the impact these storms had on personal and property damage. I also explore the possibility of differing responses between Republicans and Democrats, analyzing whether Republicans or self-identified Democrats are more likely to reassess their views on climate change following the experience of extreme weather events.

In chapter 8, "The Great Drought," which I coauthored with my former student Markie McBrayer, we explore the consequences of the devastating 2011 Texas drought on the subsequent 2012 congressional election, specifically in areas heavily reliant on the agricultural sector. In closely examining the influence of the drought's effects, we delve into the impact of distance and the here and now on electoral behavior. We highlight how experiencing the severe impacts of the drought shaped voting patterns and political outcomes in regions deeply connected to agriculture.

In the final chapter, "So What?," my concluding remarks emphasize the significance of distance in shaping our attitudes and behaviors. Adopting a big picture perspective, this chapter summarizes the argument I advance in this book: (1) drawing attention to the overarching theme of distance and its impact on our worldview; (2) making a case for recognizing how distance plays a pivotal role in shaping our perceptions, beliefs, and behaviors; and (3) offering insights for future research.

2

OUTBREAKS, EPIDEMICS, AND PANDEMICS

Zika, Ebola, and COVID-19

A cross the globe countless regions have witnessed the profound affects of outbreaks, epidemics, and pandemics on their daily lives. Once thriving communities have been reduced to shadows grappling with substantial losses and striving to regain their former vitality. Remarkably, even years after these catastrophic events, many countries continue to deal with their dire consequences. The ramifications are far-reaching, ranging from a decline in population growth to setbacks in development. Outbreaks, epidemics, and pandemics have the power to alter the trajectory of a nation's or a region's future as we all have experienced in recent times.

Despite remarkable advancements in modern medicine, the first two decades of the twenty-first century have been marred by a series of devastating global crises. From Ebola to COVID-19, and even the threat of Zika, these historical events have mercilessly dismantled the areas they have touched, leaving societies incapacitated and forced to confront the aftermath of their devastation.

When examining the most widespread recent pandemics, several common denominators emerge: low or nonexistent human immunity, the novelty of the disease, the degree of infectiousness and contagiousness, and perhaps most crucial, the extensive geographic dispersion of the virus—be it transregional, interregional, or global in scale.[1] The relationship between these events and distance is subtle yet complicated, as these crises traverse diverse groups and disproportionately affect populations.

As local and state governments and international organizations disseminate information and resources related to pandemics, individuals form perceptions regarding the severity of these large-scale events and contemplate their future actions. Alongside the public health directives issued by local authorities and organizations, distance plays a significant role in shaping our beliefs and behaviors in the face of a pandemic. If a pandemic unfolds on the opposite side of the world, concerns about its consequences and the surrounding uncertainty may arise.[2] However, until it reaches our own doorstep there may be little momentum to implement and follow mitigation methods, to really experience the danger a pandemic entails, or to fully grasp its implications for our daily lives.[3] In other words, the fear and anxiety of a pandemic have not yet materialized because the malady is still at a distance from us. Individuals' beliefs are influenced most by what they observe and feel in their immediate surroundings rather than by threats occurring across the globe.

The threat that an outbreak, epidemic, or pandemic has on an individual varies in severity depending on several factors: one's overall health, preexisting conditions, tolerance for uncertainty, anxiety level, and the specific spatial attributes of one's living environment. These attributes include factors such as residing in densely populated areas, proximity to geographic hot spots of the disease, and adherence to local mandates.[4] Geographic distance plays a crucial role in shaping the uncertainty surrounding these events. Given the proximity of an outbreak, epidemic, or pandemic, we may or may not contemplate problems associated with the danger of the virus, effective treatments, or the duration of the public health emergency. Our response may be different if we are less or more vulnerable to infection and depends on the location of the majority of cases.[5]

The COVID-19 pandemic enabled us to observe differences in individuals' perceptions and behaviors from places near the original outbreak to places on the opposite side of the globe. On December 31, 2019, the World

Health Organization's (WHO) country office in the People's Republic of China became aware of an outbreak of viral pneumonia in Wuhan, and by January 9, 2020, WHO confirmed that the outbreak in Wuhan province was caused by a novel coronavirus.[6] Between the waning days of December 2019 and the dawning days of 2020, the majority of people living in the United States remained blissfully unaware of the unfolding events in China and of the magnitude of the imminent viral blitz. Thanks to the concentrated outbreak of the coronavirus during that period in China, we now have an opportunity to examine whether geographic distance moderated individuals' attitudes. We can compare the attention given to the coronavirus by individuals living in the United States and by those living in China. To do so, I turn to Google Trends, which allows us to peek into the moderating effects of distance. Google Trends is a good tool for gauging the level of public interest in a particular issue. It employs a scale ranging from 0 to 100 to represent the search interest for a specific term or word within a given region and time frame. A score of 100 illustrates the peak of popularity, indicating a surge in searches for the term. A value of 50 indicates moderate popularity, with some individuals showing interest while others remain disengaged, and a score of 0 indicates insufficient data to measure the term's popularity, suggesting minimal interest in the search term.

Figure 2.1 presents a fascinating illustration of the search popularity for COVID-19 on Google in China (dotted line) and the United States (solid line). Despite the considerable distance between these areas, both trends exhibit striking similarities in their rise and fall. However, there is a notable difference in the timing of their peaks. China's search interest reached its high point on January 26, 2020, and the United States experienced its peak nearly two months later, around March 15, 2020, when the relentless grip of the coronavirus finally made its presence felt on our very doorstep.

Similar to previous pandemics such as the 1889 Russian flu, the 1918 Spanish flu, the 2002 SARS outbreak, and the 2009 swine flu, the geographic proximity of the COVID-19 pandemic has been closely linked to heightened emotional distress symptoms.[7] A telling example can be found in the early stages of the COVID-19 lockdown when a comprehensive

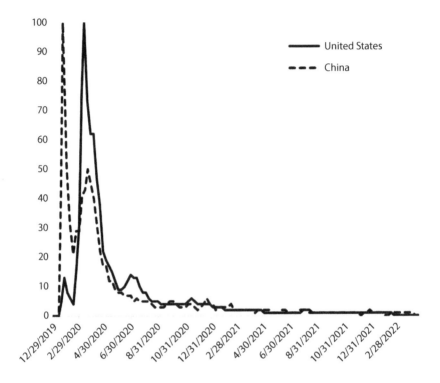

FIGURE 2.1 Coronavirus Google trends in China and the United States.

Source: Author's own date and data from Google Trends.

survey of almost 7,000 adults from the United States and Canada was conducted. The results revealed that a staggering 20 percent of participants reported elevated levels of anxiety, whereas only 2 percent had actually contracted COVID-19.[8] When the coronavirus arrived, it brought with it a significant amount of uncertainty. People become more vigilant and attentive as the virus neared our borders despite international organizations issuing warnings around the world about the dangers of a spreading virus for months in advance.

In this chapter, I first explore the shifts in public opinion surrounding the Zika and Ebola outbreaks, both prior to and following their arrival in the United States, drawing parallels with the observed dynamics of the

COVID-19 pandemic. This analysis sheds light on the impact of these infectious diseases on public perception given the temporal distance manifested in the timing of their arrival to the United States. Second, I focus on the relationship between COVID-19 and mobility patterns, considering the concentration of coronavirus-related deaths and partisanship that materialized as election returns in the 2020 presidential election.

THE ZIKA NIPPER

Zika, a virus primarily transmitted by the Aedes aegypti mosquitoes, commonly known as dengue and yellow fever mosquitoes, thrives in temperate climates.[9] The origins of Zika's surge can be traced to several theories proposing that the virus underwent mutations, transforming from an African strain to a pandemic strain in the 1990s.[10] From there it spread across the Pacific before finally arriving in Brazil. In May 2015 local transmission of Zika was first discovered in Brazil, serving as a launching point for its subsequent spread across the continent, which was primarily fueled by travel.[11]

In April 2016, the growing concerns surrounding Zika prompted Peter Hotez from Baylor College of Medicine to sound the alarm in a *New York Times* editorial titled "Zika Is Coming." Hotez's choice of a catchy title captured the mounting anxiety regarding the potential public health repercussions of the virus. He wrote, "If I were a pregnant woman living on the Gulf Coast or in Florida, in an impoverished neighborhood in a city like Houston, New Orleans, Miami, Biloxi, Miss., or Mobile, Ala., I would be nervous right now."[12] Similar to the COVID-19 pandemic, Zika sparked widespread apprehension across countries due to its uncertainty and the dissemination of alarming information through public media sources.

Just four months prior to publication of Hotez's editorial in the *New York Times*, the Zika virus was virtually absent from the radar of news media organizations. A search for the term "Zika" in the NewsBank database, which houses newspaper archives, yielded a mere 141 articles across the country in 2015, but within a year that number skyrocketed to

32,711 articles in the United States. By early September, approximately 2,400 Zika cases had been reported, and the number of cases more than doubled to 5,168 throughout the year, with the highest surge occurring between May and July.[13] Alongside the rapid spread of the virus, public anxiety experienced a significant uptick between 2015 and 2016. Figure 2.2 illustrates this point clearly. In 2015, there was noticeable variation in Zika's Google Trends across different states, as depicted in the gray-black scale (Panel A); in contrast, by 2016, this variation had almost disappeared across the United States (Panel B), indicating that Zika was a popular search term in all U.S. states. In 2015 Zika's Google Trends score was 38 out of 100, whereas in 2016 it had increased by 23 points, reaching a score of 61, reflecting the growing unease and heightened interest surrounding the virus.

As the number of Zika cases surged, a parallel rise in public anxiety followed, and 2016 witnessed a significant media spotlight on Zika, largely attributed to the Olympic Games held in Rio de Janeiro, Brazil. The media frenzy surrounding participation of athletes in the games captured widespread attention. Numerous American athletes voiced their concerns about attending the Olympics, fearing the potential risks posed by the virus. *Time* magazine reported that "fears over the Zika virus have caused numerous American athletes to alter their plans and scramble to protect their health before the upcoming Olympic Games in Rio de Janeiro."[14]

One prominent example was Hope Solo, the U.S. goalkeeper, who openly expressed her reservations in an interview with *Sports Illustrated* in February 2016. If given the choice, Solo made it clear that she would not attend the Olympics due to concerns about Zika. She emphasized her unwavering commitment to safeguarding the health of her future child, stating that she could not fathom risking the well-being of her family. Solo passionately advocated that no athlete competing in Rio should be confronted with such a dilemma, stating that she firmly believed in every individual's right to pursue parenthood while prioritizing their child's health.[15]

The media frenzy during the 2016 Olympic Games served as a catalyst for heightened public anxiety surrounding the uncertainty and rapid spread of Zika. Despite the Olympics taking place during Brazil's winter

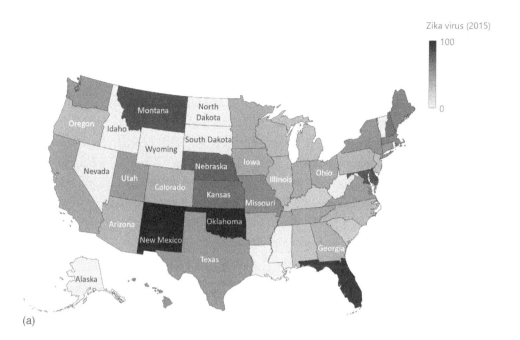

FIGURE 2.2 Zika virus search trends on Google in 2015 (*a*) and 2016 (*b*).

Source: Data from Google Trends.

season when mosquito activity tends to decrease, concerns regarding Zika remained pervasive.[16] The undeniable reality was that Zika had arrived, casting a shadow of uncertainty. But did the public's apprehension regarding Zika increase in tandem with the rising number of infections?

To explore this question, I turned to survey data for answers. The 2016 Kaiser Family Foundation Health Tracking Polls for February and June provided valuable information about this dilemma.[17] These national representative polls questioned 1,200 adults ages eighteen and above, and both surveys used identical questions, ensuring consistency and avoiding potential wording effects.[18] My primary focus centered on understanding people's anxieties regarding their personal or familial exposure to Zika. By examining these survey questions, I gained deeper insight into the evolving concerns surrounding Zika as the epidemic moved closer to us.

Figure 2.3 shows the level of concern exhibited by individuals during these two periods: in February, when Zika had not yet arrived in the United States, and in June, when Zika cases began to surge in the United States. The size of each circle indicates the level of wariness that survey respondents had about Zika's impact on them or their families. Small circles indicate no worries at all, and larger circles represent significant worries about Zika and its implications. A visual comparison between the two maps unveils interesting differences between the two time frames. Notably, the size of the circles tends to be larger in June than in February, implying that a greater number of people in specific areas had significant concerns as Zika cases surged. For instance, in Texas in February residents, on average, displayed relatively low levels of anxiety about Zika. However, in June Texans demonstrated a heightened level of worry, particularly in Houston and Dallas. As Zika cases became more prevalent and mosquitoes infiltrated urban centers and states during the warmer months, individuals became increasingly apprehensive about the potentially detrimental implications of Zika. These maps show the evolving spatial dynamics of public concern regarding Zika and their correlation with the temporal progression of the epidemic.

We can dive deeper into the connection between individuals' concerns regarding Zika and the number of infections using regression analysis.

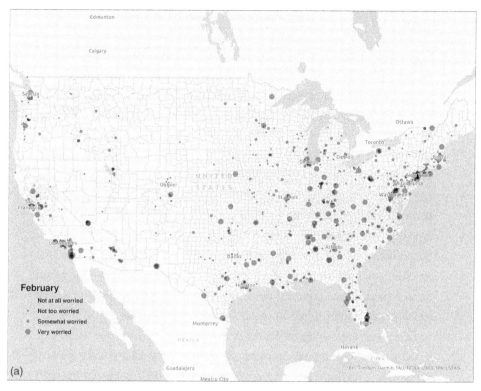

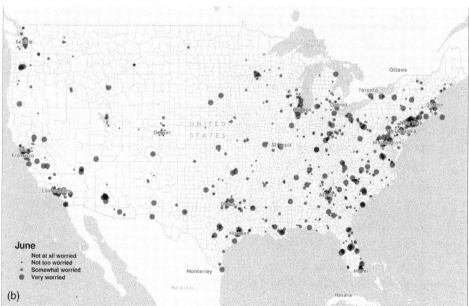

FIGURE 2.3 Survey responses to the question "How worried are you about Zika?" from February 2016 (*a*) and June 2016 (*b*).

Source: Data from the Kaiser Family Foundation Health Tracking Polls from February and June 2016.

Regression analysis is a statistical procedure widely used in the social sciences to assess associations between multiple variables. In this case, I want to build a model that explores how people's worries about being affected by Zika are influenced by the level of infections, the extent of individuals' exposure to information about Zika, their gender, education, income, and political affiliation. Essentially, I want to find out whether a correlation exists between the number of infections and the level of concern among individuals. In this case, distance is measured as the time when the threat becomes apparent. If the number of infections increase between February and June, I would expect people to be more worried in June than they were in February—a classic before and after comparison. So, if this is plausible, in June people residing in regions with a relatively higher number of infections—compared to areas with lower infection rates—would exhibit greater levels of worry regarding the potential impact of Zika than they did in February.

I ran these models separately for both February and June (see table A.2.1 in the appendix for regression tables). Figure 2.4 provides a visual summary of the outcomes derived from running linear regressions to predict the level of individuals' worries based on Zika infection rates, controlling for individuals' exposure to Zika-related information, gender, ethnicity, education, income, and self-identification as Republicans.

In general, there is a positive relationship between Zika infection levels and the level of worry among individuals. However, as shown in figure 2.4, this relationship was statistically significant in June, with a steeper slope of the line, indicating a more robust correlation, compared to February, when the relationship between Zika levels and worry was not statistically significant. Individuals residing in an area with a high number of Zika cases were 7 percent more likely to express concern about the impact on them or their families when compared to individuals in an area with low Zika numbers.

The results thus far highlight a crucial factor: timing is of utmost importance. That is, temporal distance matters. In February 2016, when Zika was practically nonexistent in the United States, infection levels did not significantly predict individuals' worries about the virus. However, as Zika became more prevalent in the United States in June 2016, individuals living

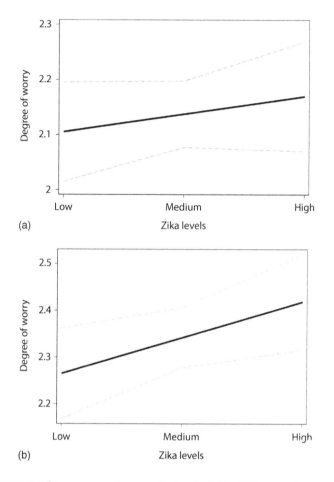

FIGURE 2.4 Linear regressions predicting individuals' degree of worry given Zika infection rates by month: (*a*) February 2016 and (*b*) June 2016.

Source: Data from the Kaiser Family Foundation Health Tracking Polls for February and June 2016.

in areas with higher infection rates were more likely to be concerned about its effects than those in regions with lower infection rates. The influence of distance is also measured in time. As threats became more tangible due to the spread of the virus and the arrival of warmer temperatures, individuals' concerns and anxiety grew.

EBOLA

The 1995 film *Outbreak* delivers an apocalyptic portrayal of a doctor's race against time to find a cure for a fictional Ebola virus that ravages California. The virus originates from a small monkey captured in a remote African jungle, which eventually finds its way into a pet store in the United States. The movie effectively captures the collective fear that surrounds the fictional town of Cedar Creek as the virus spreads uncontrollably, prompting authorities to implement unconventional measures in a desperate attempt to contain it. Remarkably, *Outbreak* bears a striking resemblance to events that unfolded in Dallas, Texas, in October 2014, albeit on a different scale, when Ebola arrived in the United States. Panic gripped the nation as news coverage became saturated, with more than 970 segments on Ebola aired on national news broadcasts during that period.[19] A story and a virus once confined to fiction were suddenly starkly real and knocking at our doorstep once again.

Extreme health events have a profound impact on our lives, often catching us off guard. When we witness such events unfold in distant nations, we may feel a sense of detachment, believing that we are immune to similar circumstances in the foreseeable future. However, once cases begin to emerge closer to home, worry and concern swiftly take hold. I must confess that I, too, fell victim to the grip of uncertainty during the 2009 H1N1 pandemic, commonly referred to as the swine flu. I made a detour to a medical supply store on my way home from work at the University of Houston. My intention was to purchase a box of N95 masks. To my surprise, the store clerk calmly informed me that I was the tenth customer that day seeking masks. In retrospect, the masks proved unnecessary, but given the prevailing uncertainty and the gradual encroachment of the H1N1 virus, it seemed like a natural response. I soon realized that I was not alone in my anxiety. People across the state and the country were succumbing to panic as the uncertainty surrounding the virus intensified.

People across the globe, however, had valid reasons for concern when it came to the Ebola virus disease (EVD), a pernicious virus known for its devastating impact and classified by WHO as one of the top eight diseases of concern.[20] EVD first emerged in 1976 near the Ebola River in what is now the Democratic Republic of Congo (formerly known as Zaire).[21] This highly infectious disease affects both humans and nonhuman primates, including monkeys, gorillas, and chimpanzees.[22] It spreads through direct contact with blood, bodily fluids, and tissues of infected animals, making it a formidable and alarming threat to public health.[23]

The 2014 West Africa EVD outbreak originated in Guinea in December 2013 and swiftly spread across Liberia and Sierra Leone by January 2014. By July of the same year, it became glaringly apparent that EVD had extended its geographic reach throughout West Africa, prompting the international community to take notice.[24] The modes of transmission and concerns surrounding biosecurity escalated as airline travel and cross-border migration facilitated the virus's dissemination.[25] Remarkably, EVD had been a pressing issue for approximately nine months before it reached the United States and Europe, where the public began to experience cognitive dissonance—a state characterized by conflicting attitudes—regarding the perceived risk of transmission versus the risk of infection, which was driven by individual fears.[26] To put this into perspective, during that time, the likelihood of contracting EVD in the United States was 1 in 13.3 million, making it less probable than being struck by lightning.[27] These statistics underscore the significant disparity between public perception and the actual risk of infection, emphasizing the influence of individual fears and the resulting cognitive dissonance in shaping people's attitudes toward EVD.

In the United States, there were a total of eleven Ebola cases, with only four individuals falling ill.[28] Compared to outbreaks like Zika, Ebola did not reach the level of a widespread epidemic. However, the locations where infections occurred received intense media coverage, accentuating the hazards and risks associated with the virus. The media emphasis played a significant role in amplifying public fears and contributed to the overall hysteria surrounding Ebola.[29] Sensationalized headlines and extensive reporting on individual cases fostered a sense of panic and anxiety among the general population. The CNN commentator and legal analyst

Mel Robbins coined a term for this phenomenon: Fear-bola. According to Robbins, "Fear-bola attacks the part of the brain responsible for rational thinking, it starts with a low-grade concern about the two health care workers diagnosed with Ebola in Dallas and slowly builds into fear of a widespread epidemic in the United States."[30]

Here I explore the role of the media in bringing Ebola to our communities and whether residing in an area with substantial media coverage of Ebola heightened individuals' fears of infection. In essence, I examine whether being in proximity to Ebola through media exposure influenced people's concerns about the virus. In other words, I explore how the media affected people's fears regarding EVD by creating a filter that changed our emotions and attitudes, illustrating how sharp apprehensions arose even in the absence of widespread infections owing to the influential role of the media and its persistent exposure to a nonexistent threat.

To shed light on this question, first I turned to a survey conducted by the Kaiser Family Foundation (KFF) in October 2014 when Ebola started gaining attention in the United States.[31] This nationally representative public opinion poll targeted 1,500 adults and encompassed a wide range of health-related questions. Notably, it included questions probing individuals' level of worry regarding the possibility of them or their family members falling ill with Ebola.

Second, I used data coming from NewsBank, a national repository that includes a vast array of news stories at the city level. NewsBank serves as a comprehensive aggregator of news stories from various media platforms, including audio, blogs, journals, magazines, newspapers, newswires, videos, and internet sources. This rich collection of media coverage allows me to examine the breadth and depth of information different segments of the population would regularly consume. Leveraging this resource, I searched for news articles referencing Ebola. Borrowing from the punctuated equilibrium theory, which shows that the level of news coverage can create policy shifts, we can assume that public opinion will also shift given the public's exposure to news coverage.[32] By joining the KFF survey with the NewsBank data, I painted a more comprehensive picture of individuals' concerns about Ebola, incorporating both personal perspectives captured through the survey and the broader impact on their attitudes via media coverage.

The findings from the Kaiser Health Tracking Poll are truly intriguing. In total, approximately 59 percent of the surveyed adults expressed varying degrees of worry that either they or their family members could contract Ebola, and the remaining 41 percent reported being relatively unconcerned. What makes these results particularly fascinating? Well, let's consider the context. Recall that in 2014 the odds of being infected with Ebola in the United States were a staggering 1 in 13.3 million. To put this into perspective, the lifetime odds of succumbing to heart disease are 1 in 6.[33] Hence, the actual risk of contracting Ebola was very small.

Despite this limited risk, levels of concern did not align with the perceived risk individuals faced. Reports emerged of children being pulled out of schools, closures of educational institutions, individuals avoiding work and public transportation, all due to unwarranted fears surrounding Ebola transmission.[34] Astonishingly, even a college located approximately sixty miles from Dallas sent a rejection letter to a Nigerian student, a country that had hardly been affected by Ebola. The rejection letter stated, "With sincere regret, I must report that Navarro College is not able to offer you acceptance for the Spring 2015 term. Unfortunately, Navarro College is not accepting international students from countries with confirmed Ebola cases."[35] These incidents highlight the significant disconnect between the actual risk of contracting Ebola and the disproportionate levels of fear and anxiety exhibited by individuals. Despite the nonexistent likelihood of infection, the perceived threat led to drastic measures and unwarranted discrimination.

How can we make sense of the fact that nearly 59 percent of adults in the United States were gripped by worry over Ebola? The answer may lie in the extensive media coverage surrounding the outbreak. In Dallas, Texas, for instance, a staggering 318 news stories specifically mentioned Ebola between September and October 2014. On a national scale, the number of news articles written about Ebola during the same period reached 15,554.[36]

Prior to Ebola making its way to the United States, media attention toward the West Africa Ebola epidemic was relatively minimal. However,

OUTBREAKS, EPIDEMICS, AND PANDEMICS

as the disease hit closer to home, media coverage soared, fueling widespread concern. Figure 2.5 illustrates the geographical distribution of articles and provides a heat map depicting the concentration of survey respondents who expressed worry about contracting Ebola. This visual representation underscores the correlation between media exposure and the heightened levels of public anxiety observed during that time.

Figure 2.5 provides evidence of a potential correlation between the fear of Ebola infection and the number of articles published in local newspapers.

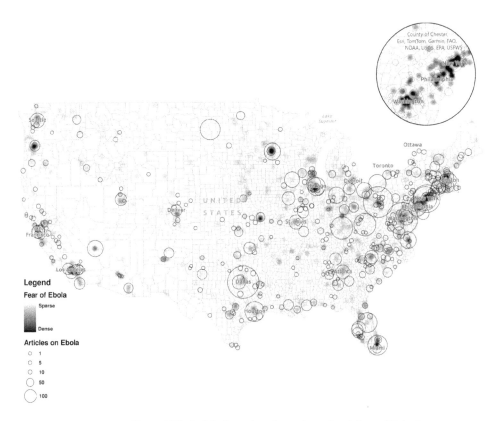

FIGURE 2.5 Fear of Ebola (*dark spots*) and number of articles published (*circles*) in the United States in October 2014.

Source: Data from the Kaiser Family Foundation Health Tracking Poll October 2014 and NewsBank.

Let's focus our attention on the Northeast region for a moment. In Washington, D.C., Philadelphia, and New York City, a notable concentration of articles were published, with the size of the circles representing these cities being larger when compared to other parts of the country—reaching the hundreds. Simultaneously, the density of individuals expressing concern about Ebola appears more pronounced around these cities, indicated by the darker spots on the map.

It is important to highlight that I am not asserting a direct causal relationship between these factors; the survey used was not designed to draw inferences at the city level. Making such an inference would be akin to committing an ecological inference fallacy, which involves using aggregate data (in this case, national survey data) to make inferences about specific cities.[37] However, there may be some patterns worthy of further exploration. Employing spatial patterns enables us to visualize potential correlations and offer a methodological perspective that can help us unravel the complexities of human behavior during times of perceived crisis.

Now that we have a preliminary understanding of the association between the number of articles and the fear of Ebola, the next step is to dive deeper into exploring their potential relationship. My primary objective is to estimate the likelihood of individuals expressing worry about contracting Ebola in relation to the quantity of articles published on the virus.

To accomplish this, I utilized the NewsBank dataset and matched the number of news stories in selected cities with the towns where the respondents resided. The dependent variable is binary, taking a value of one for respondents who expressed concern about contracting Ebola and zero for those who did not. The main predictor variable is the number of news stories published across 413 cities throughout the nation, encompassing various mediums such as audio, blog, journal, magazine, newspaper, newswire, video, and internet. In addition, I incorporated variables that account for the potential confounding factors that could influence the relationship between media exposure and fear of Ebola. These include age, education, income, and race/ethnicity. It is crucial to incorporate these demographic characteristics because they may significantly affect individuals' levels of concern about infection or their consumption of media. For instance, older individuals tend to be more vulnerable to severe viral infections, and they also tend to engage with television and print news at higher rates. It is worth noting that these mediums were the primary sources of Ebola-related stories. By considering these additional variables, I want to explore the complex interplay between the number of articles and the fear of Ebola, accounting for potential demographic disparities that may exist among different population groups.

To analyze the impact of the number of articles published on individuals' worries about Ebola, I conducted a logistic regression controlling for the factors previously mentioned. This statistical approach allows me to estimate the probability of someone expressing concern about being infected with Ebola based on the number of news articles.

The results of the regression reveal a significant relationship between the number of articles and people's concerns about Ebola (see table A.2.2 in the appendix for regression results). For instance, when only one news piece is available, the estimated probability of being worried about Ebola is 0.53. However, as the number of news stories increases to the maximum observed value of 318, the likelihood of concern about contracting Ebola rises to 0.76. This represents a substantial 43 percent increase in the probability of being concerned, indicating the impact of media coverage on shaping public apprehension.

What are the implications of these results? The significance of the results underscores the role played by media in influencing individual perceptions and worries regarding public health issues. The greater the coverage devoted to a topic, the higher the likelihood that individuals will exhibit heightened concerns about associated risks. Consistent with previous research, my findings demonstrate that the number of news articles, as a measure of media exposure, plays a critical role in generating fear among the public.[38] This aligns with studies conducted on previous epidemics, which have shown that sensationalizing the potential dangers of diseases, highlighting specific aspects of a disease, and providing continuous updates on health risks can contribute to heightened fears and anxieties among the population.[39]

The media's ability to inflict and exacerbate fear related to new viruses is particularly noteworthy, even in the absence of a real and immediate threat.

The media creates a filter that distorts reality and brings a potential threat closer to us, just as Aristotle and Aquinas argued, and becomes a shadow in the Platonian sense that molds our attitudes and responses. My findings highlight the significant role of media in shaping our perception of spatial proximity during the Ebola epidemic. The media's portrayal of the outbreak brings the issue closer to home, priming our cognitive ability to situate ourselves at the center of the crisis and amplifying our fears. Media's influence is evident through the sheer volume, rapidity, and sometimes absurdity of the content they present.[40] Through these channels, media shapes our perception of distance, frames our understanding of the epidemic, and ultimately influences our attitudes and the steps we take in response.

The extensive volume, rapid dissemination, and sensationalized nature of Ebola's media coverage in the United States significantly influenced public perceptions and understanding of the virus.[41] As John Finn and Joseph Palis describe, "the volume, the speed, the breathlessness of the media coverage of Ebola in the United States, together with the oftentimes absurdity of the content of that coverage, has played a dramatic role in not only shaping Americans' (mis)conceptions of the threat of Ebola in the United States, but also their broader geographical understanding of what was, and continues to be, an overtly spatial issue."[42]

WHEN DEATH KNOCKS ON THE DOOR: COVID-19

The saga of the COVID-19 pandemic unfolded with a pivotal phone call or email on December 31, 2019, when Chinese authorities notified the WHO country office of an alarming situation. They reported multiple cases of pneumonia with unknown origins, unresponsive to traditional treatments, and accompanied by symptoms such as fever and difficulty breathing. Within a day, the Huanan seafood wholesale market in Wuhan province was shut down, and by January 3, 2020, Chinese health authorities had already identified more than forty cases. Just seven days later, on January 10, 2020, WHO declared that the outbreak in Wuhan was caused by a novel coronavirus.[43] This announcement sent ripples of concern not only through the residents of Wuhan province but also to those connected to the city, amplifying the sense of urgency and alarm.

Upon the virus's appearance and evident danger, the United States acted. The Centers for Disease Control and Prevention (CDC) implemented passenger screenings for individuals arriving from Wuhan, China, both directly and through connecting flights to major cities such as San Francisco, New York, and Los Angeles. By January 19, 2020, the virus had already infected 282 individuals, which was confirmed through laboratory testing, primarily in China (278 cases) but also in Thailand (2), Japan (1), and South Korea (1). The following day, a Washington state resident who had recently returned from Wuhan province became the first laboratory-confirmed case of COVID-19 in the United States. This pivotal development prompted the CDC to activate its Emergency Operations Center, signaling the seriousness of the outbreak and initiating a coordinated response effort.[44]

By the beginning of February 2020, the gravity of the situation became apparent as global health organizations and governments took decisive actions. WHO declared a public health emergency of international concern, marking only the sixth time such a declaration had been made in its history. Alex Azar, the secretary of the Department of Health and Human Services (HHS), officially declared the outbreak of the 2019 novel coronavirus as a public health emergency.[45] The Department of Homeland Security (DHS) responded by rerouting flights from China to one of eleven designated airports and implemented enhanced screening measures and the possibility of quarantine. Meanwhile, Italy emerged as a COVID-19 hot spot, and its government enforced a nationwide lockdown. In the United States, the CDC began making preparations for measures that would significantly disrupt everyday life, such as school closures, workplace shutdowns, and cancellation of public events. The effects of a virus that originated on the other side of the world would start to reshape the daily activities of Americans in a matter of months.

On March 3, 2020, the CDC confirmed the presence of sixty COVID-19 cases across multiple states, including Arizona, California, Florida,

Georgia, Illinois, Massachusetts, New Hampshire, New York, Oregon, Rhode Island, Washington, and Wisconsin. The situation continued to escalate rapidly, leading to significant global developments.[46] On March 11, 2020, with 118,000 cases and 4,291 deaths reported in 114 countries, WHO officially declared COVID-19 a global pandemic.[47] Two days later the Trump administration mirrored this declaration and announced a nationwide emergency in response to the coronavirus. As the impact of the virus grew more evident, states began taking proactive measures to contain its spread.[48] By March 15, 2020, various states were implementing shutdowns to mitigate the transmission of the coronavirus. Notably, the New York City public school system implemented closures, and Ohio requested that bars and restaurants close their doors. Just four days later California issued a statewide stay-at-home order, compelling the closure of all nonessential businesses throughout the state. Between March 21 and April 7, a significant number of states followed suit and issued stay-at-home orders, although with varying degrees of restrictions. It is worth noting that the Dakotas, Arkansas, Iowa, and Nebraska were the only states that did not enforce similar mandates during this period.[49]

Within a span of just over half a year, the coronavirus made a dramatic journey from a distant city to create chaos in communities here in the United States. In mid-July, ten days after WHO confirmed airborne transmission and the spread by asymptomatic individuals, the CDC issued a crucial directive: wearing face masks when venturing outside became a vital step in curbing the virus's spread.[50] By mid-August, the devastating impact of COVID-19 was laid bare as the daily death toll surpassed 1,000, making it the third leading cause of death in the United States. The virus's relentless march continued to unfold with alarming speed. Just a day after the 2020 presidential election, the United States recorded a staggering 100,000 new cases in a single day. Following Halloween celebrations a spike in coronavirus cases emerged, casting a shadow of concern. As mid-December arrived, the reported death toll from COVID-19 surpassed the grim milestone of 300,000. However, amid the darkness, a flicker of hope emerged: Sandra Lindsay, a nurse in New York, became the first American outside of clinical trials to receive the COVID-19 vaccine. Simultaneously, a new variant, the

Alpha variant, was detected, raising fresh concerns and emphasizing the continued need for vigilance even with the advent of promising vaccines.[51]

The relentless toll of the pandemic continued in 2021, leaving no community untouched in the United States and across the globe. The new year commenced with a grim reality—400,000 deaths had already been recorded in the United States. Amid this somber backdrop, the emergence of Beta and Gamma variants in South Carolina and Minnesota added to the challenges at hand. However, there was a glimmer of hope as the Biden administration took charge, spearheading a comprehensive national strategy for the COVID-19 response. As the year unfolded, states gradually began to reopen and adapt to a new normal. Republican-led states, eager to restore a sense of prepandemic normalcy, were among the first to lift restrictions. By the end of May 2021, thirty-four states had reopened, and by the end of July, all states had followed suit.[52] Despite the increasing number of individuals receiving the COVID-19 vaccine, the nation experienced a staggering death toll that surpassed 800,000, resulting in a significant population loss, particularly among older individuals, where one in every one hundred people age sixty-five and older who became infected had succumbed to the virus.[53]

COVID-19–related deaths were influenced by various factors. In addition to the risk of infection, individuals' adherence to stay-at-home orders played a role in determining their chances of becoming infected. A study conducted by the CDC revealed that those who tested positive for COVID-19 were more than twice as likely to have dined out and more than four times as likely to have visited a bar or café.[54] Thus individuals' own actions contributed to their heightened risk of infection and potential mortality. Furthermore, underlying medical conditions or comorbidities such as diabetes, asthma, chronic lung disease, sickle cell disease, and immunocompromised states increased the susceptibility of individuals to severe illness from COVID-19. However, another formidable comorbidity affected people that transcended health and age conditions—a deeply partisan polarization that permeated society. This divisive political climate had a profound impact, shaping public perception, response, and adherence to safety measures, ultimately influencing the trajectory of the pandemic.[55]

Numerous polls have shed light on the widening partisan divide in public opinion regarding the response to the pandemic. A June 2020 poll conducted by the Pew Research Center revealed a significant gap in views on the risk posed by the coronavirus, as well as disagreements on social distancing measures and restrictions aimed at slowing its spread.[56] This divide extended to perceptions of the virus itself, as demonstrated in a July 2020 survey that highlighted stark differences in preferred news sources for COVID-19 information among Democrats and Republicans, exposing corresponding knowledge gaps.[57]

The media's role during the pandemic came under intense scrutiny, with accusations of misinformation originating from various ends of the political spectrum. The challenge for the media to provide accurate information was compounded by the rapidly evolving nature of the COVID-19 situation, fostering a sense of distrust among the public.[58] Policymakers also played a crucial role in shaping the pandemic response, often aligning their actions with their party affiliations. Democratic governors, for instance, implemented stricter policies that led to lower infection rates in their states, underscoring the partisan disparities in approaches to tackling the crisis.[59] In late May 2020, as the nation grappled with differing strategies, Modoc County's deputy director of emergency services, Heather Hadwick, defiantly stated, "we are moving forward with our reopening plan." This rural, conservative county in California defied Democratic Governor Gavin Newsom's stay-at-home order by allowing nonessential businesses and restaurants to reopen, exemplifying the divergence between state and local approaches to combating the pandemic.[60]

Trust in science, public health institutions, and expert advice became deeply divided as partisan narratives shaped public opinion on the efficacy of containment measures and the acceptance of vaccines.[61] Throughout the pandemic, government officials, particularly within the Trump administration, clashed with the scientific community, leading to a cacophony of conflicting messages that transformed the public health emergency into a bitter political battleground between Democrats and Republicans.[62] In stark contrast, other countries around the world maintained a relatively united front, with public health officials garnering broader support that resulted in much smaller partisan differences compared to those in the United States.

As the 2020 U.S. presidential election loomed, a divisive climate emerged that hindered implementation of effective strategies, further exacerbating the consequences of the crisis. The pandemic, which demanded unity and collective action, instead became entangled in partisan warfare, impeding the nation's ability to effectively navigate the challenges posed by the virus. The pandemic became fertile ground for exploiting the partisan divide, and partisanship emerged as "the core explanation for America's disastrous response to COVID-19."[63]

The pandemic had a profound impact on mobility as individuals navigated the delicate balance between safety concerns and evolving restrictions. In the United States, mobility patterns were not only shaped by public health guidelines but also by the stark partisan differences between Democrats and Republicans. Understanding the influence of partisan disparities on mobility requires recognizing the contrasting attitudes and responses exhibited by these two political groups during the pandemic. These variations, stemming from divergent ideological stances, frequently translated into distinct approaches to public health measures and government interventions.[64]

The impact of partisan differences on mobility extended beyond individual behavior. Political leaders and policymakers aligned with different parties played a crucial role in shaping mobility patterns through their decisions on reopening strategies, enforcement of restrictions, and communication of public health guidance. These partisan influences created a complex landscape in which mobility became entwined with political ideologies and beliefs.

Areas with a higher concentration of Republican voters demonstrated less reduction in mobility during the COVID-19 pandemic compared to areas with higher concentrations of Democratic voters, indicating that political affiliation played a role in shaping mobility behaviors.[65] Republicans exhibited greater resistance to altering their routines and reducing their level of mobility.[66] The differing responses and policy decision of state Democratic and Republican administrations also contributed to these disparities in mobility. Democrats generally advocated for stricter restrictions and limitations on mobility, whereas Republicans leaned toward a more relaxed approach, prioritizing individual freedoms and economic considerations.[67]

Partisanship has emerged as a paramount social identity marker, permeating various aspects of our lives and shaping our interactions with those who align or diverge from our partisan leanings.[68] During the pandemic, this pervasive partisanship intensified and transformed into a "mega-identity, with all the psychological and behavioral magnifications that implies."[69] Partisanship influenced mobility, but other factors either reinforced or superseded ideological or partisan convictions. One such factor is the impact of COVID-19 fatalities. How did proximity to increasing cumulative COVID-19–related deaths shape our mobility during the first year of the pandemic? That is, did the presence of real danger change our mobility patterns?

To answer this question, I turn to Google's COVID-19 Open Data Repository.[70] This repository stands as one of the largest databases dedicated to COVID-19, including mobility data and the cumulative number of deaths associated with positive COVID-19 cases at the county level. These metrics serve as proxies for gauging distance. For example, consider a county with a high cumulative death toll—a stark reminder of the presence of death nearby. In such cases, individuals may exercise greater caution, which may reduce their willingness to venture out. Conversely, in counties with lower cumulative death counts, the perceived risk may diminish leading to increases in mobility patterns.

Google's mobility trends also track changes in visits to grocery stores, pharmacies, parks, restaurants, and workplaces over time and in specific places. To determine whether mobility decreased or increased, mobility patterns within a county are compared to a baseline value derived from the median mobility during a five-week period from January 3 to February 6, 2020, which was before the pandemic took hold. If the mobility value is negative, it indicates a decrease compared to the baseline, and a positive value indicates an increase. Because these data lack individual-level variables, I supplemented them by merging them with the 2020 county-level presidential election results to examine the relationship between mobility,

COVID-19 fatalities, and partisanship.[71] To analyze how partisan counties were, I estimated the margin of victory for the winning presidential candidate in each county by calculating the difference between the votes for Joe Biden and Donald Trump divided by the total number of votes cast.

To explore the potential impact of partisanship on mobility, the first step is to examine how mobility was influenced in counties in which there was a significant advantage for either Trump or Biden during the first two years of the pandemic. For comparison purposes I selected Blount County, Alabama, as a county in which Trump had a substantial margin of victory; Prince George's County, Maryland, as a county in which Biden enjoyed a significant victory; and Tarrant County, Texas, in which the race was competitive and there was not a partisan bias.

Figure 2.6 shows Google's mobility index for retail and recreation places for each county spanning the onset of COVID-19 in January 2020 through

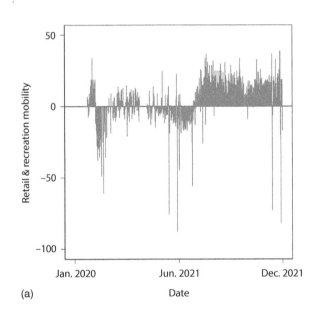

FIGURE 2.6 Google's retail and recreation mobility index for selected counties: (*a*) Blount County, AL; (*b*) Prince George's County, MD; (*c*) Tarrant County, TX.

Source: Data from Google Mobility Trends.

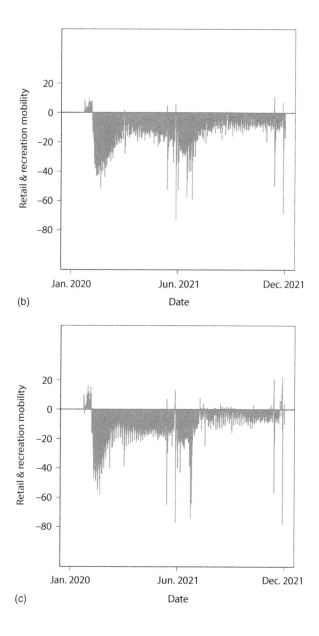

FIGURE 2.6 (*continued*)

its spread in December 2021. I chose this index due to its inherent discretionary nature; visiting retail establishments and engaging in recreational activities were not essential activities as were obtaining groceries or medications from a pharmacy.

Figure 2.6 highlights the discernible variations in mobility patterns across these counties. Blount County exhibits fluctuations in both positive and negative mobility spikes, whereas Prince George's County and Tarrant County display consistently negative mobility indices for retail and recreation, implying reduced visits to these nonessential places. The average mobility during this period in Blount County was +4; in Prince George's County it was -14; and in Tarrant County it stood at -12.

Next I modeled potential associations between mobility, county-level margin of victory for Biden/Trump, cumulative COVID-related deaths, and their interaction. I employed a fixed-effects model encompassing all counties with available data from November 4, 2020, to December 31, 2021. Incorporating state indicators in the model mitigates the risk of omitted variable bias, which may arise when crucial factors are overlooked given the nature of the data.

Figure 2.7 provides an overview of the regression findings, illustrating the relationship between the cumulative number of deaths on the x-axis and the margin of victory for either Biden (+) or Trump (-) on the y-axis (see table A.2.3 in the appendix for regression results). A contour plot shows how partisanship and the cumulative number of COVID-19 deaths influence mobility, with each line representing a specific level of movement. If the lines are close together, a small change in partisanship and COVID-19 deaths had a large effect on mobility. If the lines are farther apart, changes in the margin of victory and deaths didn't affect mobility as much. Figure 2.7 represents the mobility prediction for counties (positive values are indicated by darker shades and mean more mobility, and the opposite is true for negative values and shades) with a particular combination of cumulative COVID-19 deaths and the Trump/Biden margin of victory as a proxy for partisanship.

The findings reveal a notable disparity in mobility patterns based on the interaction between the proximity of COVID-19 deaths and the Trump/

OUTBREAKS, EPIDEMICS, AND PANDEMICS

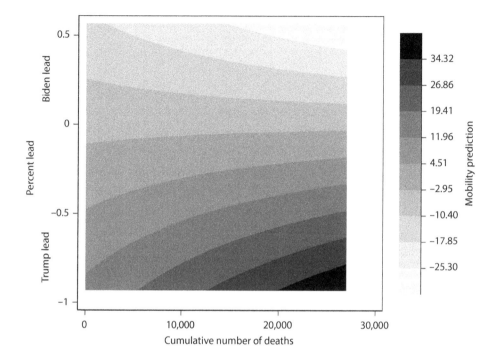

FIGURE 2.7 Relationship between cumulative deaths and Biden/Trump margin of victory.

Source: Data from Google COVID-19 Open Data Repository and *New York Times*.

Biden margin of victory. For example, the black contour line suggests that for counties in which Trump won by a landslide and had thousands of COVID-19 deaths, the predicted mobility was +34.32. However, as the number of deaths increased and Trump's margin of victory declined, the mobility predictions also decreased (i.e., the contour lines become lighter), eventually reaching Biden's counties, where he won by a significant margin and mobility predictions turned negative. This is illustrated by those counties with a high number of cumulative deaths in which Biden won by a landslide (i.e., light gray), and the predicted mobility was -25.30.

The COVID-19 crisis became intricately entangled with political campaigns and elections as voters sharply diverged along party lines in their assessments of Donald Trump's and Joe Biden's handling of the pandemic and its economic repercussions.[72] The pandemic laid bare a deep-seated polarization, not just in terms of policy responses but also in terms of public trust and perceptions. Partisan polarization proved to be the deadliest factor for Americans' health. "Deep partisan polarization created two pandemic realities in America: One where the pandemic was taken seriously and one where the pandemic was an inconvenience."[73]

This chapter centers on the analysis of various public health emergencies, shedding light on the interaction between public opinion, concerns, political dynamics, and distance. The Zika case underscores the significance of timing. In February 2016, with Zika absent in the United States, concerns were relatively low, but as infection rates soared in certain areas by June, heightened concerns emerged that were influenced by time and the illusory spatial proximity it created. The case of Ebola emphasizes the pivotal role of the media in plausibly shaping public perceptions when a virus emerges, highlighting Aquinas's *improviso* that renders public opinion irrational in the face of a viral threat. The COVID-19 case reveals the influence of party affiliation on pandemic responses, which exhibited variation across different locations. Examining mobility patterns in counties supporting Trump versus those supporting Biden demonstrates that places are more than physical locations; they are intricately shaped by the interplay of social and geographic factors, as conceptualized by Enos.[74] When faced with a real and clear danger, partisans sought guidance on the best course of action during COVID-19 to minimize potential losses whether in lives or in their previously held political beliefs, as Saint Augustine observed.

3

BOMBS AND GUNS

Boston, Paris, and El Paso

The Federal Bureau of Investigation (FBI) classifies terrorism in two distinct categories: international terrorism and domestic terrorism. International terrorism involves violent acts committed by individuals or groups affiliated with foreign terrorist organizations or state-sponsored nations. Domestic terrorism involves violent acts carried out by individuals or groups with the goal of advancing ideological objectives originating from within the country, such as political, religious, social, racial, or environmental factors.[1] Both types of terrorism share a common objective: to instill fear in individuals who are not directly targeted by the attacks.[2]

Since the tragic events of 9/11, the United States has faced numerous terrorist attacks carried out by both international and domestic actors. These attacks have varied in nature, from the shoe bomber incident in December 2001 in which an al-Qaeda operative attempted to detonate a bomb hidden in his footwear during a flight from Paris to the January 6, 2021, attack on the United States Capitol by a mob of President Donald Trump's supporters seeking to disrupt the certification of electoral votes from the 2020 election. The impact of these attacks has been long-lasting, leaving scars on the nation's psyche and institutions.

Another tragedy occurred at the Robb Elementary School in Uvalde, Texas, on May 24, 2022. During this barbaric event, a lone gunman took the lives of nineteen innocent children and two teachers, further highlighting the ongoing threat of terrorism within the country.

Human beings possess the inherent ability to experience anxiety and fear, which emerge in response to a perceived threat. This emotional response is facilitated by two interconnected mechanisms. The first mechanism resides within the amygdala, a small, almond-shaped structure located in the temporal lobe of the brain. The amygdala serves as a detector of motivational relevance and plays a crucial role in processing and generating fear-related emotions.[3] The second mechanism operates through the contextual information surrounding an event or individuals, which is known as the "context." This context encompasses various circumstances in both time and space that influence our perception and evaluation of potential threats. As illustrated in chapter 2, context can be shaped either by time, making us feel that a threat is near such as in the Zika case, or by being exposed to media frames that bring a nonexistent threat to our doorsteps, such as the Ebola case. It is through these contextual lenses that our fears are calibrated and shaped. These two mechanisms, the amygdala and context, work in tandem to ensure that we are equipped to effectively process and respond to fear-inducing stimuli, which enables us to take precautions to protect ourselves from potential dangers.[4] The counties with a significant number of COVID-19 deaths that were won by Biden in 2020 illustrates this (see chapter 2).

On the night of November 19, 2022, a scene of terror unfolded at Club Q in Colorado Springs, Colorado. In a brazen act of violence, a heavily armed assailant burst into the nightclub brandishing an assault rifle. During the chaos and panic, two patrons emerged from the middle of the crowd: Richard Fierro and Thomas James, both veterans with a tremendous amount of courage. Without a moment's hesitation, Fierro and James sprang into action, confronting the gunman head on and swiftly neutralizing the threat. Their heroic efforts saved countless lives, preventing the tragedy from escalating further. Tragically, five innocent souls perished, and eighteen others were wounded, a stark reminder of the devastation that could have unfolded.[5]

Reflecting on the traumatic ordeal, Fierro humbly attributed his brave actions to pure instinct, highlighting the indomitable human spirit that propels individuals to act selflessly in times of crisis: "It's just a reflex. You go! You run towards the danger. You stop the activity. You don't let anyone get hurt."[6] Fierro's words exemplify the remarkable courage and firm determination that can arise in the face of unimaginable adversity. Just days later, in Palm Coast, Florida, another incident of violence shook that community. Inside the Smiles Nite Club, chaos erupted when a regular suddenly unleashed a hail of bullets, targeting innocent bystanders. In the face of imminent danger, two individuals demonstrated extraordinary bravery and quick thinking. Paul Ibelli, a patron, and Dave, a bartender, swiftly subdued the armed assailant and disarm him, thereby averting another tragedy.[7] Remarkably, neither Ibelli nor Dave possessed any formal military training. Instead, it was their instinctual response, fueled by a determination to protect and preserve life, that empowered them to confront and neutralize the threat.

In moments of extreme crisis such as these, our responses to fear take on different forms. When faced with an immediate and life-threatening situation, our primal instincts present us with three primary options: fight, flee, or freeze.[8] These reactions are direct consequences of the stress we encounter, triggering intricate changes in our nervous and hormonal systems. These alterations prepare us to confront the danger head on, escape from it, or freeze.

However, when the threat is not imminent, we have a range of choices, and our response to fear is more nuanced. In these scenarios, the amygdala does not sound the alarm, our sympathetic nervous system remains inactive, and the release of adrenaline and cortisol into our bloodstream is not prompted. Instead, the context in which we find ourselves plays the main role in shaping our response to potential threats.[9]

As noted by Aristotle and Aquinas, the interaction between context and distance heavily influences our fears, highlighting the significance of these factors in our understanding and interpretation of the world around us. Context provides the framework through which we "shape and define the perception of sensory traces . . . and assign meaningful cues to spatial locations," which enables us to navigate and make sense of our environment.[10]

The interplay between distance and context plays a fundamental role in constructing our memory frames and influencing our expectations of future events. This connection enables us to access crucial information that helps us navigate ambiguous situations and to adjust our behavior or attitudes accordingly.[11] When we contemplate future expectations based on past experiences, our memory engages the availability heuristic, which assigns significance based on proximity.[12] As a result, events that may seem distant in time or space can be perceived as closer and more likely to occur in the future, transforming fear into Aquinas's *improviso* and inducing a sense of anxiety regarding potential future outcomes (see chapter 1).

TOO CLOSE FOR COMFORT?

At 6:50 A.M. on February 1, 2017, the forty-fifth president of the United States, Donald J. Trump, took to Twitter to address the contentious debate surrounding his controversial executive order on immigration. His tweet, which garnered significant attention and analysis, succinctly conveyed his administration's perspective on the issue: "Everybody is arguing whether or not it is a BAN. Call it what you want, it is about keeping bad people (with bad intentions) out of the country!" In 117 characters, Trump encapsulated the core principles guiding his administration's approach to immigration and national security. By singling out seven Muslim-majority countries as potential sources of risk, Trump emphasized the imperative of safeguarding the United States from the perceived threat of foreign terrorism. His message resonated with a commitment to combat what he termed "radical Islamic terrorism" by leveraging fear as a catalyst for what he considered bold and resolute action.[13]

Between 2007 and 2021, the world was rocked by an astonishing 60,500 incidents of terrorism. These acts of violence were particularly prevalent in regions plagued by political instability and ongoing conflicts. However, a remarkable trend emerged in the West, including the United States, where terrorist attacks decreased by a staggering 70 percent.[14] Although the impact of these attacks is undeniably brutal and inhumane, the probability of an American falling victim to a terrorist attack perpetrated by a refugee stood at the incredibly low odds of 1 in 3.64 billion. Similarly, the chances of being killed in an attack by an undocumented migrant were just 1 in 10.9 billion. To offer some perspective, the likelihood of winning the Mega Millions jackpot of $1.3 billion on July 29, 2022, was a mere 1 in 302.6 million, while the chances of drowning while bathing in a bathtub were estimated to be 1 in 403.[15]

The probability of winning the Mega Millions is higher than the likelihood of falling victim to a terrorist attack or being killed by an undocumented migrant. So why do we continue to worry about terrorist attacks? The answer lies in the psychological impact of such events and our limited ability to grasp their extremely low probabilities. Despite the statistical improbability, the possibility of a terrorist attack evokes deep discomfort, fear, and anxiety within us. The notion of such an attack lingers in our minds, much like the idea of winning the lottery, even though we recognize the minuscule likelihood of the latter.

The never-ending stream of political news inundating us may provoke overwhelming anxiety (e.g., the case of Ebola discussed in chapter 2). Each report of a terrorist attack amplifies our fears, causing us to question the likelihood of such atrocities unfolding in our own lives. Even though it is challenging to distinguish between the probability of a distant event and its potential occurrence in our own backyard, there is a stark contrast between the impact of a domestic terrorist attack and that of an international one—a distinction that is pivotal to our comprehension of terrorism and how we perceive it as an abominable act in our proximity or one far removed from us.

BOSTON VERSUS PARIS

To start pealing the complex layers between domestic and international terrorism, I turn to data from the Omnibus surveys conducted by the Pew

Research Center. These surveys, administered in April 2013 and January 2015, explored individuals' levels of news consumption regarding two significant terrorist incidents: the 2013 bombing during the Boston Marathon and the 2015 shootings at a newspaper office in Paris, France.[16] In addition to these surveys, the Pew Research Center has compiled an extensive repository of information encompassing a multitude of terrorist attacks worldwide in recent years.[17] By leveraging this wealth of data, comparisons can be drawn between attacks that struck close to our own communities and those that unfolded in more distant places both from a cultural and a spatial perspective.

Between January 2000 and the Charlie Hebdo shootings in January 2015, a time marked by the alarm of suspected terrorists in the United States, a total of forty-two terrorism incidents occurred.[18] To gain insight into the impact of cultural and spatial distance on public perception, I first classified each event from the Pew Research Center based on its proximity to the United States in terms of cultural distance, which encompasses values such as democratic principles, due process, market economy, and freedom of the press. These values create a sense of closeness between the United States and other countries that share these ideals. When terrorist attacks strike countries perceived as being culturally close to us, the public's concern about the potential for catastrophic terrorism on U.S. soil is sustained. For example, people in the United States were extremely concerned about a terrorist attack following the tragic bombings of the London transit system on July 7, 2005.[19] The recency of the London attack triggered a psychological phenomenon known as recency bias, leading people to assign greater significance to recent events and overestimate the likelihood of their recurrence. The London attack also highlighted the vulnerability of transportation systems, resonating with people worldwide. The targeting of public transportation raised awareness of the potential for similar attacks in other cities, elevating concerns about personal safety during commutes. Both the U.S. 9/11 attacks of 2001 and the London transit system bombing in 2005 involved coordinated suicide bombings, intensifying fears of replication in other locations and heightening public apprehension about future acts of terrorism.[20]

The coding process I used for this analysis was straightforward and involved categorizing each current terrorist incident based on its spatial location and cultural proximity. For instance, the Boston Marathon bombing was classified as an internal event, occurring within the United States, and as culturally proximate because it took place in a location that shares similar values with the United States (it is the same place). In contrast, the bombing and shooting in Norway in 2011, which resulted in the deaths of more than ninety people, was classified as an external event, happening in a country far from the United States. However, due to its cultural similarity to the United States, it was coded as culturally proximate. The 2008 bombing at a Marriott hotel in Pakistan, which claimed the lives of more than fifty people was coded both as an external incident because it occurred outside the United States and as culturally distant because that location is not culturally close to the United States.

In total, twenty-two terrorist incidents covered in the Pew Omnibus survey were near the United States, and twenty incidents occurred far away.[21] In terms of cultural proximity, thirty-three events were classified as close to American values, and nine events were distant from those values. Figure 3.1 illustrates both coding strategies. An interesting finding is that there is a significant difference of approximately twenty percentage points ($p < 0.05$) between closely following internal/close events and external/distant events. In addition, individuals were found to be fourteen percentage points ($p < 0.05$) less likely to express concern about external/distant events than internal/close events.

At face value, these patterns show that our level of concern regarding a possible terrorist attack is higher when the threat is in close proximity to our own lives and has the potential to directly affect our well-being. This aligns with the observation made by Saint Augustine many centuries ago highlighting the profound effect that events closer to us have on our possessions, aspirations, and relationships (see chapter 1). It is innate human nature to prioritize the safety and security of ourselves and our immediate circles, and this inclination is reflected in our responses to potential dangers.

Individuals have a tendency to prioritize their attention toward events that unfold in their immediate surroundings, be it spatially or culturally.

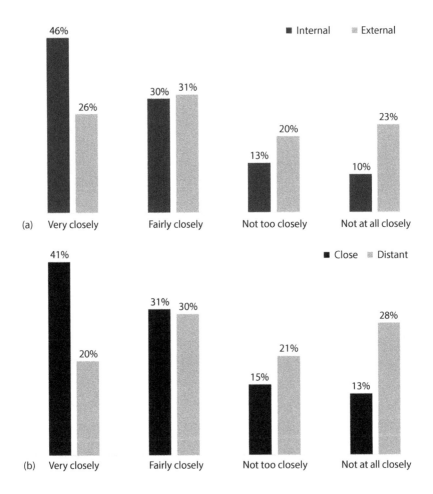

FIGURE 3.1 The difference in how closely terrorist attacks news stories were followed based on (*a*) geographic distance and (*b*) cultural distance.

Source: Author with data from the Pew Research Center.

However, the analysis conducted thus far does not provide a comprehensive understanding of the magnitude of our fears regarding the potential occurrence of a terrorist attack in the future. Next I focus on exploring the connection between news consumption and the level of public concern surrounding a terrorist attack. For this analysis, I turn to the 2020 American

National Election Studies (ANES), which provides a more detailed and nuanced analysis of the relationship between these variables.[22]

ANES is a comprehensive nationwide survey targeting adults that combines online surveys and live video and telephone interviews to ensure a representative sample. Among the array of questions, ANES investigated individuals' concerns regarding the likelihood of a terrorist attack happening within the United States in the near future. To gauge these concerns, respondents were prompted to assess their worry level on a five-point Likert scale, ranging from extremely worried to not at all worried. ANES also asked respondents the frequency with which they engage in governmental and political affairs news, offering a five-point Likert scale to measure their levels of information, ranging from always to never. I included this question as a proxy measure of individuals' awareness and knowledge regarding current events.

On average, survey participants expressed a moderate level of concern regarding the possibility of a terrorist attack occurring within the United States in 2020. Moreover, people displayed a notable level of engagement and attentiveness toward government and political affairs information. To explore the relationship between apprehension about a potential terrorist attack and the extent of focus on governmental and political affairs news, I conducted a multivariate regression analysis with the former as the dependent variable and the latter as the primary predictor. To accommodate potential variations in viewpoints among survey respondents, I incorporated factors such as political party affiliation (ranging from strong Democrat to strong Republican), income (ranging from less than $9,000 to $250,000 or beyond), educational attainment (ranging from less than a high school diploma to professional degrees), and gender (female/male).

After running the regression analysis (see table A.3.1 in the appendix for regression results), the findings reveal a statistically significant association between increased news attention and a heightened concern about a future terrorist attack: increasing attention to current events is associated with a 0.09 point increase in individual worries on a five-point scale (β = 0.09, $p < 0.05$). This finding aligns with the work of Brigitte Nacos, Yaeli Bloch-Elkon, and Robert Y. Shapiro in which they shed light on the impact of proximity on fear, exemplified by the heightened perception of another attack among New Yorkers following the 1993 World Trade Center bombing and the 9/11 terrorist attacks, two internal and close events shown in figure 3.1.[23] Nacos, Bloch-Elkon, and Shapiro also emphasize how media coverage of these events serve as a reminder of the atrocities that can occur during terrorist attacks. In 2020 alone, people in the United States were exposed to more than 6,000 newspaper articles and news stories mentioning terrorist attacks: equivalent to approximately sixteen articles per day. Exposure to these reports alone influences our perception of the potential risks associated with such incidents even though no substantial threats of a terrorist attack occurred in 2020 and only two National Terrorism Advisory System alerts were issued.[24]

Our opinions and perceptions are not shaped solely by the media we consume; they are also influenced by the cues provided by political leaders. The way leaders respond to terrorist attacks can have a significant impact on how we perceive potential future risks. John Zaller argues that "when elites uphold a clear picture of what should be done, the public tends to see events from that point of view."[25] With this in mind, let us examine the readouts of phone conversations by President Obama following two terrorist attacks in 2015: one in Turkey and one in France. By analyzing these public statements, we can gain valuable insight into how leaders perceive the distance of these attacks. It is evident that the impact of terrorist attacks extends beyond their immediate physical location and can have far-reaching consequences that shape our understanding and reactions.

On October 10, 2015, a tragic incident occurred in Ankara, Turkey, where two suicide bombers, believed to be affiliated with the Islamic State of Iraq and Levant (ISIL), detonated bombs at the central rail station. This devastating attack took the lives of 105 people who were peacefully participating in a political rally.[26] Nearly a month later, on November 13, 2015, ISIL terrorists carried out a coordinated series of suicide bombings and mass shootings across Paris, France, and its suburbs, resulting in the death of more than 130 innocent individuals.[27]

In the aftermath of these horrifying events, President Barack Obama engaged in phone conversations with Turkish President Tayyip Erdogan and French President Francois Hollande. The White House press secretary provided summaries of these conversations, which offer valuable insights into the leaders' perceptions and responses, which are highlighted in italics in table 3.1.

The readouts from the calls with the presidents of Turkey and France share a similar length, with the former summarized in seventy-six words and the latter in eighty words. Both calls also express condolences and offer support in the fight against terrorism. Although it may appear that there are no substantial differences between them, to gain a deeper understanding of any potential variations I used sentiment text analysis. This technique evaluates the emotions, opinions, and attitudes conveyed in the text.

TABLE 3.1 Readout of President Barack Obama's calls to leaders of Turkey and France after terrorist attacks in their countries

CALL WITH PRESIDENT ERDOGAN OF TURKEY[1]	CALL WITH PRESIDENT HOLLANDE OF FRANCE[2]
The President spoke today with Turkish President Recep Tayyip Erdogan *to offer condolences for the terrorist attacks* that killed at least 86 and wounded over 200 people at a peace rally in Ankara today. The President conveyed *his deepest personal sympathies for those killed and injured* in these heinous attacks, and affirmed that the *American people stand in solidarity* with the people of Turkey in the *fight against terrorism* and shared security challenges in the region.	President Obama spoke by phone this evening with President Hollande of France to *offer the condolences of the American people for the horrific terrorist attacks* in Paris earlier this evening. The President reiterated the *United States' steadfast, unwavering support for the people of France, our oldest ally and friend*, and reaffirmed the offer of any necessary support to the French investigation. The two leaders pledged to work together, and with nations around the world, *to defeat the scourge of terrorism*.

Source: Obama White House, emphasis added.

[1] National Security Council, "Statement by NSC Spokesperson Ned Price on Today's Terrorist Attack in Ankara, Turkey" (Washington, DC: The White House, 2015), https://obamawhitehouse.archives.gov/the-press-office/2015/10/10/statement-nsc-spokesperson-ned-price-todays-terrorist-attack-ankara.

[2] Barak Obama, "Statement by the President on the Attack in France" (Washington, DC: The White House, 2015), https://obamawhitehouse.archives.gov/the-press-office/2015/01/07/statement-president-attack-france.

Using computer algorithms, the overall sentiment of the text is labeled positive, negative, or neutral based on indicators of joy, anger, satisfaction, disappointment, or other emotions.

After running both texts through sentiment analysis software, intriguing disparities between Erdogan's and Hollande's calls emerge. Erdogan's call had a positivity tone of 75.4 percent, and Hollande's call boasted a striking 85.8 percent positivity tone. These discrepancies become apparent when we examine the highlighted words in the readouts. The conversation with Erdogan emanates a sense of camaraderie between allies but lacks the intimacy that permeates Hollande's call. Hollande's conversation exudes a much more personal and intimate vibe, as if it were a heartfelt exchange between longtime friends. These subtle cues could have significant implications for how the public perceives the cultural proximity between the United States and other nations.

A rich history of intellectual and philosophical exchange exists between the United States and France. Renowned French philosophers and thinkers such as Voltaire and Jean-Jacques Rousseau undeniably influenced American intellectual thought. Furthermore, the United States and France share fundamental values and principles, including democracy, human rights, freedom of expression, and the pursuit of individual liberties. Although cultural differences certainly exist between the two nations, the profound cultural closeness between the United States and France remains evident. This closeness is characterized by historical ties, artistic exchanges, shared values, and mutual influence.

Conversely, due to their disparate histories, languages, and traditions, the United States and Turkey have experienced limited direct interactions until recent times. These limitations shape how these two cultures are perceived and understood.

The data presented thus far reveal two noteworthy patterns. First, individuals who demonstrate a heightened level of interest in government affairs and political news are more likely to hold concerns regarding the occurrence of future terrorist attacks in the United States. Second, perceptions of cultural proximity can be swayed by signals emanating from political leaders, with positive sentiments being expressed toward a particular nation following a terrorist attack. In essence, it is reasonable to infer that people direct greater attention toward events that possess spatial and cultural proximity to their own lives.

In the next section, I focus on the concept of spatial proximity, scrutinizing how individuals alter their behavior when confronted with the immediate ramifications of a terrorist attack. Here I explore changes in individual behavior after mass shootings in Texas.

TO CARRY OR NOT TO CARRY? TEXAS LICENSE TO CARRY AFTER MASS SHOOTING

The FBI lacks an official definition for mass shootings, a fact that may catch some people off guard. The bureau has established a definition for mass murder, however: "a number of murders (four or more) occurring during the same incident, with no distinctive time period between the murders."[28] The baseline for this definition was revised in 2013 through Public Law 112–265, and it now encompasses incidents in which three or more victims are killed.[29] Therefore, any occurrence in which a minimum of three individuals are murdered within a continuous time frame and at a specific location can be categorized as a mass shooting.

From 1982 to 2022, a staggering toll of mass shootings unfolded across thirty-seven states, claiming the lives of more than 1,000 individuals and leaving an additional 1,500 wounded.[30] Despite discrepancies in definitions, one undeniable fact emerges: we have witnessed an alarming surge in mass shootings in the United States in recent years, with an annual growth rate of 32 percent. This trajectory has engendered a disheartening phenomenon of desensitization, rendering us numb to the frequency of these avoidable tragedies in which a perilous sense of complacency prevails, accompanied by a failure to fully grasp the profound gravity that accompanies these events.[31]

The Lone Star State has witnessed numerous incidents of mass shootings. The earliest systematic record with a national focus originates from

Mother Jones magazine in the mid-1980s, but their database has diligently chronicled cases since 1982, ensuring regular updates to its dark and sad collection.[32] Among the chronicles lies a disturbing event that unfolded in June 1984, when a thirty-nine-year-old man unleashed a shooting spree in an upscale nightclub in Dallas, Texas. His heinous act claimed the lives of six individuals and was driven by his anger over a woman's rejection. Before the Texas First Baptist Church massacre in Sutherland Springs, where a twenty-six-year-old former U.S. Air Force airman mercilessly ended the lives of twenty-six worshipers during Sunday services, the Killeen massacre of October 1991 held the gruesome distinction of having the highest number of fatalities. As reported by the *New York Times*, a troubled thirty-five-year-old man, described as "impatient and troubled," drove his pickup truck into a Luby's cafeteria and unleashed a barrage of gunfire that extinguished the lives of twenty-four people.[33] Another heart-wrenching chapter unfolded on May 24, 2022, when an eighteen-year-old gunman, armed with an AR-15–style rifle, perpetrated a mass shooting at Robb Elementary School in Uvalde, Texas. This senseless act of violence claimed the lives of nineteen innocent children and two teachers, forever marking it as the deadliest school shooting since the heartbreaking tragedy at Sandy Hook Elementary School in Connecticut in 2012. The memories of that horrific day, where twenty children and six adults fell victim to unfathomable evil, still resonate.

In the wake of a tragic mass shooting, the public's response echoes with fear, grief, and a resounding call for decisive action to confront the persisting scourge of gun violence. People grapple with a collective trauma, and the emotional weight of these events bears heavily on their hearts. The American Psychological Association illuminates the distressing aftermath of mass shootings: heightened levels of anxiety and fear grip people of all ages, especially children who harbor genuine concerns regarding the threat of an attack within their schools.[34] The once unthinkable fear of being ensnared in a mass shooting has insidiously entwined itself into the fabric of our reality, instilling worries about personal safety and triggering a distressing inclination toward avoiding public spaces.[35] In the digital age, social media platforms have emerged as vital outlets for individuals to channel and express their immediate reactions. Through real-time updates, these platforms offer a glimpse into the profound emotional impact of mass shootings on the collective psyche. Analyzing Twitter data following acts of violence in Atlanta, Boulder, Las Vegas, and El Paso, one bears witness to the raw emotions that emerge as people deal with the overwhelming horror in an effort to make their voices heard in the face of such appalling acts of violence.[36]

Within a cacophony of "thoughts and prayers" from the National Rifle Association and elected officials, a resounding cry for action and policy reforms reverberates throughout the public. The demand for stricter gun control measures, enhanced access to mental health services, and intensified surveillance of social media to identify potential threats grows ever louder.[37] These pleas surge in the aftermath of every mass shooting, a testament to the mounting frustration felt by the public. But in the intricate landscape of Texas, the pursuit of gun control reform proves to be a complex endeavor.

Since 2009, the University of Texas *Texas Tribune* (UT/TT) polls have consistently revealed a noteworthy trend: a substantial segment of the Texas population, ranging between 40 and 50 percent, consistently support stricter gun laws. The remaining 60 to 50 percent either express support for the existing legislation or support even less restrictive measures.[38]

Despite the desire for greater firearms regulation by a significant number of Texans, the realization of such measures hinges on the actions undertaken by the state legislature, where stricter gun laws remain aspirational for those looking to safeguard themselves through limiting firearm accessibility. Complicating this predicament is the fact that the Republican-controlled legislature aligns itself with the minority who are advocating for less stringent gun laws. This is manifest in their stance on policies that expand the permissible areas for firearms, broaden eligibility criteria for gun possession in educational institutions, and grant the right to openly carry firearms without a permit. Within this cocktail of policies, spatial proximity emerges as a pivotal factor influencing the call for stricter gun laws. People residing in closer proximity to mass shooting sites exhibit a greater inclination to support stringent gun control measures than their counterparts residing farther away. A June 2022 UT/TT poll conducted shortly after the Robb Elementary mass shooting illustrates this divide. It shows a higher proportion of residents in the San Antonio and El Paso areas, which have borne witness to the tragic events in Uvalde, Sutherland Springs, and El Paso, favor stricter gun laws than residents in north central Texas, Amarillo, and Lubbock.[39]

The residents of Uvalde were engulfed by a mix of anger and frustration as they grappled with the aftermath of a botched police response. Among those who hurried to the scene to aid their loved ones was Ruben Ruiz, a school district police officer and the husband of a teacher at Robb Elementary School. Heartbreakingly, his noble intentions were thwarted when fellow police officers intercepted him, disarmed him, and forcibly escorted him away from the school premises.[40] This chain of events elicited shock, grief, and an unwavering demand for accountability within the community, but reactions throughout the state of Texas showcased a wide spectrum of responses. Public discourse surrounding gun policies and strategies for addressing mass shootings surged to the forefront, with experts underscoring the imperative of comprehensive solutions rather than engaging in narrow debates.[41] As the dust settled, a report published by a Texas House of Representatives investigative committee shed light on a litany of failures and an overall negligent approach exhibited by the responding officers, further deepening the sense of dismay and righteous indignation.[42]

Following a mass shooting a distinct response emerges that diverges from the customary offering of "thoughts and prayers" or calls for stricter gun control laws. This alternative reaction manifests in people seeking the acquisition of firearms as a means of self-protection. The Trace, a nonprofit news agency committed to reporting on gun violence nationwide, has uncovered a notable surge in gun sales following such tragic events. Texas, too, bears witness to this trend, as Caroline Covington's analysis for the *Texas Tribune* illuminates. In the aftermath of the El Paso, Santa Fe, and Sutherland Springs shootings, the number of background checks conducted for firearm purchases soared by almost 10 percent, underscoring the tangible impact of these incidents on the public psyche.[43]

In Texas, existing laws grant gun owners the right to store their firearms within the confines of their vehicles and residences. Furthermore, as of 2021, individuals who are at least twenty-one years old and meet the federal and Texas legal requirements for handgun purchases and possession may exercise the privilege of openly carrying a firearm, as outlined in HB-1927, commonly known as the "constitutional carry bill." Not all Texans can openly carry, people with recent convictions for specified felonies—including assault, deadly conduct, terroristic threats, or disorderly conduct—within the past five years are prohibited from openly carrying firearms. In addition, certain spaces are designated as off limits for firearm possession under Texas law. This includes schools and educational facilities, higher education institutions, as well as areas where school-sponsored activities are taking place. Open carry is also expressly prohibited at specific locations, such as polling places, courts, racetracks, airport security zones, bars, professional sporting events, correctional facilities, hospitals, nursing homes, mental health facilities, amusement parks, and public meeting rooms of government agencies. In addition, private establishments such as supermarkets, gyms, shopping malls, and stores hold the authority to prohibit the open carry of weapons by posting signs explicitly stating that entry into their premises with openly carried weapons is strictly prohibited, in accordance with Section 30.07 of the Texas Penal Code.[44]

Purchasing a firearm and openly carrying it may not be the optimum strategy for individuals seeking self-protection because HB-1927 imposes certain limitations on the locations where firearms can be carried. Conversely, obtaining a Texas License to Carry (LTC) offers a broader range of options within the confines of the law. This license gives specific protections to its holders, including unintentional firearm possession in secured airport areas, authorization to carry in government meetings, and the ability to bear arms in private establishments or institutions of higher education where open carry is otherwise prohibited.

Do individuals exhibit a higher likelihood of applying for an LTC following a mass shooting near their neighborhood? To answer this question I use data from the Texas Department of Public Safety (DPS), which routinely compiles and publishes a comprehensive array of statistics related to concealed carry applications, including gender, race, and zip code.[45]

To begin the analysis, I examine the issuance of concealed weapons permits from a broader perspective. Over the span of fiscal year 2016 to 2022, the Texas DPS granted a total of 2,407,656 licenses. Notably, the years marked by the disruptive impact of the COVID-19 pandemic (2020–2021) witnessed a remarkable surge in firearm licenses issued, with a staggering 860,429 permits granted. This figure accounts for more than one-third of the total licenses issued during this period, illustrating the significant influence of the pandemic on the demand for LTCs. The spike during this period is truly remarkable, with a momentous 182 percent increase from 2019 to 2020–21 (see figure 3.2).

One of the most interesting observations from the data over the course of this period was a 6 percent increase in the number of licenses granted to minorities while the number of permits issued to whites decreased by 2 percent. Even taking into account the significant decrease in applications between 2021 and 2022 due to the open carry rule that went into effect on

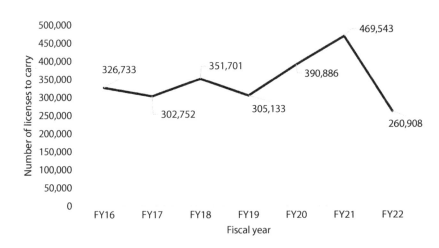

FIGURE 3.2 Total number of Licenses to Carry (LTCs) in Texas in fiscal year 2016 to 2022.

Source: Data from Texas Department of Public Safety.

September 1, 2021, Blacks saw an 11 percent increase in applications, followed by multiracial individuals (7 percent) and Asian-Pacific Islanders (5 percent). This growth was largely fueled by a 20 percent increase in permits granted to Black women. Gun violence affects individuals from all walks of life, but evidence suggests that certain minority communities may face disproportionate impacts. Studies have highlighted the disparities and higher rates of gun violence within minority communities, particularly in urban settings.

Extensive research consistently highlights a distressing reality: communities of color endure disproportionately high levels of gun violence when compared to the broader population.[46] The statistics speak volumes. Blacks, for instance, face a harrowing truth—they are at least four times more likely to fall victim to gun-related fatalities than the general population, and a staggering twelve times more likely to do so than their white counterparts.[47] These alarming disparities in gun violence rates serve as a catalyst, driving an increase in applications for licenses as individuals seek means to protect themselves and their communities from the pervasive threats they face (see figure 3.3).

Allow me to restate the question: Is there a correlation between proximity to a mass shooting and an upsurge in applications for concealed handgun permits? To shed light on this question, I want to focus on the Walmart shooting in El Paso on August 3, 2019. In this incident, twenty-three people died and twenty-six others were wounded at the hands of a convicted gunman who embarked on an eleven-hour drive from the outskirts of Dallas to El Paso. The shooter's explicit motive was to target immigrants and Latinos. Prior to the attack he published a 2,300-word manifesto titled "The Inconvenient Truth," which was riddled with white supremacist rhetoric, espoused opposition to "race mixing," and urged immigrants to return to their countries of origin. The shooter's deranged mind was fueled by a racist motivation—to instill fear in the Latino community in El Paso where the population is 82 percent Latinx and across the nation. His own words bear testimony to this intent: "The reason behind this attack is the Hispanic invasion of Texas. They are the ones responsible, not me. I am just safeguarding my country from the cultural and ethnic substitution that has resulted from this invasion."[48]

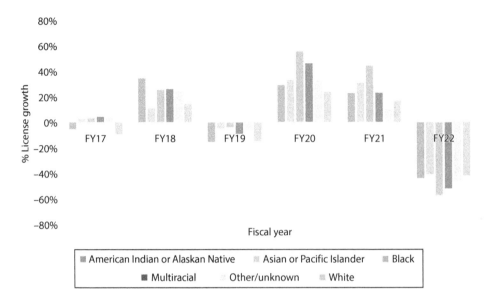

FIGURE 3.3 Percent growth in Licenses to Carry in Texas by race and fiscal year.

Source: Data from the Texas Department of Public Safety.

Figure 3.4 unveils the striking bivariate relationship between the issuance of License to Carry permits in 2019 and 2020. The map serves as a visual depiction, contrasting the number of licenses granted within each zip code of the City of El Paso relative to the location of the mass shooting. Employing a bivariate color scheme, the map effectively portrays a grid adorned with four distinctive hues, strategically highlighting the highest and lowest values within the dataset. Notably, the presence of a black grid signifies a robust correlation between the number of LTCs issued in 2019 and 2020. For instance, focus on the noteworthy statistics within zip code 77934. In 2019 this particular area witnessed the issuance of 346 LTCs. Fast forward to 2020 and an impressive 513 licenses were granted—a notable growth of 48 percent. These figures illustrate the palpable increase in demand for LTC permits within this specific region.

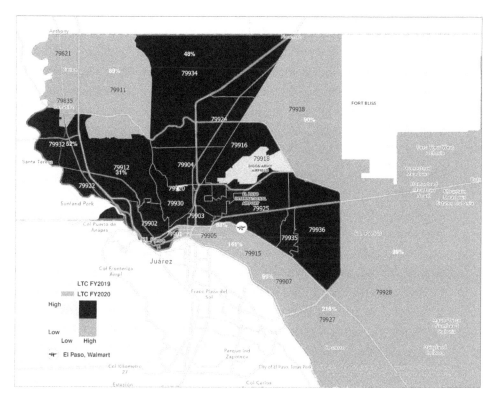

FIGURE 3.4 The increasing number of LTC permits in El Paso from 2019 to 2020.

Source: Data from the Texas Department of Public Safety.

The lower right quadrant, depicted in a distinctive dark gray shade, illuminates the zip codes wherein the number of licenses issued experienced a significant surge in 2020 compared to 2019. Take, for instance, zip code 79925—the location of the mass shooting. The striking statistics reveal a remarkable increase of 218 percent between 2019 and 2020. The license count soared from 90 to 286 in the aftermath of this tragic incident, signifying a profound shift in the demand for licenses within the affected community.

Texas was not alone in experiencing this trend. The terrorist attack that unfolded in San Bernardino, California, provides another illustration of this phenomenon. On December 2, 2015, a heavily armed couple unleashed a deadly shooting spree at a social service center, resulting in the tragic loss of at least fourteen lives and leaving seventeen others wounded.[49] Adding to the gravity of the situation, the attackers had publicly declared their allegiance to the Islamic State on social media just moments before perpetrating the attack. The incident took place during a Christmas party hosted at the Inland Regional Center, a facility dedicated to serving individuals with disabilities.[50]

In the aftermath of the San Bernardino shooting, a notable pattern emerged.[51] Among the residents of San Bernardino, gun sales experienced a substantial 85 percent surge, surpassing the overall statewide increase of 35 percent in California. Similarly, following the mass shooting in El Paso, the issuance of concealed firearms licenses witnessed a remarkable 66 percent rise. The number of firearm licenses granted skyrocketed from 4,709 in 2019 to 7,810 in 2020. When analyzing the average number of licenses within El Paso's zip codes, a significant discrepancy emerged. For 2019 the average stood at 181 licenses, and in 2020 it surged to 300—a difference of 119 ($p < 0.05$), suggesting that an external shock was the driving force behind this growth. The rest of the state and other areas experienced a 27 percent increase in the number of licenses issued during this time—a substantial jump but one that paled in comparison to the surge witnessed in El Paso.

In this chapter I have presented evidence highlighting the influential role of space and time in shaping our attitudes and behaviors. It underscores the profound impact that the specific location and timing of events can have on our emotional responses. This analysis revealed that significant shocks, such as terrorist attacks or mass shootings, can serve as catalysts, triggering a cascade of cognitive appraisals that deeply influence our attitudes and behaviors as we grapple with the anticipation of potential future harm. Although this analysis does not establish causation, the observed correlations undeniably reflect genuine connections between space, time, and our emotional states. Moreover, the intricate interplay between our external and internal environments is analyzed, shedding light on how contextual factors and emotions hold sway in the formation of our attitudes. Building on this crucial insight, chapter 4 explores the role of spatial distance in shaping our attitudes toward social movements.

4

PROTESTS

#BlackLivesMatter

Embedded in the fabric of the U.S. Constitution, the First Amendment safeguards the far-reaching right to free speech, which goes beyond mere verbal expression to include the rights to peacefully assemble and petition, in other words the right to protest, which lies at the very core of a functioning democracy.[1] The right to protest is an indispensable conduit for citizens to voice their opinions and hold those in positions of power accountable. Although at times it may seem noisy and disruptive, the right of peaceful assembly can foster deep social change and preserve individual rights.

Protests have been a part of our nation's history since the latter half of the seventeenth century. It is through these demonstrations that ordinary citizens have ignited institutional change. From the transformative Boston Tea Party of 1773, defying the British government's taxes on tea imports, to the Black Lives Matter movement of 2020, protesting police brutality against communities of color, these demonstrations bear witness to the continuing search for civil rights, gender equality, women's enfranchisement, income inequality, antiabortion, and climate change. Protesters fight for justice, demand change, and disrupt the status quo.

Peaceful protests provide a vital avenue for political participation. The civil rights movement, for example, compelled the White House to prioritize the pressing issues of racial segregation and voting rights.[2] Similarly, protests during the Vietnam War fueled the demand for increased congressional hearings, guaranteeing that the concerns of the people were heard by those in power. Protests have the potential to change the status quo and shape public opinion. In the 1960s, for instance, white Southerners residing in districts where protests against segregation unfolded were more inclined to lend their support.[3] However, the scale, intensity, and local context of these demonstrations also influence people's attitudes toward social movements. In some cases, political hostility is created based on the magnitude and the distance people are from the location of the protest.[4] In other cases, attitudes vary based on the demographics and the intensity of protest activities.[5] Sometimes an "on-the-ground effect" moderates support for the protesters.[6]

In this chapter I draw on the rich data derived from the American National Election Studies (ANES) of 2020. I examine the impact of spatial distance from a demonstration on individuals' attitudes toward the Black Lives Matter movement. I also explore how these attitudes sway people's perceptions regarding the most effective approaches to deal with urban unrest, particularly concerning their proximity to a demonstration and the dynamics of distance and its influence on people's sympathy levels toward the Black Lives Matter movement. In particular, I want to explore whether this sympathy, or its absence, plays a pivotal role in shaping individuals' decision-making processes concerning the resolution of issues tied to racism and police violence and how their perspectives align with the maintenance of law and order during urban unrest.

SOCIAL JUSTICE AND THE BLACK LIVES MATTER MOVEMENT

The year 2014 wrote itself into the annals of history with a tragic event—the shooting of eighteen-year-old Michael Brown by a white police officer in Ferguson, Missouri. The shooting ignited protests against the excessive and disproportionate use of deadly force by police against minorities and gave rise to the nationwide social movement known as Black Lives Matter (BLM), which aimed to bring attention to and address the mistreatment of Blacks and other minorities by law enforcement.

Six years later a series of fatal shootings further fueled the movement. Among the tragic cases that shook the nation in 2020 was the killing of Ahmaud Arbery, a twenty-five-year-old Black man mercilessly gunned down while jogging in Brunswick, Georgia, on February 23. Months later, the release of a video depicting two white men pursuing and ultimately ending Arbery's life reverberated across the nation, capturing national attention and stirring widespread outrage. Another case that shocked public opinion was the tragic death of Breonna Taylor—an innocent twenty-six-year-old Black woman—during the execution of a "no-knock" warrant at her apartment in Louisville, Kentucky. Taylor was met with an onslaught of gunfire by the police, including five fatal shots. This devastating incident further fueled the fire and solidified the urgent need for change within the criminal justice system.

May 25, 2020, will forever remain fixed in our memory: a cell phone video captured the horrifying killing of George Floyd, an unarmed Black man, at the hands of a white police officer in Minneapolis, Minnesota. This event became the catalyst that ignited a nationwide "conversation" about policing in America and the treatment of minorities, shining a searing spotlight on the quandary of Black Americans whose encounters with law enforcement are marred by an egregious lack of respect and a distressing pattern of excessive force.

Merely two days later we received news of yet another death. Tony McDade, a Black transgender man, was fatally shot by a police officer in Tallahassee, Florida. This thrust into the limelight the intersectional nature of police violence and the alarming and disproportionate impact it inflicts on transgender people of color.

The deaths of Michael Brown, Ahmaud Arbery, Breonna Taylor, George Floyd, and Tony McDade reverberated with an intensity that transcended boundaries, galvanizing the Black Lives Matter movement. These killings sparked impassioned protests against police violence and the systemic racism that engulfed the country. These tragedies became stark reminders of the enduring problems of racial profiling, use of force by law enforcement, and the pervasive systemic injustices that plague Black and other marginalized communities. Communities across the country and the world passionately demanded a profound shift that guarantees justice, dismantles barriers, and wholeheartedly embraces inclusivity and equality under the law.

The haunting reality of people of color falling victim to law enforcement persists, with countless cases left undocumented due to a dearth of reliable statistics. An eye-opening investigation conducted by the *Washington Post* uncovered a staggering truth: FBI data on police shootings were underreported by more than 50 percent. The primary reason behind this alarming discrepancy lies in the fact that police departments are not mandated to report such incidents to the federal government.[7]

From 2015 to January 2023, the statistics reveal that 8,166 individuals met a tragic fate, fatally shot during encounters with police officers. It is important to note that half of those shot were white, but there is a disproportionate impact on Black Americans. Despite constituting only 14 percent of the U.S. population, Black Americans face more than double the likelihood of being shot by police than their white counterparts. Similarly, Latinx also bear the brunt of this injustice, enduring a disproportionate toll of police shootings.[8]

Given the essence of our laws, values, and historical struggles, the BLM movement emerged as a morally and politically justified response to these egregious injustices. However, the movement found itself entangled in a web of political polarization. The vital issue of equal treatment before the law—the core of their cause—was silenced in the noise of partisan battles fought by talking heads on cable news channels.

"I CAN'T BREATHE"

The video capturing George Floyd's death shook us to our very core—an unsettling testament of police brutality and deep-rooted racism. The indelible image of a white police officer cruelly kneeling on the neck of a defenseless Black man already restrained and pleading for his life illuminated the injustices that people of color endure on a daily basis. In those horrifying moments, the phrase "I can't breathe" echoed with chilling clarity. George Floyd voiced those words more than twenty times, but his desperate pleas were met with indifference as the police officer mercilessly pressed his knee against Floyd's neck for an agonizing nine minutes. The cruelty persisted even after Floyd became unresponsive.[9] This revolting act became a spark, igniting a fervent wave of protests and unleashing a storm of unrest that reverberated not only across the United States but also around the globe. The phrase "I can't breathe" became a resounding cry for all those who fight for social justice and meaningful police reform. It serves as a powerful reminder that every individual—irrespective of their race, ethnicity, sexual orientation, or background—must be treated with dignity, respect, and fairness.

In the demonstrations sparked by the tragic killing of George Floyd, a striking contrast emerged—a narrative of calm and peaceful protests during the day were transformed into chaotic nights shadowed by acts of aggression, with incidents of gunfire, theft, and destruction.[10] In reaction to this turn of events, a harmonious collective voice arose, with governors, municipal authorities, and police chiefs grappling with the intensifying unrest. In Minneapolis, Minnesota, for example, protesters were met with a heavy hand. Tear gas and rubber bullets were used as law enforcement sought to disperse crowds. In tandem, Minnesota Governor Tim Walz took decisive action, activating the National Guard to restore order, and a loud tweet from President Donald Trump delivered an ultimatum to protesters: "These THUGS are dishonoring the memory of George Floyd, and I won't let that happen. Just spoke to Governor Tim Walz and told him that the Military is with him all the way. Any difficulty and we will assume control but, when the looting starts, the shooting starts. Thank you!" Trump's choice of words bore a striking resemblance to the racist rhetoric employed by former Miami Police Chief Walter Headley during the civil rights movement in the 1960s to discredit it.[11]

In analyzing the government response, a noteworthy pattern emerged: once protests turned violent, law enforcement's response transcended the boundaries of partisan affiliations. Democratic-run cities such as New York and Philadelphia found themselves entangled in clashes between protesters and police. Pepper spray and arrests became the norm as law enforcement sought to regain control.[12] However, behind the veil of political rhetoric, a palpable partisan divide existed. Democrats, for the most part, recognized the protests as catalysts for change, emphasizing the urgent need to address systemic racism and societal inequality. In contrast, although some Republicans acknowledged the concerns raised by the movement and acknowledged racial disparities within policing, many viewed the protests through a negative lens.[13] Senator Tom Cotton of Arkansas fueled the controversy with his op-ed in the *New York Times* advocating for the utilization of military force to suppress the protests.[14]

A seismic wave of protests against police brutality emerged in 2020, producing a wide range of opinions and reactions that starkly revealed the deep divisions within the public falling along party lines. Democrats and Republicans found themselves rooted in opposing views, intensely held and fueled by their respective ideologies. Although contrasting in nature, these views converged in their determination and conviction.[15] Despite political differences unity emerged. Across racial and ethnic lines, majorities from diverse backgrounds lent their support to the BLM movement, accentuating a shared acknowledgment of the urgent need for change.[16] This broad recognition echoed globally, transcending borders and resonating with countless individuals who viewed the protests as a response to the systemic racism and pervasive police violence suffered by Black Americans and marginalized communities. In South Africa, members of the Economic Freedom Fighters took to the streets, staging a demonstration outside the U.S. Consulate in Sandton, standing in solidarity with BLM.[17] Even magazines typically centered on celebrities, fashion trends, and beauty tips, such as *Marie Claire*, rallied behind the global movement, shedding light on the profound impact it carried.[18] In Brazil, demonstrators in Rio de Janeiro joined the global community, raising their voices against racial violence and inequality, and in Sweden citizens in Stockholm stood united, participating in protests as evidence of their solidarity.[19]

After Floyd's tragic murder, support for the BLM movement and the urgent call for police reform surged, aligning with a pronounced increase in public attention toward the BLM agenda.[20] However, as with any powerful movement, opposing voices emerged that were critical of the protests and voiced concerns about the violence, property damage, and disruption associated with some demonstrators.[21] These individuals questioned the underlying goals of the protests, contending that the issue of police brutality was exaggerated or that the protests were fueled by obscure political agendas rather than by a genuine concern for social justice.[22] In the heart of the nationwide protests against police brutality and systemic racism, former Fox News host Tucker Carlson incited further tension with a statement that intensified an already delicate situation. Carlson's claim that the protests were "definitely not about Black lives" garnered widespread criticism because it undermined the fundamental significance of the BLM movement and the profound importance of addressing the pervasive problem of police violence against Black individuals. Many perceived Carlson's remarks not only as racially insensitive but as actively harmful, particularly considering the enduring racial disparities that continue to afflict our society.[23]

During the chaotic summer of 2020, one truth emerged: public opinion stood sharply divided, and individuals on both sides of the spectrum were expressing firm and intense emotions. This division begs these fundamental questions: Did proximity to the protests and individuals' stance on the BLM movement have an impact in shaping their attitudes toward the most effective approaches to address urban unrest? Would they favor employing force or advocate for reforming the existing status quo?

ADDRESSING ROOT CAUSES OF RACISM VS. LAW AND ORDER

On July 3, 2020, the *New York Times* published an article titled "Black Lives Matter May Be the Largest Movement in U.S. History."[24] In their article the authors exploited the power of the Crowd Counting Consortium—an innovative collaboration that aggregates publicly available data on crowd sizes across the United States supplemented by meticulous aerial photography. Working in tandem with Edwin Chow of Texas State University, the reporters revealed a staggering peak on June 6, 2020, with an approximate participation of 500,000 individuals joining nearly 550 demonstrations sprawled across the nation. By mid-July, their analysis suggested an astounding range of fifteen to twenty-six million people who had protested in the United States based on survey estimates, making it the largest mobilization in the nation's history. According to the Crowd Counting Consortium, a more conservative approximation indicates that over 9,600 demonstrations occurred throughout the United States from May to July 2020 with a cumulative participation of approximately 2.5 million individuals—a testament to the profound impact of the BLM movement (see table 4.1).

Despite these staggering statistics, support for the BLM movement experienced a gradual decline over time, leaving a picture of shifting sentiments in its wake.[25] Insights from a September 2020 poll conducted by the Pew Research Center sheds light on this changing landscape. In the aftermath of the protests triggered by the shooting of Jacob Blake, a majority of U.S. adults (55 percent) still expressed varying degrees of support for the movement—a noticeable drop from the robust 67 percent recorded in June.[26] Examining the nuances within this decline, the impact was particularly discernible among white and Hispanic adults. In June, a solid 60 percent of white adults and an impressive 77 percent of Hispanics offered their support to the movement. However, three months later, these figures diminished, with only 45 percent of white adults and 66 percent of Hispanics continuing to give their support. In stark contrast, the support among

TABLE 4.1 Average marchers and total demonstrations, May–July 2020

	MAY	JUNE	JULY	TOTAL
Average marchers	401,704	2,061,315	97,026	2,560,044
Total events	1,439	6,756	1,497	9,692

Source: Author's data and data from the Crowd Counting Consortium.

Black adults remained strong, with approximately 87 percent continuing to champion the cause.[27]

In a conflict along party lines, the gap between support for the BLM movement widened, highlighting the contrasting perspectives embedded in the political landscape. There was a substantial decline in support by those identifying as Republicans or leaning toward the Republican Party, plummeting from 37 percent in June to a mere 16 percent by September 2020. Conversely, sentiments among Democrats and individuals aligned with the Democratic Party showed a relatively steady trajectory throughout this period. Their commitment to the BLM movement remained resilient, with an enduring 92 percent expressing support in June and a decline to 88 percent by September.[28]

The contrasting views held by Democrats and Republicans are apparent, and understanding the impact of protests on public support for a social movement and its objectives requires a close examination of distance and context. For example, when individuals feel empowered by the protests, a sense of solidarity with the movement tends to emerge, whereas those who perceive the protests as menacing are more inclined to adopt an opposing stance, having reservations toward social change in the aftermath.[29]

The influence of distance and context on public support and attitudes toward social movements and their goals cannot be overstated. Proximity has the potential to shape individuals' sentiments toward the BLM movement and their perspectives on urban unrest. Those near protest locations may have had a firsthand experience, leading to reinforced emotions and strong opinions regarding the movement and the underlying issues. In contrast, individuals farther away may rely more on media coverage to shape their viewpoint, having less direct contact with the events. Supporters of the BLM movement may be more inclined to view the protests as a necessary tool to draw attention to systemic problems and advocate for police reform, whereas those who lack sympathy for the movement may perceive the protests as disruptive and unnecessary and support any means to maintain law and order.

Distance and context may exert considerable influence over people's perceptions of the BLM movement and their attitudes toward the protests.

Proximity to events can evoke intense reactions and shape opinions, and media coverage may play a significant role in shaping the viewpoints of those with limited direct contact. These factors contribute to the divergence in views on the movement and the strategies used to address social issues and maintain order.

In terms of context, the racial composition of communities is a crucial factor that may influence individuals' support for the BLM movement. Studies suggest that people living in racially diverse areas tend to exhibit more favorable attitudes toward racial justice movements such as BLM.[30] The role of violence in shaping public support is also significant. Residents of areas that have experienced higher levels of violence may be less supportive of social movements and more inclined to view the protests as destructive and counterproductive.[31] However, research findings on this matter are mixed, with some studies revealing that exposure to violence during protests increases support for social movements.[32]

It is important to recognize that people's attitudes toward urban unrest are multifaceted and depend on various factors, including political ideology, preexisting beliefs about the effectiveness of protests in bringing about change, and other individual-specific elements. Media coverage also plays a significant role in shaping public opinion. The way protests are portrayed in the media can undermine the goals of social movements and influence how the public perceives these demonstrations.[33] The classification of protests as violent or peaceful, legitimate or illegitimate, can profoundly sway public opinion and the responses of policymakers.

When media coverage focuses on the radical or violent aspects of a protest, Summer Harlow emphasizes that this can delegitimize the cause and question the legitimacy of the protesters' grievances. Conversely, protests that align with the status quo or support conservative values are more likely to receive positive media coverage, which can legitimize their grievances and garner greater public support. Harlow's research reveals a striking disparity in media coverage between conservative protests and Black Lives Matter protests. According to Harlow, "articles about conservative protests—like those against immigration or LGBT rights, or those supporting Trump and gun rights—are less likely to be negatively labeled as 'riots' compared to other types of protests. In contrast, Black Lives Matter protests are more likely to be framed as riots, with news coverage focusing more on the violence, property damage, and confrontations with police."[34]

In the larger context, the interaction between factors such as racial composition, exposure to violence, and personal beliefs greatly shapes individuals' perceptions of the BLM movement and their stance on protests and urban unrest. The media further contributes to this dynamic by framing protests in a way that aligns with established norms or political ideologies. Selectively highlighting certain aspects can distort the public's perception of these events.

PUTTING EVERYTHING TOGETHER

Figure 4.1 provides a visual depiction of the spatial clustering and offers insights into areas of high concentration relative to neighboring units in comparison with overall data patterns. The circles indicate hot spots where there is a notable concentration of individuals who hold favorable views toward the BLM movement. Figure 4.2, in contrast, maps the spatial clustering among people who believe in employing all available means to maintain law and order during urban unrest.

The maps provide interesting insights into the perspectives of residents in various cities across the United States. In Boston, New York, Washington, D.C., Chicago, San Francisco, and Seattle, a higher likelihood of expressing positive sentiments toward the BLM movement is evident. The data reveals statistically significant hot spots in these cities, indicating strong support with 99 percent confidence intervals (see figure 4.1).

In the South and Midwest, however, Dallas, Naples, Columbus, Nashville, Charlotte, and Jefferson demonstrate hot spots in which individuals believe that addressing issues of racism and police violence necessitates employing any means necessary to maintain law and order (see figure 4.2). These results are crucial given the bimodal nature of attitudes toward the BLM movement. The data reveals that 19 percent of respondents reported a value of zero degrees on the feeling thermometer, indicating negative sentiments

FIGURE 4.1 Hot spot analysis of people who hold positive views about the Black Lives Matter ratings.

Source: Data from ANES 2020.

FIGURE 4.2 Hot spot analysis of people who think the use of all available force is the best way to deal with urban unrest.

Source: Data from ANES 2020.

toward the movement. Conversely, 15 percent reported a value of 100 degrees, indicating positive sentiments. The mean value of the feeling thermometer was 53 degrees, suggesting a relatively neutral overall sentiment toward the movement, a finding supported by the median value of 60 degrees.

After examining the survey data regarding attitudes toward racism and police violence, the difference in opinions among respondents becomes clear. Approximately 35 percent of participants expressed the belief that addressing racism and police violence is extremely important in effectively tackling urban unrest. In contrast, 18 percent of respondents leaned toward the viewpoint that employing all available means to maintain law and order is necessary, suggesting a prioritization of security over resolving police violence and issues of racism. Only 13 percent of participants assumed a neutral stance, representing a lack of a decisive opinion. These results highlight the intriguing spectrum of perspectives regarding the approach to combating racism and police violence. Although a significant portion of respondents exhibit a willingness to confront these issues head on, a distinct minority leans toward using more aggressive law enforcement measures to address urban unrest.

Next I examined the relationship between the management of urban unrest and the public's stance on the BLM movement. To investigate this, I employed a statistical method called two-stage least squares (2SLS) regression. This approach is useful when addressing endogeneity, which occurs when the predictors in a linear regression are potentially mutually related. In simpler terms, it helps navigate situations in which variables are entwined, making it challenging to determine their relationship. The 2SLS regression estimates the relationship between the variables. The first step is to identify a set of predictors that have an impact on the endogenous variable but remain unaffected by it. In the second step, these variables are used to predict the endogenous variable. The primary objectives are twofold: mitigating bias stemming from endogeneity and generating more accurate estimates of the relationship between the variables.[35]

In the first stage (see table A.4.1 in the appendix for regression results), I identified a range of variables that predict the public's attitudes toward the BLM movement, measured on a scale from 0 to 100. These variables encompassed diversity, party identification (spanning from strong Democrat to strong Republican), race (including white, Black, Hispanic, Asian, Native American, and multiracial), age (ranging from eighteen to eighty years), income (spanning from less than $9,000 to over $250,000), news attention (ranging from always to never), education (ranging from less than high school to professional), and gender (female and male).[36]

In the second stage (see table A.4.2 in the appendix for regression results), I used the predicted values of BLM as a variable in the equation that gauges individuals' attitudes toward addressing urban unrest, which range from 1 (solving problems of racism and police) to 7 (using all available force to maintain social order). In addition, I incorporated the distance between the respondent's state and the protest site to explore how proximity might influence attitudes.

After running the 2SLS regression, two key findings emerged that deserve attention. First, as expected, the results indicate that individuals with a more positive disposition toward the BLM movement are less inclined to endorse the use of all available force to maintain law and order, whereas those who are further removed from the protests are more likely to support the use of force in managing urban unrest.

Distance encompasses more than just geographic proximity. As discussed in chapter 1, distance also includes emotional closeness or distance that significantly influences our attitudes and actions. Individuals who possess a strong emotional connection to the BLM movement, indicating a positive attachment to its cause, are less inclined to endorse extreme measures for maintaining order. In contrast, individuals who experience spatial distance are more prone to endorsing force to suppress urban unrest. These findings underscore the crucial role played by both emotional and geographic proximity in shaping our perceptions and attitudes toward social issues. They highlight how our emotional and spatial connections or detachments can profoundly affect our stances on matters of societal importance.

To provide visual insights into the relationship between use of force to address urban unrest (y-axis) and geographic distance in kilometers (x-axis), figure 4.3 portrays data from respondents with varying levels of emotional attachment to the BLM movement separately. The first panel

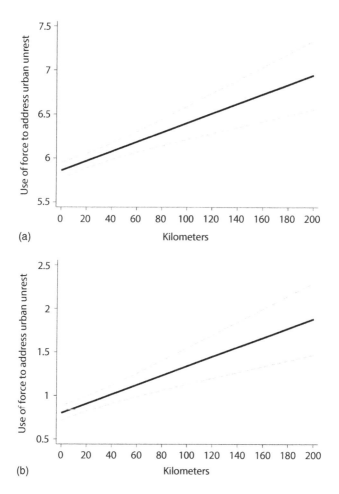

FIGURE 4.3 Linear prediction of using all available force to deal with urban unrest and distance given the coldest (*a*) and warmest (*b*) feelings toward the BLM movement.

Source: Data from ANES 2020.

presents data from respondents who exhibited colder sentiments toward BLM at the lowest point of the feelings thermometer, 12 degrees, and the second panel presents data from those who held warmer sentiments toward BLM, 96 degrees on the feelings thermometer scale. Notably, the slope for individuals with colder feelings toward BLM (falling within the teens range on the thermometer) is steeper compared to those with warmer feelings (falling within the 90 degree range on the thermometer), and these figures highlight their differences.

Individuals close to the epicenter of a demonstration and who had the coldest feelings toward BLM significantly supported the use of all means to address urban unrest (5.9 out of 7 points on the support scale). As the distance from the demonstration location increased, so did the preference for employing force to confront issues related to racism and police brutality.

Individuals with warmest sentiments toward BLM exhibited a slight positive correlation between increased distance from the demonstration location and a higher level of support for employing force in addressing urban unrest, but the degree of support remained relatively low, which the difference in scales between the two graphs indicates. An interesting pattern is that individuals with the warmest feelings toward BLM and in close proximity to where demonstrations took place generally do not endorse the use of force (0.8 out of 7 on the support scale), whereas those living further away from the protests display a marginal inclination to support the use of force in managing urban unrest (scoring 1.9 out of 7 on the support scale).

Overall the findings I present in this chapter underscore the crucial importance of distance and emotions in shaping individuals' attitudes toward social issues. The interaction between distance and emotion establishes a distinctive framework for a specific social phenomenon, encompassing both tangible and intangible aspects of societal constructs. Both distance and emotion seem to shape our encounters with protests and influence our affective responses toward the use of force.

In chapter 5, I describe an additional facet of distance in much more detail: culture. I investigate the manner in which our perspectives on a particular group of individuals vary in accordance with our perceptions of them when their presence in our lives become noticeable after an external shock.

5

ONE SIZE DOES NOT FIT ALL

Attitudes Toward Immigration

Limiting immigration has been deeply ingrained in the American ethos, just like baseball and apple pie. Since the late 1800s, the public has perceived immigration as a multifaceted nuisance: a threat to individual values, republican self-governance, and the living standards of urban workers. Moreover, it has been regarded as an obstacle to labor organization and a drain on vital public resources such as health care and education.[1] Researchers have examined public attitudes toward immigration from diverse economic and noneconomic perspectives. From an economic perspective, immigration is widely regarded as a direct liability to the material well-being of native-born citizens, including both the lower and upper ranks of the income distribution. Those positioned at the lower rungs of the socioeconomic ladder may perceive immigration as an immediate threat to their own prosperity when they find themselves competing with immigrants for jobs and access to public resources. In contrast, individuals situated at the upper stratum of society may bear the financial repercussions of immigration because they shoulder the burden of financing immigrants' utilization of public services.[2]

Noneconomic theories, in contrast, propose that individuals who share a common culture with incoming migrants are more likely to hold pro-immigration views compared to those lacking similar cultural affinities.[3] For instance, some argue that Hispanics generally exhibit more favorable attitudes toward Latin American immigration than do non-Hispanics.[4] Scholars like de la Garza and colleagues suggest, however, that the disparities in immigration opinions between Latinos and Anglos depend more on the former's relative socioeconomic position than on their national origin.[5] In a different vein, individuals who experience a sense of alienation from mainstream society and harbor isolationist perspectives on U.S. foreign policy are less inclined to support higher levels of immigration than those who do not feel estranged and possess more globalist views on the United States' role on the global stage.[6]

Even prior to the formation of the United States by the thirteen colonies, immigration policies with varying degrees of restrictiveness were in place, excluding migrants based on factors such as religion, poverty, criminal records, disease, and the potential to become a burden on the state.[7] However, throughout the nation's history, key factors shaping public opinion and immigration policies have revolved around various divisions: whites versus nonwhite migrants, radical immigrants versus defenders of American values, Protestants versus Catholics, and Anglo-Saxons versus Southern and Eastern Europeans, Asians, and Latin Americans.

At its core, our immigration policy is founded on the underlying narrative of "us versus them," which is not entirely surprising. Immigration, by definition, implies the movement of individuals or groups from one country to another, often with the aim of establishing permanent or temporary residence in a foreign land.[8] This definition inherently incorporates issues of race and ethnicity because people from diverse ethnic and racial backgrounds migrate to countries with distinct cultural and racial compositions.

The birth of the United States is linked with a particular ethnic population, the Anglo-Saxon, and a specific set of moral and ethical values rooted in Protestantism, which despite diversity increasing over the last decades resist adaptation. The foundational creation of the United States implicitly divides society into "us," the in-group (i.e., the "legal heirs" of the founders) who are closely connected to our heritage, and "them," the out-group (immigrants who do not belong to the Anglo-Saxon Protestant group) who may be perceived as distant from us. The "us vs. them" boundaries become even more evident when individuals are segregated into groups and when group boundaries do not align, that is, when there is no overlap in terms of race, ethnicity, language, religion, values, and so forth.[9]

These boundaries are also exacerbated when the well-being of our own group is perceived as being threatened, symbolically or literally, and individuals are continually reminded of these perceived threats (e.g., through heightened airport security, national threat warnings, or anti-immigrant rhetoric). In both cases members of the in-group may develop negative attitudes toward those in the out-group due to misconceptions regarding the size and impact of the out-group on either our values or well-being.[10]

Another lens through which the distance between boundaries can be aggravated is by analyzing how the ethnoracial characteristics of the in-group interact with their attitudes toward immigration by exploring whether the in-group perceives immigration as a positive or negative force for the country, and how these attitudes map to the ethnoracial characteristics of the out-group.

Research has consistently demonstrated that individuals tend to evaluate members of out-groups based on their perceived similarity or dissimilarity to the in-group, particularly in relation to race and ethnicity.[11] In the context of immigration, this means that the perceived differences between the in-group and the out-group can significantly influence attitudes toward immigrants, as well as the policies and practices concerning immigration. For instance, individuals who perceive immigrants as sharing similarities or closeness with themselves in terms of race or ethnicity may be more inclined to hold positive attitudes toward immigration. They might also be more likely to support policies that foster integration and the inclusion of immigrants in society. Likewise, individuals who perceive immigrants as distant or dissimilar from themselves may be more prone to holding negative attitudes toward immigration and endorsing policies that impose restrictions or exclusions on immigrants.[12]

The demographic composition of an immigrant wave can trigger various behaviors within the in-group. Studies have shown that people tend to overestimate the size of the out-group in response to such changes.[13] This exaggerated perception of the out-group's size can foster an increased sense of threat, leading to more negative evaluations of the group.[14] In simpler terms, the more visibly distinct and distant an immigrant group appears to be from the native population in terms of cultural or ethnoracial differences, and the more it is perceived to jeopardize the well-being and values of the broader society, the greater is the likelihood of negative judgments being made.

My primary focus in this chapter is to explore the interaction between the race and ethnicity of the in-group and the race and ethnicity of prospective immigrants to the United States. This interaction serves as a vital predictor in understanding present attitudes toward immigration, particularly among non-Hispanic whites, Blacks, Hispanics, and Asians. My objective is to investigate whether external shocks that emphasize the differences between immigrant groups and the mainstream population lead to an overestimation of the size of these groups due to heightened perceptions of potential threats.

BEFORE AND AFTER THE HART-CELLER ACT

Earlier immigration policies not only determined who was allowed to enter the country but also played a significant role in shaping the demographic makeup of the United States. As highlighted by Desmond King, these policies indirectly contributed to the development of a distinct "northwestern European vision" of American identity and nationality.[15] By selectively defining the boundaries of national identity, immigration policy inevitably influenced individuals' attitudes toward who is part of the in-group and who is part of the out-group.

Prior to 1965, in an era of racial segregation, the American public was used to predominantly European immigration. Around 95 percent of the spots allocated by the national origins quota system of the 1920s were designated for Europe, with the United Kingdom, Ireland, and Germany receiving approximately 70 percent of those places.[16] The remaining 5 percent were allotted to immigrants from the rest of the world.

However, the 1965 amendments to the Immigration and Nationality Act marked a significant turning point. These amendments abolished the quota system and eliminated nationality as a criterion for admission. As a result, immigration policy placed individuals from all nations on an equal footing. In the following decades, the foreign-born population experienced substantial growth after a period of decline between 1910 and 1970. Since then the foreign-born population has consistently increased at an average rate of 18 percent per decade. All in all, between 1850 and the latest U.S. Census of 2020, the foreign-born population exhibited a growth rate of 0.10 percent per decade, particularly following the pivotal changes implemented in 1965 (see figure 5.1).

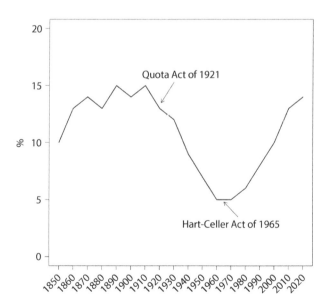

FIGURE 5.1 Percentage of the foreign-born population, 1850 to 2020.

Source: Data from the U.S. Bureau of the Census.

The enactment of the Hart-Celler Act and subsequent immigration laws marked a pivotal moment, opening the doors of the United States to new waves of immigration from regions beyond Western Europe. Although the explicit ethnic and racial biases of the 1920s immigration laws were no longer present, public opinion on immigration was implicitly influenced by the ethnic and racial composition of the "new immigrants" arriving in the United States. Economic concerns and apprehensions regarding cultural change played significant roles in shaping this opinion. Many Americans believed that the substantial influx of immigrants from Southern and Eastern Europe was negatively affecting wages and employment opportunities for native-born workers. There was also a prevailing sentiment that these immigrants were not assimilating into American culture at a pace deemed satisfactory.[17]

During this era, public opinion toward immigration was multifaceted, with different groups advocating for varying degrees of restriction or leniency in policies. Attitudes toward immigration were not solely determined by factors such as race and ethnicity; they were also influenced by religious affiliation, with certain groups facing higher levels of discrimination and prejudice than others.[18]

As illustrated in figure 5.2, the foreign-born population experienced an increase following the 1970s. However, the proportion of European immigrants entering the United States continued its downward trajectory. Figure 5.2 shows the relative shares of immigrants from Europe (solid line), Latin America (dashed line), Asia (dotted line), and other regions of the world (dot-dash-dot line) in relation to the total foreign-born population.

From 1850 to 1960, European immigrants constituted approximately 86 percent of the total foreign-born population in the United States, and immigrants from Latin America and Asia accounted for around 3 percent and 2 percent, respectively. However, a notable shift occurred in the 1970s after implementation of the Hart-Celler Act. During this period, immigrants from Latin America accounted for approximately 37 percent of the foreign-born population, and those from Asia comprised around 20 percent. Europeans averaged about 35 percent during this period.

By the year 2000, a clear trend emerged. Over half (51 percent) of the foreign-born population entering the United States arrived from Latin

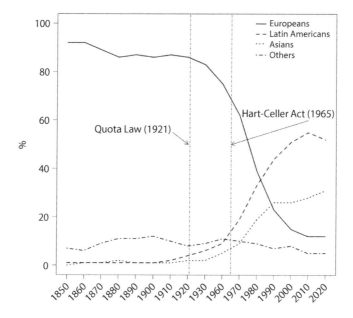

FIGURE 5.2 Population from different regions of the world as a proportion of the total foreign-born population, 1850 to 2020.

Source: Data from the U.S. Bureau of the Census.

America, and 26 percent came from Asia. In contrast, European immigrants accounted for only 15 percent. A decade later immigration from Latin America reached a tipping point and began to decline, and immigration from Asia continued to rise.

Figures 5.1 and 5.2 provide powerful evidence of two distinct patterns. First, there was a significant surge in the proportion of the foreign-born population after 1965, particularly due to the Hart-Celler Act. Second, following this legislation, migration flows from Latin America and Asia continued to increase, and European migration flows experienced a decline. These patterns give rise to the question of whether public opinion regarding immigration underwent substantial changes in response to the new migration flows from Latin America and Asia. In other words, did attitudes toward immigration shift because of these evolving demographic trends?

ONE SIZE DOES NOT FIT ALL

AND AMERICA SAYS...

Figure 5.3 shows the critical shifts in public opinion that occurred after 1965. For instance, between 1965 and 1995, there was a remarkable increase in the percentage of individuals favoring reduced immigration, soaring from 33 percent to 66 percent (represented by the dashed line), and the proportion of those supporting maintaining current immigration levels (represented

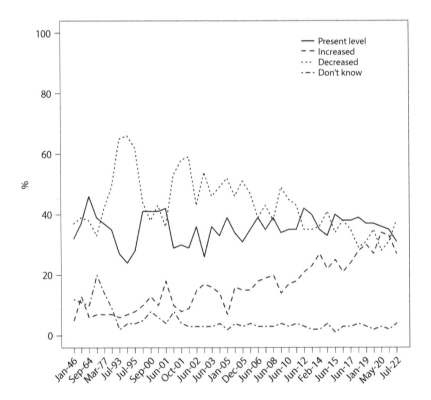

FIGURE 5.3 Public attitudes toward the levels of immigration that should be permitted.

Source: Data from Rita. J. Simon and Susan H. Alexander, *The Ambivalent Welcome: Print Media, Public Opinion, and Immigration* (Westport, CT: Praeger, 1993) and iPOLL from the Roper Center for Public Opinion Research.

by the solid line) declined by 15 percentage points. Public opinion toward immigration underwent further changes following the terrorist attacks of 9/11, manifesting an increased negativity and a surge in opposition toward immigration. The terrorist attacks created an atmosphere of fear and suspicion toward immigrants, particularly those hailing from Muslim-majority countries, thereby influencing public attitudes on immigration.[19] Moreover, the government's response to the attacks, exemplified by implementation of the Patriot Act and establishment of the Department of Homeland Security, intensified scrutiny and imposed greater restrictions on immigration, thereby shaping public opinion even further.[20] From December 2001 until 2022, attitudes toward immigration levels exhibited significant fluctuations. As of June 2023, public sentiment was divided: 31 percent advocating for maintaining immigration levels at their current state, 26 percent favoring an increase in immigration levels, and 41 percent expressing a desire to see a decrease in immigration levels.

What happened after 1965? Why did the percentage of individuals who favor reducing immigration increase? Plausible answers to these questions can be found in the transformations observed in the ethnoracial composition of migration flows. Between 1960 and 1990 a remarkable correlation of 0.98 and 0.97, respectively, existed between the proportion of Latino and Asian immigrants and the proportion of those supporting a reduction in immigration. This strong correlation suggests that Americans' attitudes toward immigration may have been influenced by the reception of these new migration flows. This new wave of immigration fundamentally altered the face of contemporary migration and society overall by introducing a distinct ethnic and racial component to the foreign-born population, which had been comprised predominantly of white Europeans prior to the 1960s.[21]

The U.S. decision to embrace non-European immigration brought about a massive shift in public opinion across America. The prevailing sentiment was to impede or restrict the immigration of individuals who, due to their background and experiences, were perceived as unable to assimilate into the American mainstream. These individuals were deemed as not belonging to the in-group and were perceived as distant from a defined set of values associated with being white, Anglo-Saxon, and Protestant, similar to the sentiments of the 1920s.[22] During the early and mid-1990s, anti-immigrant sentiment was widespread and manifested in numerous public opinion polls. However, beginning in 1995 opposition to immigration began to decline. By 2000 the level of opposition dropped to 38 percent, comparable to the era prior to the Immigration Reform Act of 1965. Nonetheless, immigration once again ascended to the forefront of the national agenda in 2000, reclaiming its position as a top issue of concern.[23]

Thirty-five years after the Hart-Celler Act, U.S. society had grown accustomed to living and working alongside individuals who didn't necessarily belong to the traditionally defined in-group, and this shift was reflected in the political arena. During the Republican Party convention, George W. Bush's remarks on immigration came as a surprise to many and shed light on his administration's stance. In his speech, Bush argued in favor of a compassionate and pragmatic approach to immigration that upholds the rule of law. Drawing inspiration from John F. Kennedy's *A Nation of Immigrants*, Bush emphasized that immigrants have always played a vital role in America's history and asserted that the nation should continue welcoming those who arrive to work hard and contribute to the country.[24] Furthermore, Bush strongly criticized the notion of "nativism"—the belief that only individuals native to a country should be regarded as true citizens. He contended that such an approach contradicts the values and historic trajectory of the nation. Instead, Bush advocated for a guest worker program that would enable temporary workers to fill jobs in the United States that Americans may not wish to pursue. He believed that this approach would not only benefit the U.S. economy but also provide opportunities for those seeking employment.

However, following Bush's controversial victory in 2000 and the subsequent change in his administration's stance on immigration, public opinion took a swift turn. In a June 2001 Gallup poll, 41 percent of the American public expressed a desire to reduce immigration, and 42 percent favored maintaining current immigration levels. The sentiment, however, shifted dramatically after the 9/11 terrorist attacks. An October 2001 Gallup Today poll revealed that 58 percent of the public believed immigration should be reduced, 30 percent favored maintaining current levels, and only 8 percent of the American public supported an increase in immigration.[25]

The shift in public opinion may have been due to the fact that the terrorists behind the 9/11 attacks had entered the country on temporary visas, sparking concerns about the effectiveness of the immigrant vetting process. The devastating events prompted a significant increase in the scrutiny of immigration policies, leading the government to implement new security measures aimed at addressing potential vulnerabilities within the system.[26]

Following 9/11 immigration faded from the political forefront, and the Bush administration redirected its focus toward new priorities arising from the terror attacks. It wasn't until 2004 that immigration once again took center stage as a national issue. During that time, the Bush administration proposed a "reform" package designed to tackle the perceived "problems" associated with immigration. The president's proposal emphasized the positive contributions of immigrants to American society, and it included the introduction of a guest worker program alongside heightened border security measures. Although some applauded the plan as a bold and necessary step toward addressing an urgent concern, others criticized it as excessively lenient and detrimental to American workers and to national security.[27]

Critics of the plan, including some within Bush's own party, contended that it would reward illegal behavior and potentially encourage further illegal immigration in the future. They also voiced concerns about its impact on American jobs and wages, arguing that the plan would enable employers to hire cheaper foreign workers at the expense of American workers. The response to Bush's proposal from many Democrats and immigration advocates was tepid. Senator Ted Kennedy, representing Massachusetts, expressed cautious optimism regarding the administration's involvement in immigration matters, hoping that it stemmed from genuine intentions rather than political considerations.[28] The push for immigration reform also faced opposition from influential conservative commentators and media outlets who portrayed it as a threat to American sovereignty and security. For instance, radio host Rush Limbaugh argued that the plan would result in an influx of individuals from third-world countries who would resist assimilation into American culture and potentially bring crime and disease to the nation.[29]

Despite varying perceptions regarding the White House's motivations, there was a lack of legislative activity on the immigration issue for nearly two years. It wasn't until President Bush once again advocated for immigration changes that the focus shifted toward stricter border enforcement rather than the guest worker program initially proposed in 2004.

By the end of 2005, the immigration debate had gained significant momentum, capturing the attention of the American public. A November 2005 poll conducted by the Pew Research Center revealed that only 2 percent of the public spontaneously identified immigration as the country's primary concern.[30] However, by March 2006 the percentage of individuals voluntarily recognizing immigration as the most pressing issue grew by 1 percent.[31] In May of 2006 this figure surged to a substantial 13 percent.[32]

This increase in public attention can be attributed, in part, to the escalating national significance of the immigration issue, which gained prominence through the efforts of politicians, political activists, media coverage, and the effect immigrant marches had in 2006. Despite the heightened importance of immigration as a national concern, the proportion of Americans advocating for a reduction in immigration continued to decline. By June 2006 public opinion reached a near equilibrium, with the nation evenly divided on whether immigration should be increased (39 percent) or decreased (39 percent) for the benefit of the country (see figure 5.3).

ONE SIZE? TWO SIZES? OR MAYBE THREE?

To what extent does distance influence attitudes toward immigration? Do people react differently to groups that are geographically, racially, ethnically, linguistically, or culturally closer than to those that are more distant? Culture is dynamic and ever evolving, but its geographical dimension must not be disregarded. The presence of disparities in race, ethnicity, language, religion, and other factors across various groups is inevitably shaped by the influence of spatial distance. If the spatial proximity between different regions were reduced, these disparities would either cease to exist or significantly diminish, leading to a higher level of congruence among groups. Conversely, when significant spatial distance separates groups, their differences may not be readily apparent until the lack of congruence between the out-group and the in-group becomes evident, thereby bringing them closer together and amplifying the perceived distance and its impact.[33]

There are numerous ways to operationalize this complex interaction. Here, I have chosen to investigate the interaction between racial and ethnic disparities among various immigrant groups, aiming to assess the distance between "them" and "us." Specifically, I analyze the perceptions of different immigrant groups, including Europeans, Latin Americans, Asians, Africans, and Arabs by asking a number of questions about these groups.[34] I also explore their perceived influence on immigration in the United States by asking a more general question.[35]

In this chapter, I draw on data from Gallup's Minority Rights and Relations poll, spanning two years, which provides valuable insights into migration levels from different countries and people's overall perceptions of immigration.[36] These data enable me to examine the impact of distance on attitudes toward immigrant groups that may be viewed as threatening, especially in the aftermath of external shocks that have reduced their proximity.

The first year of analysis is 2002, occurring nine months after the September 11, 2001, terrorist attacks, and the second year is 2006, beginning approximately one month after a series of large-scale protests and demonstrations in support of immigration reform across the United States. These protests were primarily driven by concerns among immigrants and their supporters regarding proposed immigration legislation, specifically the Border Protection, Antiterrorism, and Illegal Immigration Control Act. This act aimed to criminalize unauthorized immigration and impose severe penalties on employers for hiring undocumented workers. The protests, organized by labor unions, civil rights organizations, and immigrant advocacy groups, were largely peaceful. The largest demonstration was held in Los Angeles and reportedly attracted up to one million participants.

These demonstrations played a significant role in shaping the political discourse on immigration reform and in preventing the passage of more restrictive laws.[37]

Focusing on these two events, I could evaluate whether increased differences between a particular immigrant group (such as Arabs after 9/11 and Latin Americans after the 2006 marches) leads to more negative attitudes. I am examining the impact of an external shock on a particular immigrant group, not comparing these two events across time. Survey data capturing such questions in the aftermath of external shocks are rare, and by focusing on 2002 and 2006 I could ascertain how attitudes toward different groups evolve as they move closer or farther away in perceived proximity to these events.

To analyze these dynamics, I employed an ordered logistic regression model. This statistical method, also known as ordinal regression, assesses the relationship between an ordinal dependent variable (one that can be ranked or ordered meaningfully, such as "too many," "about the right amount," "too few") and one or more independent variables. In simpler terms, an ordered logistic regression helps us understand how changes in the independent variables influence the likelihood of being in a higher category on the dependent variable.

Gallup's samples provide a representative picture of the sociodemographic characteristics of non-Hispanic whites, non-Hispanic Blacks, and Hispanics. Income disparities were evident across these groups, with the median income of non-Hispanic whites ranging from $30,000 to $50,000 and the median income of Hispanics generally in the $20,000 to $30,000 range. Education levels also varied: Hispanics tended to have lower educational attainments than non-Hispanic whites or non-Hispanic Blacks.

Most respondents in the study were employed either part-time or full-time, and a majority of non-Hispanic whites and Hispanics expressed satisfaction with the state of affairs in the United States during those periods. Urban areas were predominantly inhabited by non-Hispanics Blacks and a significant proportion of Hispanics, whereas approximately half of non-Hispanic whites resided in suburban areas. It is interesting that a substantial 70 percent of Hispanics believed immigration was beneficial to the country, compared to 63 percent of non-Hispanic whites and 54 percent of non-Hispanic Blacks.

To comprehensively examine attitudes toward immigration, the model incorporates various control variables that were demonstrated to play a role in previous research. These variables include education, gender, age, income, political ideology, marital status, presence of children under age eighteen, life satisfaction, generational status, party affiliation, employment status, satisfaction with the national situation, church attendance, region of residence, and urban, suburban, or rural living conditions. Of utmost importance, the model captures individuals' perceptions of immigration's impact on the country, encompassing whether they view it as positive, negative, or a combination of both, and also considering respondents' race or ethnicity.

ATTITUDES TOWARD IMMIGRATION AFTER 9/11

Figure 5.4 provides a comprehensive view of the expected responses based on different scenarios related to immigration (see table A.5.1 in the appendix for regression results). The top row represents the outcomes when the dependent variable relates solely to immigration without specifying any particular immigrant group. Subsequent rows focus on specific regions of the world. For example, the Europeans' row illustrates the expected responses when the dependent variable refers to immigrants from European countries coming to the United States. The solid black line represents the probability of stating that there are too many immigrants from Europe, and the solid gray line indicates the probability of perceiving the number of European immigrants as appropriate. The dashed dark line illustrates the probability of expressing the view that there are too few immigrants from this particular region. These rows provide a visual representation of the probabilities associated with different perspectives on immigration levels from specific parts of the world.

Figure 5.4 reveals distinct patterns: individuals who think immigration is bad for the country tend to believe that there is an excess of immigrants, regardless of their geographic origins. Those with positive views on immigration and their contributions to U.S. society are more inclined to perceive

ONE SIZE DOES NOT FIT ALL

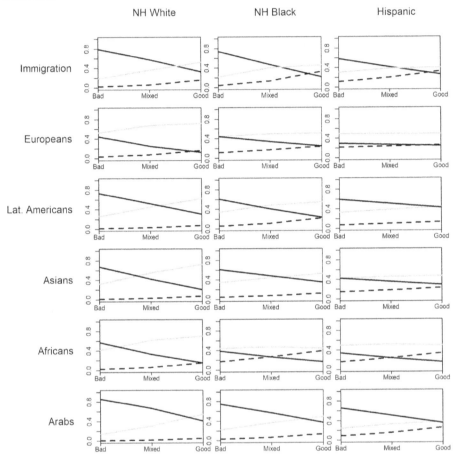

FIGURE 5.4 The results of the 2002 ordered logistic regression model related to immigration.

Source: Data from Gallup Minority Rights and Relations Poll 2002.

the influx of immigrants into the United States as appropriate. These findings may not come as a surprise. When people perceive immigration positively, viewing it as less of a threat, they tend to consider the number of immigrants arriving as "about right."

ONE SIZE DOES NOT FIT ALL

Despite these clear trends, notable nuances are worth exploring. Following the September 11, 2001, terrorist attacks, respondents with negative attitudes toward immigration were particularly inclined to express the belief that there was an excessive number of immigrants arriving in the United States from Arab countries, surpassing immigrants from other groups. Among these respondents, white individuals were most likely to hold this viewpoint, followed by Blacks and Hispanics. The ethnic, cultural, and religious distance between whites and Arabs make them the most distinct groups with the greatest degree of separation. In contrast, Hispanics, potentially showing solidarity with other immigrant communities, demonstrate the lowest inclination to assert an excessive influx of immigrants from Arab countries into the United States. Black perspectives on the number of immigrants from Arab countries fall in the middle and are similar to those of whites and Hispanics. This middle ground could reflect religious solidarity because Black Muslims constitute one-fifth of the entire U.S. Muslim population.[38]

The perception of threat probably played a significant role in shaping attitudes toward Arab immigrants, especially when the in-group felt threatened. The perceived disparities in culture, religion, and politics between the in-group and Arab immigrants further intensify these feelings of threat, resulting in negative attitudes toward them.[39]

The terrorist attacks of September 11, 2001, were a horrifying and highly publicized event that left an indelible mark on my memory. At that time, I lived on the Upper West Side of New York City, near Columbia University. I vividly recall that tragic day. In the morning I made a trip to the now-defunct Fairway Supermarket on 125 Street. As I arrived, a fleet of police cars raced down Henry Hudson Parkway toward Lower Manhattan. Curiosity got the better of me, and I asked a security guard about the situation. The response left me bewildered: "We are under attack." I immediately dismissed this response simply because it was beyond my comprehension. Being a student, I couldn't afford a TV or a monthly cell phone plan, and I relied on a prepaid phone that served as a landline and was never taken outside. Upon returning to my apartment, I was stunned to find multiple missed calls from my mother, who was worried about my safety. After calling her I hurried to Columbia University to gather the latest news through television and the internet. The atmosphere at the School of International and Public Affairs, usually bustling, was filled with an eerie silence as everyone grappled with disbelief. The entire city seemed dazed, struggling to come to terms with the barbaric events that had just unfolded. The images on the television screen were chilling, leaving a lingering sense of unease. Many other New Yorkers had similar emotions, and these collective experiences triggered an immediate shockwave that disproportionately targeted a specific group.

Although Arab immigrants constitute a small fraction of the overall immigrant population, they became subject to suspicion in the aftermath of the September 11 attacks.[40] Regrettably, the association of the attacks with Arab groups and individuals led to unwarranted scrutiny despite the fact that the vast majority of Arabs condemn violence and terrorism.[41] Negative attitudes toward Arab immigrants were further fueled by the media's portrayal of Arabs as violent, which were coupled with a lack of familiarity with Arab culture and customs. These representations provided fertile ground for the growth of stereotypes and prejudice.[42]

ATTITUDES TOWARD IMMIGRATION AFTER THE 2006 MARCHES

In contrast to the tragic events of September 11, 2001, which brought attention to an outsider group through these acts of violence, the immigrant demonstrations of 2006 illuminated the long-standing historical presence of Latinos in the United States. These demonstrations acted as a powerful catalyst, revealing the previously unseen growing political and social influence of immigrant communities. Moreover, they exposed the existing divisions and tensions surrounding immigration and identity issues within the United States.[43]

Figure 5.5 shows the expected responses related to immigration (see table A.5.2 in the appendix for regression results). Given the disparities between non-Hispanic whites and Hispanics, it comes as no surprise that non-Hispanic whites who held negative views regarding the impact

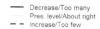
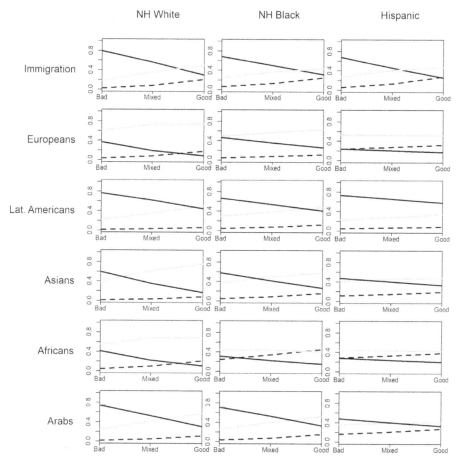

FIGURE 5.5 The results of the 2006 ordered logistic regression model related to immigration.

Source: Data from Gallup Minority Rights and Relations Poll 2006.

of immigration on the country were the most likely group to believe that there were excessive numbers of immigrants from Latin America (0.77). However, it is perhaps unexpected that Hispanics also expressed a similar sentiment about an excessive influx of immigrants (0.73).

Immigration from Latin America exhibited a steady rise from the 1970s, reaching its peak in 2010. However, the portrayal of the 2006 immigrant demonstrations in the media and political discussions surrounding anti-immigrant legislation (i.e., H.R. 4437) served to strengthen the perception of Latino immigrants as a threat to the established way of life. Conservative media outlets focused on the unrest caused by the protests, highlighting the perceived negative consequences of illegal immigration on the economy and on national security. They painted the demonstrators as lawbreakers, using the rallies as evidence to advocate for stricter immigration controls. In essence, conservative media outlets underscored the disconnect between the in-group and the out-group. In contrast, liberal media outlets highlighted the vast number of peaceful protesters and emphasized the vital role immigrants play in the fabric of American society. They emphasized immigrants' contributions to the economy and celebrated the diversity they bring to the United States. This symbolic threat, in turn, likely led non-Hispanic whites to adopt a hostile attitude toward Latino immigrants.[44] As observed in other regions worldwide, racial or cultural prejudice deepens the divide between groups and plays a significant role in shaping attitudes toward immigrants from ethnically diverse countries.[45] The media also played a pivotal role by perpetuating a negative image of immigrants, aligning them with a narrative of threat, which contributed to more hostile attitudes.[46]

Throughout history, a substantial number of Latinos, particularly Mexican Americans, have expressed concerns about undocumented immigration from Latin America. Various factors contribute to this sentiment. One primary concern is the potential displacement of Mexican American workers by undocumented immigrants. Mexican American workers face challenges when competing with undocumented individuals who are willing to accept lower wages and fewer benefits. In addition, some Mexican Americans worry that the negative stereotypes and prejudices held by mainstream American society toward all Mexicans, regardless of their citizenship status, can be reinforced by the presence of undocumented immigrants. This reinforcement fosters an environment of suspicion and hostility toward all Latinos, including those who have lived in the United States for multiple generations.[47] This dynamic further fuels the overall apprehension among

Latinos regarding the impact of undocumented immigration on their community and the broader perception of Latinos in the United States.

In this chapter I provided a perspective on the role of distance in shaping attitudes toward immigration. First, I focused on how the racial and ethnic characteristics of immigrants entering the United States affect the viewpoints of individuals who approach immigration from a geographically bounded standpoint. Although public opinion on immigration generally follows a similar pattern in the absence of specific group references, a lack of congruence between racial or ethnic groups leads to more negative sentiments toward out-group members. Group distance typically fuels attachment to one's own group and fosters hostility toward members of other groups. This effect becomes particularly pronounced when there is limited overlap between groups and when immigrants are perceived as potential threats to the values and well-being of the in-group.

Second, the visibility of immigrant groups increases the manifestation of negative social emotions toward them. This heightened visibility draws them closer and exposes them to public scrutiny. Following the September 11, 2001, terrorist attacks, there was a heightened belief among the public that there were excessive numbers of immigrants from Arab countries. This suggests that people responded to perceived threats to their own well-being. Similarly, after the 2006 immigrant marches, both Hispanic and non-Hispanic white respondents were more inclined to believe that there were too many Latino immigrants. Non-Hispanic whites expressed negative sentiments toward Latino immigrants as a response to a symbolic threat that seemingly compromised values associated with patriotism and cultural assimilation. And Hispanics reacted negatively to Latino immigration due to their relative position within U.S. society.[48]

Overall, in this chapter I explored the relationship of distance from an ethnoracial and cultural standpoint and its impact on attitudes toward immigration, shedding light on how various factors shape perceptions and emotions concerning immigrant groups. In chapter 6, the focus shifts to another aspect of immigration: the border wall between the United States and Mexico. I examine how geographic distance interacts with partisanship to shape people's opinions on the infamous border wall.

6

FROM A DISTANCE

Partisanship, Public Attitudes, and Geographic Proximity Toward the U.S.-Mexico Border Wall

A five-hour drive south from Houston on U.S. 59 will lead you through Freer, Texas, where you will encounter one of the many Border Patrol interior checkpoints. As you approach, the first indicator of entering the "borderland" is a modest building resembling construction site trailers and a metal roof structure offering shade to Customs and Border Patrol officers. This checkpoint is approximately sixty-five miles from the controversial border wall that stretches across more than a third of the continental border between the United States and Mexico.

Although the concept of a border wall between the United States and Mexico is not new, the fragmented construction of this barrier has become a highly contentious political matter. The first piece of fencing along the U.S.-Mexico border was constructed in 1854, shortly after the Gadsden Purchase of 1853.[1] However, the modern debate on the wall gained significant attention in the early 1990s. Both Republican and Democratic administrations have had a complex relationship with the wall, with varying levels of support and opposition. For example, the Clinton administration took significant steps by constructing substantial portions of the wall in Laredo, Texas, and San Diego, California. In 2005, during the Bush administration, the Real ID Act was signed into law, which included provisions allowing for the construction of additional fencing along the U.S.-Mexico border. This was followed by the Secure Fence Act of 2006, which provided further authorization and funding for the construction of hundreds of miles of fencing.[2]

In 2013, the Border Security, Economic Opportunity, and Immigration Modernization Act was passed by the Senate, with support from every Democrat. The bill included a significant allocation of $20 billion for border wall construction. However, it did not pass the House of Representatives, preventing its implementation.[3]

It was during the 2016 presidential campaign that the border wall truly emerged as one of the most divisive issues in American politics. Shortly after meeting with the president of Mexico, Enrique Peña Nieto, candidate Donald Trump made a bold statement at a rally in Phoenix, Arizona. He proclaimed, "We will build a great wall along the southern border—and Mexico will pay for the wall 100 percent."[4] Trump's words not only set the tone for his campaign but also ignited intense budgetary battles in Congress in the years that followed, exacerbating the partisan divide among the public.

Scholars have explored the relationship between the border wall and public opinion, but most research has focused on national security, border policing, or illegal immigration within the context of the "war on terror."[5] At first glance, this gap in research may seem surprising. After all, immigration-related issues are highly partisan, and the impacts of the wall are geographically bound. Many studies include party identification as a control variable, but it has "not been a central feature in research on immigration attitudes," with a few notable exceptions.[6] Equally surprising is the relatively theoretical treatment of geographic distance, considering the actual location and impact the wall has on the lives of border residents.[7]

Despite the prominent role of the wall in recent politics, our understanding of public opinion remains limited. Building on my previous work, I take a deeper look into the influence of partisanship and geographic distance and their interaction in shaping public attitudes toward the border wall. As discussed in chapter 1, distance interacts with other factors such as partisan perceptions and attitudes, which in turn mold our attitudes toward the wall. Those who reside near the wall have a direct understanding and firsthand experience of the border's "here and now." They witness its unique characteristics and the impact it has on their daily lives.[8] Individuals living far away from the wall perceive it through a distant lens, relying on decontextualized, generalized, and prototypical characteristics that may align with their partisan beliefs and the nationalized, partisan discourse on immigration.[9]

PUBLIC OPINION AND THE BORDER

The border wall plays a pivotal role in shaping public opinion on immigration policy. To some, it stands as the final defense against perceived threats from "others," as chapter 5 illustrated in the case of race and ethnicity. But for many others the wall represents an unwelcome nuisance tainted by partisan ideologies. Geographic distance emerges as a determining factor in people's support for the wall and acts as a switch that either illuminates or extinguishes previously held beliefs. Border residents directly witness the reality and significance of the wall, whereas those living farther away remain detached from its real impact.

The U.S.-Mexico border, as we know it today, is a product of historical correction that took place in 1896 to rectify mapping errors from the U.S.-Mexican War of 1849–1855. However, it is not merely a line drawn by Washington, D.C. and Mexico City to separate two nations. Rather, it is a dynamic permeable membrane shaped by centuries of movement and interaction among Indigenous peoples, Spaniards, Mexicans, and Americans.[10]

Contrary to popular belief, the U.S.-Mexico border is not a war zone.[11] In fact, on average, violence is lower on the border than in other parts of the country.[12] In addition, the militarization of the border is not an isolated phenomenon. Police departments nationwide have been on a trajectory of militarization since the 1970s. Therefore, rather than being an anomaly, the militarization of the border aligns with the prevailing national trend.

The deployment of the National Guard at the border may be perceived by some as an alarming indicator of the sometimes chaotic environment experienced by border residents on a daily basis. However, troop deployments to the border have been occurring since President William Taft, who sent troops to the Texas border during the Mexican Revolution.[13] The political rhetoric surrounding the border and the wall has been heavily influenced by former President Trump's dark views and policy solutions, in which the wall is presented as the sole option for taming the perceived apocalyptic chaos at the border.

However, this rhetoric is not unanimously embraced. Border mayors from Brownsville to El Paso, as well as officials in other border states, strongly opposed the border strategy imposed by the Department of Homeland Security, particularly when the federal government seized land to construct a fence.[14] This disagreement is not surprising: the border represents a dynamic social institution that fosters interdependence and mutually beneficial interactions on personal, cultural, and economic levels between neighboring communities.[15] People on either side of the border are influenced by and rely on their interactions with one another.[16]

The construction of a wall symbolizes a significant disruption to the social, political, and economic dynamics that thrive at the border. Most, if not all, interactions occurring in the border region create a shared identity that blends Mexican and American values, forging a unique space where "us" and "them" coexist as equals.[17] Such a distinctive border identity may not be evident in places far removed from the border, where differences between groups, such as Hispanics and non-Hispanics, become more pronounced.[18] The lack of similarities become more apparent when group boundaries lack congruence, with limited overlap in terms of race, ethnicity, language, and nativity.[19]

Proximity to the border fosters a physical and emotional connection that may transcend previously held beliefs such as partisanship, shaping individuals' collective identity.[20] In contrast, those with less direct contact lack the here and now experience of the border within their immediate reality. Consequently, their attitudes toward the wall are shaped by decontextualized information, replacing substantial evidence with preexisting partisan beliefs.

Partisanship exerts an individualizing effect on attitudes.[21] Partisans tend to rely on information that aligns with their party's positions, enabling them to form judgments on policies, political controversies, or simply understand their immediate political landscape through the lens of their party's perspectives.[22] As examined in chapter 1, the perceptual screen created by party identification[23] is further amplified by geographic distance, increasing the selectivity in interpreting policy positions to align with existing partisan views. Party labels interact with geographic distance by providing crucial information to individuals living far from a specific event, place, object, or person, helping partisans adopt positions that harmonize with both their own values and their party's ideology.[24]

Think of partisanship as the reflective surfaces and colored glass pieces within a kaleidoscope, with distance serving as the mechanism responsible for their movement. As we rotate the kaleidoscope, the images change, altering our perspective. The interplay between partisanship and distance is strikingly evident at the border. An example of how these mechanisms may be at play can be found in more than two dozen cities, counties, and Native American tribes that have passed resolutions opposing the wall project.[25] Hundreds of miles away from the border the former Iowa Representative Steve King has ardently advocated for its construction since 2006.[26] Thus partisanship and geographic distance to the U.S.-Mexico border interact to shape individuals' support for building a wall.

Context and place play a crucial role in shaping interactions.[27] As the distance from the border increases, self-identified Republicans are more likely to support the construction of a border fence along the U.S.-Mexico border. On average, Republicans residing far from the border have limited direct contact with the border, its residents, and the social and political landscape surrounding the wall. This lack of direct interaction with the here and now weighs down the potential for their prejudices to be challenged through meaningful engagement. In this context, Republicans far away from the border tend to align themselves with their party's nationalized stance on immigration.[28]

DO DISTANCE AND PARTISANSHIP IMPACT ATTITUDES TOWARD THE WALL?

To examine the impact of distance, partisanship, and their interaction on shaping individuals' attitudes toward the border wall, I utilize data from the Pew Research Center's February 2017 Political Survey, which surveyed adults residing in the United States.[29] The main dependent variable assesses individuals' endorsement or resistance toward constructing a wall spanning the complete Mexico-U.S. border. The question presented holds significant significance because it directly acknowledges the specific geographical area where the barrier would be erected, thereby offering a crucial element for examining the practical consequences of distance on public opinion regarding the wall. This differentiation distinguishes it from prior studies that used variables lacking a definitive geographic reference point.

My primary predictors in this study are the geographic distance from each respondent's place of residence to the border, their partisanship, and the interaction between these two factors. Distance is measured in two ways: (1) The log of the driving distance between a respondent's residence and various border-crossing points along the U.S.-Mexico border, and (2) the log of the Euclidean distance, also known as the "as-the-crow-flies" distance, from each respondent's residence to the international border between Mexico and the United States.[30] The use of the as-the-crow-flies distance compensates for any potential bias that may arise from the selection of specific border crossing points. It provides a more comprehensive representation of the actual geographic proximity between the respondent's residence and the international border. Despite the high correlation between the two distance measures, calculating the driving distance provides valuable precision for the estimates.[31] It serves as a psychological anchor that individuals would likely employ when thinking spatially.[32] As creatures of habit, we naturally consider routes and shortcuts when navigating from one place to another. For instance, when planning a trip to the supermarket from home, we subconsciously evaluate streets, stop signs, and traffic lights to determine the shortest route. This ingrained thought process demonstrates the significance of considering driving distance as a variable in this study to conceptualize and envision a destination accurately.

To estimate the driving distance, I calculated the distance between each respondent's zip code's longitudinal and latitudinal coordinates and the most frequently used border crossing points along the U.S.-Mexico border, moving from west to east. These points were selected because of their size and unique dynamics, which are influenced by international commerce and daily migration.[33]

As a robustness check—an approach that enhances confidence in the accuracy of variable measurements—I conducted additional analysis to estimate the as-the-crow-flies distance. This measure was determined by calculating the shortest distance between the longitudinal and latitudinal coordinates of each respondent's zip code and the U.S.-Mexico international boundary line. Building upon the work of Regina Branton and Johanna Dunaway, I identified the shortest distance from each respondent's zip code to one of the nineteen designated border crossing points, as well as the shortest distance from each zip code to the U.S.-Mexico international boundary line itself.[34] Figure 6.1 provides a visual representation of the geocoding results, displaying the locations of each survey respondent, the designated border crossing points, and the U.S.-Mexico international boundary line.

Partisanship is a dichotomous variable (1= Republican, 0 = Otherwise) measuring the differences in attitudes arising between Republicans and Democrats and Independents, including partisan leaners who hold attitudes similar to those of declared partisans.[35] Partisanship measures the differences among those who potentially hold more conservative views on immigration-related issues versus those who hold more liberal views on them.[36] From a theoretical perspective, geographic distance to the border, partisanship, and their interaction serve as proxies for encapsulating the processes that shape public attitudes toward the border wall.

In addition to these key predictors, several control variables influence individuals' attitudes toward immigration-related matters. These controls include age, gender, and socioeconomic indicators such as income and education. They aim to account for any differences in opinion that may arise

FROM A DISTANCE

FIGURE 6.1 Border-crossing points along the Texas-Mexico border.

Source; Data from Pew Research Center.

between individuals occupying different positions on the socioeconomic ladder. For instance, those at the lower end may perceive immigration as a direct threat to their well-being because they compete for jobs and public resources with immigrants.[37] Whereas those at the higher end of the socioeconomic spectrum might bear the financial burden of immigration's impact on public services.[38] Consequently, individuals at either extreme may be more inclined to support the construction of a border fence to safeguard their financial interests.

Additional control variables include race/ethnicity (non-Hispanic white, non-Hispanic Black, other racial identification, Hispanic) and nativity (Hispanic foreign-born). These controls address any differences that may exist between individuals sharing a common culture and those who do not possess similar cultural affinities.[39] As presented in chapter 5, research has demonstrated that Hispanics tend to exhibit more favorable attitudes toward Latin American immigration than do non-Hispanics.[40] To account for this ethnic context, the study incorporates the Mexican share of the county's total population, derived from the U.S. Census, as a proxy for the frequency with which respondents encounter the immigration debate.[41] It is worth clarifying that I am by no means suggesting that the entire Mexican-origin population consists of immigrants.

I also incorporate the total crime index provided by EASI at the zip code level to account for the safety concerns faced by both border and nonborder residents in their daily lives. EASI's crime index amalgamates the probabilities of eight serious crimes, including murder, rape, robbery, assault, burglary, larceny, motor vehicle theft, and arson. A crime index score below 92 indicates that the likelihood of criminal activities occurring in a specific zip code is lower than the national average. To illustrate, the average crime index in border states stands at 87, whereas it reaches 95 in nonborder states.[42]

THE EVIDENCE: ACT I

I estimate people's probability of supporting the wall given their proximity to the U.S.-Mexico border, partisanship, and their interaction while taking into account demographic and socioeconomic variables (see table A.6.1 in the appendix for regression results). The results indicate that individuals who live far away from the border are less likely to support building a fence along the Mexico border. The coefficients are not significant, however, so distance at face value does not help us understand people's attitudes toward the border wall.

Republicans are also more likely to support the wall, but the coefficients are not significant, meaning that being a Republican per se does not determine whether you support or oppose the wall. Foreign-born Hispanics, as well as non-Hispanic Blacks, are less likely to support the wall with Mexico, which is in line with previous findings. This finding may be surprising to some, but African Americans' collective policy is simply in line with the Democratic Party's national position, as suggested by Dan Hopkins.[43] Older individuals, those who approved of the way Donald Trump handled his job, and those who believe that the wall would effectively deter migrants from entering the country without inspection are more likely to support building a wall along the border with Mexico. The other controls (including income, education, the percent of the Mexican-origin population at the county level, and crime) do not seem to impact public opinion.

When I interact geographic distance with partisanship, a very different picture is revealed. Recall that I am interested in investigating how both geographic distance and partisanship condition people's attitudes toward the wall.[44] Overall, the interaction suggests that distance interacts with Republicans' attitudes toward the wall: as distance increases, so does the probability of supporting building a wall along the U.S.-Mexico border ($p < 0.05$). Figure 6.2 plots the predicted probabilities with 95 percent confidence intervals of favoring building a fence along the U.S.-Mexico border for self-identified Republicans. The figure shows that as distance increases so does the probability of favoring building a fence along the border.

What does this finding mean? Consider what happens as geographic distance to the border increases. For instance, a twenty-fold increase in distance from the border ($q = 100/5$) increases the odds of a Republican favoring the construction of the wall by 3.97 ($20.^{460}$) when using driving distance and by 3.74 when using Euclidean distance ($20.^{440}$). The odds of supporting building a fence along the border with Mexico are 19.51 ($q = 2,565/4=641$; $641.^{460}=19.51$) times higher for a Republican living in Aroostook County, Maine (the farthest place from the border, given the data) than for a Republican living in Yuma County, Arizona (the closest place to the border, given the data).[45]

An important question remains: Are these findings truly valid? In simpler terms, do we compare individuals who possess similar characteristics in terms of socioeconomic status, race, ethnicity, and so forth but differ only in their partisanship and relative proximity to the border? To address this question, I draw on the rationale behind the potential-outcomes model.[46] This model can be viewed as an expansion of the conceptual framework used in randomized experiments but is adapted for nonexperimental data.[47]

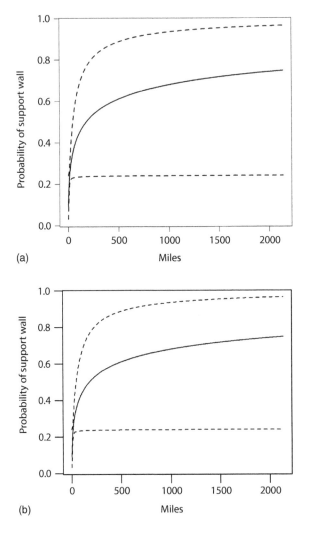

FIGURE 6.2 Predicted probabilities for a self-identified Republican of favoring building a wall along the U.S.-Mexico border (and 95 percent confidence intervals) as a function of (*a*) driving distance and as a function of (*b*) Euclidean distance from the border.

Source: Data from the Pew Research Center.

In essence, I aim to mimic the conditions of an experiment in which the researcher has full control over the experimental setup. Of course, when working with observational data, we can only approximate those ideal conditions. Nonetheless, my objective is to achieve comparable results that lend support to my findings.[48]

The strategy I use here allows for a multivalued treatment that varies across four levels of distance.[49] (See table A.6.2 in the appendix for regression results and tables A.6.3–A.6.6 for diagnostics.) At level 0, observations are limited to within 100 miles of the U.S.-Mexico border. This threshold corresponds to the distance that allows the Border Patrol to conduct internal checkpoints, as outlined in Section 287(a)(3) of the Immigration and Nationality Act. Level 1 comprises observations of Republicans residing between 100 and 500 miles from the border. For instance, cities like San Antonio lie approximately 150 miles away from Laredo, whereas Lafayette, Louisiana, is situated roughly 530 miles from Laredo. Moving to Level 2, I focus on Republicans residing between 500 and 1,000 miles from the border. To provide an example, Portland, Oregon, is approximately 1,000 miles away from San Diego, California. Finally, Level 3 encompasses Republicans residing more than 1,000 miles from the border. For instance, Helena, Montana, is situated around 1,400 miles from Nogales, Arizona. The model estimates the average impact of distance on the probability of supporting the construction of a border fence for Republicans who do not reside at the border compared to individuals who do reside at the border. In other words, I analyze Levels 1 to 3 in relation to Level 0.[50]

The findings demonstrate a clear pattern: when compared to individuals residing at the border (Level 0), Republicans living between 100 and 500 miles away (Level 1) are 3.75 times more likely to express support for the construction of a wall. Similarly, Republicans residing more than 1,000 miles away from the border (Level 3) exhibit a 5.40-fold increase in the likelihood of supporting the wall compared to those living at the border (Level 0).

As distance from the border increases, Republicans (in contrast to Democrats and Independents) display a stronger inclination to back the construction of a fence along the U.S.-Mexico border. It becomes evident that both geographic distance and partisanship play crucial roles in shaping public attitudes toward the wall. Distance serves as a necessary factor that facilitates direct contact and reduces prejudices.[51] In other words, at the border individuals encounter a unique reality when they experience firsthand the presence of the border wall, along with its far-reaching implications on familial, economic, and community aspects. This lack of perceptual separation reinforces the connection between proximity and attitudes toward the wall. As the distance from the border grows, there is a notable decline in both the quantity and quality of direct information available to individuals (see table A.6.7 in the appendix that interacts distance and crime to show that the latter has no statistically significant impact on predicting individuals' attitudes toward the wall). The physical separation imposes a barrier that hinders individuals' ability to fully comprehend the intricacies of the border. Consequently, their understanding becomes reliant on decontextualized and stereotypical information, which can be influenced by partisan biases. Although geographic distance alone may not determine people's attitudes, it serves as a medium through which individuals either encounter or remain distant from the realities of the border within their own lived experiences.

ALL DEPENDS ON THE EYE OF THE BEHOLDER

Geographic distance or proximity to the border provides individuals with different levels of understanding regarding the various aspects surrounding the border. Individuals who live in close proximity to the border and the wall directly witness the reality of the border, with fewer filters obscuring their observations. They observe lower crime rates compared to the national average, understand the reliance on economic trade between the United States and Mexico, experience enriching cultural exchanges, and maintain familial connections, among other factors.

Numerous studies highlight the influence of issue framing on public attitudes, revealing that the way in which specific matters are framed can shape people's perspectives.[52] Given this it is pertinent to explore whether people's support for the wall depends on how it is framed: being framed as an economic issue or as a national security concern are the most common frames. It also raises the question of whether support for the wall varies depending on how far individuals perceive themselves to be from the border. In chapter 1, I discussed how our understanding of the world is influenced by distance relative to a particular phenomenon and whether we are near or far away from the phenomenon.

Brian Reed, a senior producer with *This American Life*, worked on a compelling story about undocumented immigration in the remote town of Homer, Alaska.[53] Homer is a city of 5,709 residents, of which 96.5 percent were born in the United States, including Puerto Rico, and 3.5 percent were born abroad, and most of those are naturalized U.S. citizens.[54] Homer is far from the U.S.-Mexico border. The driving distance from Homer to Tijuana, Mexico—the nearest southern border point—is 3,959 miles. It would take approximately 65 hours and 23 minutes of nonstop driving (equivalent to around three full days) to reach Tijuana from Homer.

In 2016 the residents of Homer found themselves embroiled in a highly contentious City Council meeting, which became one of the most heated debates in the town's history. During the meeting, residents expressed their anxieties and fears surrounding immigration. One resident conveyed their concerns this way: "You bring in illegals, okay, by definition, they're criminals. Okay, they live in the underworld. They don't have a stake in the game as we do. About the first time somebody gets raped or killed, I hope they come straight after the Homer City Council and sue the city to the point of bankruptcy. If you make this a magnet for that type of people, then, you know, shame on you." The statements by Homer residents summarized the arguments of Aquinas, Aristotle, and St. Augustine: "It's as if we're enacting a play that reflects our deepest anxieties, but none of it is based on anything real. It's built upon what-ifs, differing perspectives, potential occurrences in other places, and fear. Fear of something becoming real. Yet none of it is grounded in actual events happening here."[55]

These exchanges raise a fundamental question: Why did immigration-related issues cause such upheaval, nearly tearing the fabric of the town apart, despite their absence in reality? The answer lies in the anxieties and fears rooted in an imagined future in which the "threats" of immigration become tangible. Homer residents perceived themselves as being closer to or more exposed to the potential negative impacts of immigration than they actually were. When we believe that an unknown evil is in close proximity, our anxieties and fears take on an entirely different nature than when we perceive that the danger is distant (see chapter 1).

Brian Reed reported that the residents of Homer were plagued by concerns over an unforeseen and imagined harm that could manifest within their own community.[56] Their worries extended beyond the ethnoracial aspects of immigration and encompassed the potential erosion of their way of life, customs, and worldview. In this context, whether interpreted literally or metaphorically, the wall can be viewed as the manifestation of Aristotle's hope—a barrier shielding them from the perceived negative consequences of immigration, such as the financial burden on taxpayers or potential threats to national security. The wall becomes a symbol of reassurance, providing a sense of security and alleviating anxieties.

As discussed in chapter 1, whether grounded in reality or constructed in our imagination, we seek ways to reduce our fears and concerns and avoid danger. Moreover, our worries and fears may be fueled by tangible dangers, past experiences, personal and political biases, or anticipation of future threats, all of which are influenced by our perceived distance from the presumed source of danger.

DOES DISTANCE PERCEPTION IMPACT ATTITUDES TOWARD THE BORDER WALL?

Individuals who imagine or perceive themselves to be closer to the border are more likely to support the construction of the wall because they may associate proximity to immigration with an increased likelihood of experiencing negative fiscal consequences or potential threats to national security. To examine the impact of distance perception on individuals' attitudes toward the border wall, I use data from the 2016 Cooperative Election Study. I created a set of experimentally designed vignettes, randomly assigned to respondents, that present different contexts framing immigration as either a fiscal burden or a national security threat.

The first vignette prompts respondents to express their support or opposition to building a wall along the U.S.-Mexico border, highlighting the significant financial costs incurred by U.S. taxpayers due to undocumented immigration.[57] The second vignette focuses on framing immigration as a matter of national security and asks for respondents' stance on the wall in this context.[58] For comparison purposes, I have providing an additional vignette that does not reference national security or immigration's fiscal impacts.[59]

Each of these experimental scenarios measures respondents' support or opposition to constructing a fence or physical barrier along the U.S.-Mexico border and poses the following question: "Thinking now about the border wall, do you favor or oppose building a fence or physical barrier along the U.S.-Mexico border?" Similar to the previous section, the question emphasizes the specific geographic location of the proposed wall, providing a fixed reference point for respondents.

To construct the primary predictor, participants were asked about their perceived distance from the U.S.-Mexico border: "How far, in miles, do you estimate you live from the U.S.-Mexico border?" Subsequently, I calculated the driving distance between the longitudinal and latitudinal coordinates of each respondent's zip code and the key border crossing points along the U.S.-Mexico border, following the same methodology I used previously. Figure 6.3 provides a visual representation of each respondent's zip code and the nearest driving route to the border, illustrating the geographic context.

Finally, I estimated the over/underestimation of distance by subtracting respondents' perceived geographic distance from the actual driving distance from their zip code to the border. Multiple routes could be taken from each respondent's residence to the U.S.-Mexico border, and I selected the shortest distance to ensure conservative estimates and to avoid overestimating respondents' perceived distance. Given that I am subtracting the actual

FIGURE 6.3 Nearest driving route to border crossing points along the Texas-Mexico border.

Source: Data from Cooperative Election Studies.

driving distance from respondents' perceived distance, the resulting values can be either negative or positive. A negative value indicates that respondents perceive themselves as being closer to the border than they actually are, whereas a positive value suggests that they perceive themselves as being farther away from the border than they are. Subsequently, I created a dichotomous variable to indicate whether respondents underestimated or overestimated their proximity to the border. Specifically, a value of 1 signifies an underestimation, and a value of 0 represents an overestimation.

In addition to the main predictor, I included other variables related to public opinion toward the wall to control for any potential confounding effects that may exist between individuals' attitudes toward the wall and geographic distance. I included ideology (1= very liberal . . . 5 = very conservative), gender (1 = female, 0 = male), age (18–90 years), race/ethnicity (1 = white, 2 = Black, 3 = Hispanic, 4 = Asian, 5 = Other), education (1 = no high school . . . 6 = graduate), income (1 = <$10K . . . 17 = >$150K), if they are registered to vote (1 = Yes, 0 = No), if they planned to vote for then candidate Trump (1 = Yes, 0 = No), if they are employed (1 = Yes, 0 = No), and if they own a home (1 = Yes, 0 = No).

THE EVIDENCE: ACT II

I estimated the likelihood of individuals supporting the construction of the border wall based on their perceived proximity to the border (see table A.6.8 in the appendix for regression results). This analysis was conducted across three experimental conditions: fiscal impact, national security, and no framing context.

The findings reveal that individuals who perceive themselves as living closer to the border exhibited a higher probability of supporting building of a fence than those who believe they live farther away from the U.S.-Mexico border. However, among the three experimental conditions, only the national security context yields a statistically significant coefficient. However, the perceived distance in the fiscal burden and no framing experiments align with the expected theoretical direction: that is, those who imagine a threat to be near to them because they believe they were closer to the border were more likely to support building the border wall.

To present the results in a more digestible manner, I apply Andrew Gelman's and Jennifer Hill's "divide by 4 rule."[60] This rule allows for the interpretation of the predictive difference corresponding to a unit difference in the main predictor. According to this rule, individuals who perceive themselves as being closer to the border than they actually are were approximately 36 percent (1.44/4 = .36) more likely to support the wall based on concerns related to national security when compared to individuals who believe they are farther away from the border.

Regarding the control variables, the results suggest that self-identified conservatives, in contrast to self-identified liberals, and those who intended to vote for Donald Trump in the 2016 election are more likely to express support for the wall. This aligns with the findings presented in the previous section.

Why do the results matter? Who truly cares about people's opinions regarding the border wall? And why should we consider geographic distance? These questions can be answered through two critical perspectives that shed light on the significance of these findings.

First, the results bring attention to the weight of immigration-related matters for residents living in border areas, revealing a complex interplay between opinions and policies. This connection unveils a partisan divide between Democrats and Republicans, as well as internal divisions within the Republican Party itself. This divide also appears to be influenced by spatial distance and the availability of information specific to different localities. However, in general, those directly experiencing a particular place or the consequences of policies within a geographically bounded region possess richer contextual knowledge and direct experiences (see chapter 1). This equips them to make more informed judgments about these policies, independent of their partisanship. Those who are further removed from the border tend to rely more on partisan cues, potentially limiting their understanding of the nuanced realities.

Second, the results demonstrate that our perception of where we reside in relation to events unfolding elsewhere plays a significant role in shaping public attitudes. Our distance perception influences our anxieties, fears, and how we perceive potential threats that could affect our way of life. For some individuals, the border wall represents a source of hope, a defense against their imagined fears, particularly when framed within the context of national security. This resonates with the precise messaging of the Trump campaign during the 2016 election.

Overall, the findings from this chapter suggest that polarization extends beyond mere partisan or ideological boundaries. Actual and perceived geographic distance can exacerbate this problem by amplifying how we perceive imagined threats and their potential impact on our lives. This, in turn, influences our attitudes and behaviors, underscoring the far-reaching consequences of these dynamics.

In chapter 7, I shift my focus from immigration to another pressing issue: climate change. I explore the impact of experiencing extreme weather events on individuals' perceptions of climate change. By examining the tangible realities of the here and now of climate change, I aim to shed some light on how these firsthand experiences shape people's outlook and understanding of this global environmental challenge.

7

THE PERFECT STORM

Attitudes toward climate change are as diverse as the individuals who hold them. Some people firmly believe that climate change represents a pressing critical issue that demands immediate action to diminish greenhouse gas emissions and transition toward a more sustainable way of life. Others hold the belief that climate change is a natural occurrence, consistently observed throughout Earth's history, and that human activities alone are insufficient to cause significant alterations.[1] Another segment of society is skeptical of the scientific consensus on climate change, casting doubt on the credibility of the data and the methods employed to analyze it. In a nutshell, some perceive climate change as a fabricated deception, a hoax, or a conspiracy theory, and others acknowledge the changing climate but attribute it to factors other than human influence.

Attitudes toward climate change arise from a multitude of factors, including partisan affiliations, ideological beliefs, educational achievements, race, and geographical location.[2] In shaping these perceptions, personal encounters with climate change through the experience of extreme weather events (that is, the here and now) can exert a significant impact.[3] The first-hand experience of being evacuated due to a 500-year flood—a flood event with a mere 0.2 percent probability of happening—enables individuals to grasp otherwise abstract concepts and bridge the gap between understanding climate change through the detached lens of media outlets or previously held beliefs and personally encountering it.[4]

Personal experiences with extreme weather events can exert substantial influence over perceptions, beliefs, attitudes, behaviors, and policy support regarding climate change.[5] The impact of these experiences can be profound and transformative; personal encounters play a pivotal role in shaping climate change beliefs, making them susceptible to variation.[6] For instance, when individuals face recurrent extreme weather events, the magnitude of their impact is intensified when accompanied by personal or financial losses. A recent survey conducted in Florida and Texas by Gabrielle Wong-Parodi and Dana Rose Garfin had compelling findings. It revealed that adverse encounters with hurricanes lead to heightened perceptions of risk regarding specific climate hazards. Moreover, these experiences prompted individuals to engage in adaptive behaviors and exhibit increased support for interventions aimed at mitigating the effects of climate change.[7] Personal experiences with extreme weather events hold the potential to serve as catalysts, inspiring both the adoption of climate change mitigation and adaptation behaviors.[8] These events also have a profound influence on individuals' perceptions, beliefs, attitudes, behaviors, and support for climate change–related policies.[9]

In this chapter, my focus is on the profound influence of multiple extreme weather events on the attitudes of Houstonians toward climate change. I investigate the complex connection between personal experiences with these devastating storms and the likelihood of accepting climate change as a contributing factor in their occurrence.

THE STORMS

MEMORIAL DAY FLOOD: 2015

A slow moving storm system was to blame for the devastating Memorial Day flood in Houston in 2015. Heavy rain poured down from Monday

THE PERFECT STORM

night, May 25, until the morning of May 26.[10] In the span of just ten hours, some areas of the city received a staggering twelve inches of rain, amounting to approximately 162 billion gallons of water.[11] To put this into perspective, the average American uses around 82 gallons of water per day at home, which means that the amount of rain that fell in Houston over those two days is equivalent to nearly six days of water usage for 333 million people or filling 3.2 billion bathtubs.[12]

The persistent rainfall resulted in extensive flooding throughout Houston, with numerous bayous and creeks overflowing their banks. The Memorial area, known for its affluent neighborhoods, was particularly hard hit. The Buffalo Bayou, which runs through this area, reached unprecedented flood levels, causing severe damage to homes and businesses along its banks.[13] The effects of the flood were evident across the city, with scenes of submerged pickup trucks and tractor trailers near the medical center and abandoned cars piled up on freeway shoulders like something out of an apocalyptic movie. Downtown Houston, usually bustling with traffic, saw water-covered streets instead. The situation led to 531 water rescues; some individuals failed to heed the warnings of the Federal Emergency Management Agency's (FEMA) 2003 "Turn Around, Don't Drown" public education campaign, and others were caught off guard.[14]

The economic impact of the Memorial Day flood was astonishing. Considered one of the costliest floods in U.S. history, it caused more than $460 million in damages.[15] Nearly 2,000 homes were damaged, and more than 7,000 Houston residents sought disaster assistance from FEMA.[16] Tragically, seven lives were lost, some dying in their own vehicles.[17]

The Memorial Day flood of 2015 marked the beginning of a series of severe storms that not only prompted increased efforts to enhance the region's flood protection infrastructure but also served as a catalyst for shifting attitudes toward climate change. In that year, Rice University's Kinder Houston Area Survey, a long-standing annual poll of more than 50,000 Houston residents, revealed an interesting divide among the population: 45 percent of Houstonians attributed climate change or global warming to normal climate cycles, and 49 percent believed it was caused by human activity.[18] However, this pattern underwent a transformation in the next two years as Houstonians experienced the impact of two more severe storms.

TAX DAY FLOOD: 2016

Paying taxes is our civic duty, but it's safe to say that no one eagerly anticipates the annual ordeal. As if to add insult to injury, Tax Day on April 15, 2016, delivered a merciless blow to Harris County. A deluge of extraordinary proportions fell on the area, with rainfall measuring a staggering 7.75 inches. The aftermath? A mind-boggling 240 billion gallons of water, equivalent to filling 4.8 billion bathtubs.[19] This flood surpassed the notorious Memorial Day flood of 2015 by approximately 80 billion gallons and left behind a trail of pure devastation. The *Houston Chronicle* immortalized the chaos with images of residents kayaking down Memorial Parkway, a bustling four-lane road near downtown Houston that had been transformed into a watery freeway. The city stood no chance against the relentless rain, which tragically claimed five lives and left more than 744 homes and 400 apartments flooded.[20] The main culprit of this storm: climate change.

Although a single weather event cannot be definitively linked to climate change, experts show that the looming threat of a warmer atmosphere lies in its potential to spawn more intense rainstorms and subsequent floods.[21] When coupled with urban development that destroys ecosystems, this can become disastrous for a city like Houston.[22]

HARVEY: 2017

The Prelude

On September 13, 2008, Hurricane Ike unleashed its fury on Galveston Island, situated about an hour's drive south of downtown Houston. The impact was unprecedented, with the highest storm surge recorded on the island since 1915, accompanied by sustained winds clocking in at 110 miles per hour. A staggering $27 billion in damages included $15 billion in insured losses. In 2008 this hurricane stood as the third costliest hurricane in U.S. history, trailing only Hurricane Andrew and Hurricane Katrina.[23]

As fate would have it, I found myself caught in the middle of this stormy ordeal. I had just returned from a conference in San Salvador, El Salvador, aboard Continental Flight CO827, which landed in Houston at 4:30 P.M., a mere nine and a half hours before Ike's catastrophic arrival. A hurricane novice, I had not prepared myself for this daunting experience. Upon reaching home from the airport I was met with shuttered supermarkets, and my only food option was to purchase a dozen Ensure protein shakes from an open pharmacy. As I drove to my home, the streets were ghostly empty, which fueled my growing unease. Regret began to trouble me for not having taken the storm seriously enough. Upon reaching home, I quickly filled the bathtub with water, just in case. I began reaching out to friends, gauging their plans for evacuation, but their responses painted a bleak picture. The notion of enduring a grueling fifteen-hour ordeal on congested highways outweighed the perceived safety of fleeing due to what had happened during Hurricane Rita.

That night I slept through the whole storm without even hearing the wind, completely exhausted from the day's events. The following day there was no electricity, but I still had water and gas and enough food to last a couple of days. Unlike Hurricane Harvey, which was a rain event, Hurricane Ike carried most of its power through tremendous winds. The aftermath left a trail of destruction, with power lines scattered across the ground. It was a painstaking four to five days before electricity was finally restored in my area, situated approximately sixty-five miles north of Galveston. Supermarkets swiftly reopened their doors, alleviating the initial panic, and life on the mainland gradually began to regain a semblance of normalcy. At the same time, Galveston embarked on its journey of rebuilding and healing, a resilience ingrained in its very core since the catastrophic events of 1900.

When Hurricane Harvey struck in 2017, it became evident that we were dealing with an entirely different beast. Fortunately, this time around everyone had ample opportunity to prepare. Like countless others, I diligently tracked the storm's trajectory through various weather apps, counting on reliable updates from Houston's Space City Weather, a source of information untainted by the usual sensationalism. As a scholar driven by numbers, I found myself captivated by the intricate storm forecast models, which primed Harvey's slow and frightening approach. Residing on the highest floor of a three-story apartment building, I found peace in the relative safety it provided against any potential flooding. However, the situation was far graver for friends in nearby neighborhoods. Their homes stood close to the brink of being under water, particularly those in the vicinity of the Brazos River. Although the neighborhood was shielded by a protective levee, the ever-present threat of its breach remained, leaving us all vulnerable to the specter of prolonged flooding that could persist for weeks on end.

The Postlude

On August 25, 2017, the destructive force of Hurricane Harvey fell on Rockport, Texas, unleashing a devastating rampage that left no corner untouched. As a Category 4 hurricane, its fury was relentless, and it was accompanied by a tragic loss of life. But the storm's cruelty extended beyond its initial impact and unleashed a cascade of torrential rain on the Houston metropolitan region and its surroundings. For four consecutive days, a ruthless nonstop downpour released an astonishing one trillion gallons of water.[24] To put this staggering volume into perspective, it would be equivalent to filling 20 billion bathtubs to the edge, leaving a wake of unprecedented flooding and never before seen damage. The economic toll inflicted by Hurricane Harvey was nothing short of astounding, with damage totaling $128 billion. This catapulted it to the unenviable rank of the second most expensive natural disaster in American history, surpassed only by the devastating Hurricane Katrina. The car and truck devastation produced by the hurricane was equally shocking, obliterating nearly one million vehicles along the Texas Gulf Coast. To understand the magnitude of this destruction, the number of ruined cars in Texas exceeded the total vehicle count in the entire state of Utah in 2021.[25]

Within the boundaries of Harris County alone, the hurricane's fury left more than 200,000 homes and apartments in shambles. Tragically, the storm also claimed the lives of sixty-eight people, leaving countless families shattered by grief. The sheer magnitude of the disaster forced more than 37,000 souls to seek refuge in shelters during the chaos.[26]

The Houston region bore the brunt of nature's rage, enduring a relentless assault of rain. Between the Memorial Day flood, the Tax Day flood, and the devastating peak of Hurricane Harvey, 74 inches of rainfall had flooded the area.[27] The cumulative impact of these three monstrous storms in which infrastructure crumbled, homes were reduced to wet paper, and businesses were left in ruins exacted a toll that surpassed imagination, with a price tag exceeding $128 billion. To put this figure into perspective, it eclipses the combined GDP of both Costa Rica and Panama for the year 2021.[28]

CLIMATE CHANGE AND STORMS: WHAT SAY YOU?

How does firsthand experience of the devastating aftermath of these storms influence one's perception of the role of climate change? To shed light on this question, let's first look into the data. The Memorial Day flood struck on May 25, 2015. The 2015 Kinder Houston Area Survey (KHAS) was conducted between February 2 and March 4, 2015, which provided a valuable snapshot of public sentiment prior to the flood's occurrence. The Tax Day flood inflicted chaos in the Houston area on April 15, 2016. The KHAS survey was conducted between January 25 and March 3, 2016, capturing residents' views before the storm.

The colossal Hurricane Harvey made landfall on August 25, 2017, and the KHAS survey took place between January 24 and March 1, 2018, gauging the aftermath of the monstrous storm. Given the timing of the storms and when the KHAS surveys were done, we can consider the 2015 KHAS data as our baseline, reflecting attitudes prior to the first massive storm and seven years after Hurricane Ike in 2008. Within this survey wave, respondents' viewpoints on the primary cause of climate change were probably aligned with their fundamental beliefs at the time. The

THE PERFECT STORM

subsequent data from 2016 and 2018 offer insight into how Houston residents' attitudes may have shifted following exposure to weeks before the Tax Day flood and after Hurricane Harvey, respectively, carving a mark on their collective attitudes.

Let us now consider some statistics that illuminate the evolving attitudes of Houston area residents regarding the primary cause of climate change. Table 7.1 shows an intriguing trend, painting a vivid picture of shifting beliefs. In 2015, a mere 52 percent of Houstonians attributed climate change to human activity, and the remaining 48 percent attributed it to natural climate cycles. However, the landscape transformed significantly after the cataclysmic impact of Hurricane Harvey in 2017. In the wake of this disaster, a noteworthy transformation in beliefs emerged. The proportion of Houstonians who acknowledged human activity as the primary cause of climate change surged to 62 percent, marking a significant 19 percentage point increase. The percentage of individuals attributing climate change to normal climate cycles plummeted by 21 percentage points, changing from 48 percent to 38 percent. These statistics underscore the potential influence of experiencing the here and now of extreme weather events on individuals' understanding and acknowledgment of human contributions to climate change.

How can we make sense of this profound shift in perspective? The attitudes we hold toward climate change are not shaped by a single force but by a complex interaction of diverse factors. Sociodemographic and economic factors, political affiliations, geographical location, and distance all

TABLE 7.1 What do you believe is the primary cause of climate change or global warming?

YEAR	HUMAN ACTIVITIES (%)	NORMAL CLIMATE CYCLES (%)
2015	52	48
2016	57	43
2018	62	38

Source: Houston Area Surveys, 2015–2018.

contribute to the formation of our beliefs. A key driver of climate change attitudes lies in the level of public awareness and comprehension surrounding the reality, causes, and inherent risks of this phenomenon. Greater understanding tends to fuel heightened concern and a greater inclination to support necessary actions to address climate change.[29] In addition, sociodemographic factors such as gender, age, education, income, and ethnicity exert their influence on individuals' perceptions of climate change.[30] These factors shape the lens through which we view climate change issues and contribute to the diversification of perspectives. Geography also plays a pivotal role in shaping climate change attitudes. Those residing in areas more susceptible to the impacts of climate change, such as coastal regions, often hold more heightened concerns than their counterparts living in less vulnerable territories.[31] The immediacy and tangible risks associated with climate change's manifestations can foster a sense of urgency and awareness. Furthermore, one's perception of personal impact plays a significant role in determining climate change attitudes. Individuals who believe they will bear direct consequences from climate change are more inclined to support mitigation efforts.[32] The recognition of a personal stake in the matter bolsters the commitment to actively address the challenges posed by climate change.

Political ideology also serves as a robust predictor of climate change attitudes, with a clear difference between Democrats and Republicans. Democrats consistently exhibit a higher likelihood of acknowledging the reality of climate change and endorsing the need for decisive action to combat its effects.[33] Throughout the past decade, the contrasting views held by Democrats and Republicans regarding the threat posed by climate change have become increasingly pronounced. According to the Pew Research Center, a majority of U.S. adults (54 percent) recognize climate change as a significant threat to the nation's well-being, but this proportion has declined slightly from 2020 although it remains higher than it was in the early 2010s. Notably, a substantial 78 percent of Democrats now perceive climate change as a major threat to the nation's well-being, marking a significant surge from the 58 percent recorded a decade prior.[34] In stark contrast, a mere 23 percent of Republicans view climate change as a significant

THE PERFECT STORM

menace, a figure that echoes their stance from a decade ago. This persistent polarization highlights the profound divide between the two major political parties regarding the urgency and gravity of climate change's impact.

The Houston region has been no stranger to severe storms, but Houstonians' attitudes toward climate change are similar to those in other states. In 2016, approximately 20 percent of Democrats downplayed the seriousness of climate change, whereas 52 percent perceived it as a significant and imminent threat. In contrast, 56 percent of Republicans viewed climate change as a less pressing concern, and a mere 17 percent considered it a major threat. A significant portion of both Democrats and Republicans fell somewhere in the middle, facing varying degrees of concern.[35] However, the landscape of Houstonians' climate change perceptions underwent a transformation following Hurricane Harvey. The hurricane acted as a catalyst, generating notable shifts in the attitudes of both Democrats and Republicans. In 2018, a few months after the storm, Democrats displayed heightened concern regarding climate change: only 14 percent regarded it as a negligible matter, and a resounding 60 percent deemed it a highly serious threat. A notable 26 percent fell within the spectrum of mixed views. Among Republicans, a similar trend emerged, with 59 percent considering climate change to be of minimal consequence, 19 percent acknowledged it as a significant and imminent threat, and the remaining 22 percent perceived climate change as a somewhat serious issue.

Although these changes appear modest in scale, their impact was significant. Houstonians' shifting perceptions of climate change following the devastation of Hurricane Harvey underscore the vital role distance plays. Their firsthand experience with monstrous storms was shaping individuals' understanding and viewpoint on climate change. Recognizing the severity of climate change is one thing, but understanding its underlying causes is another.

Within the scientific community a consensus exists regarding the primary driver of climate change: human activities. Emissions stemming from the burning of fossil fuels stand at the forefront, accompanied by economic development, population growth, and alterations in forest coverage. The release of greenhouse gases—including carbon dioxide, methane, nitrous oxide, and chlorofluorocarbons—into the atmosphere remains the chief culprit, trapping heat that is warming the planet.[36] Human actions that engender greenhouse gas emissions encompass the combustion of fossil fuels, deforestation, and specific agricultural practices such as livestock farming.[37] Natural phenomena such as volcanic eruptions and fluctuations in solar radiation also contribute to climate change, but to a lesser extent.[38] Although acknowledging the existence of natural factors that influence climate dynamics, it is the acceleration of anthropogenic greenhouse gas emissions that has spearheaded the most notable and expedited transformations.[39]

Experiencing a storm from a distance pales in comparison to the profound impact of being engulfed in its fury and witnessing one's possessions being submerged in several meters of unforgiving water. We may catch glimpses of the storm's aftermath through media coverage or distant observation, but the true magnitude of its devastation eludes us unless we confront its destructive force firsthand. The physical, economic, and emotional toll inflicted by a natural disaster defies quantification and can inflict enduring attitude and behavioral changes on individuals and communities. As my colleague at Rice University, Lacy M. Johnson, states, the "catastrophic flooding does not touch people's lives equally."[40] Hence, the obligated question: What degree of devastation must individuals endure to transform their perspectives on climate change?

THE HARVEY MODULE

The 37th Annual 2018 Kinder Houston Area Survey emerges as a charming resource, focusing on responses concerning income inequalities, demographic shifts, and the lasting impact of monstrous storms.[41] Administered to 1,507 participants seven months following Hurricane Harvey, this survey provided a crucial window of time in which individuals grasped the full scope of the storm's consequences, effectively mitigating the influence of recency bias in their responses. Recency bias, a cognitive phenomenon, underscores the human inclination to give greater weight to recent events when answering surveys. This inclination has the potential to distort survey results and yield biased conclusions.[42] To illustrate, consider a hypothetical survey gauging participants' satisfaction with their internet service. If an individual encountered an internet outage on the day preceding the survey, their satisfaction rating might be lower than it would have been had the outage not occurred so recently. Although no scientific threshold for quantifying the impact of recency effects has been determined, seven months provides ample time for individuals to retain vivid recollections of the chaos wreaked upon their life during Hurricane Harvey. The phrase "cada quien habla de la feria según como le fue en ella" (each one speaks about the fair according to how it goes for them) resonates, encapsulating the notion that individuals often express their thoughts and opinions through the lens of their personal experiences and circumstances. In the case of Hurricane Harvey, this sums up the profound impact firsthand experiences with the storm's devastation hold, which influence individuals' perspectives.

A total of 28 percent of the survey respondents disclosed that their homes had incurred some degree of damage. Within this group, 15 percent said that the necessary repairs had been successfully carried out within a month's time, and 9 percent said that the restoration process would extend beyond a month, presenting a more complicated journey toward recovery. Approximately 1 percent shared the tragic news that their homes had been irreparably destroyed. The impact of Harvey extended beyond homes, and 13 percent of the participants indicated damage to their personal vehicles, amplifying the scope of the storm's reach. Moreover, the survey explored whether respondents had encountered any instances of home flooding within the five years preceding Hurricane Harvey. Approximately 6 percent answered in the affirmative, signifying that their residences had previously fallen victim to flooding, further underscoring the recurring nature of the risk faced by certain individuals and communities. These figures paint a real picture of the tangible consequences experienced by Houston area residents, exposing the vast challenges and losses sustained as a result of the storm's relentless offensive.

THE PERFECT STORM

Modeling Attitudes Toward Climate Change

Allow me to reframe the central question of this chapter: How does a firsthand encounter with the devastating repercussions of these storms affect the inclination of individuals to recognize climate change as a contributing factor? In this section, I explore this question through the lens of partisanship.

To tackle this question, I focus on an analysis of the 2018 Kinder Houston Area Survey that centers on self-reported damage. By constructing an additive scale, I take into account whether participants' homes had suffered flooding in the five years preceding Hurricane Harvey, if their residences endured home damage during the storm, and whether their personal vehicles were affected. This scale attempts to gauge the extent of personal and direct experiences among Houston area residents after Hurricane Harvey. The scale goes from 0 to 4, with 0 meaning respondents' homes did not flood over the past five years nor did their homes or vehicles sustain any damage during Harvey, and 4 meaning that respondents experienced flooding in the past five years and their homes and vehicles suffered damages during Harvey. It is worth noting that the scale is only measuring how much damage Houstonians suffered during Harvey, it is not creating a new construct using variables that may be related but that measure different factors.

Harvey left an indelible mark on everyone's life, but the severity and proximity of its impact varied significantly. For instance, residing on the top floor of a low-rise building shielded me from harm, whereas just a few miles away numerous homes were subject to severe flooding. Although both my neighbors and I can claim to have "experienced" Harvey, our encounters diverge markedly, potentially influencing our attitudes in distinct ways.

As discussed previously, there is a clear link between party identification and conflicting beliefs concerning the existence and causes of climate change. Therefore, party identification stands as my second crucial predictor variable, encompassing participants' self-identification as either Republican or Democrat.

In addition to the damage scale and partisanship, I incorporated FEMA's housing assistance data, which provides insights into the cumulative damage

THE PERFECT STORM

reported at the zip code level. Expanding the scope to account for how different groups may experience the damages of Harvey, I included respondents' race and ethnicity, total household income, highest level of educational attainment, age, and gender. Recognizing that our attitudes can be shaped by the experiences of those around us, I also devised a social damage scale ranging from 0 to 4. This scale reflects whether individuals' extended social network—comprised of family members, close friends, or neighbors who are not part of their immediate household—endured damage to their homes or vehicles. By incorporating this social dimension, I can capture the potential influence of witnessing the ramifications of these storms on individuals within our immediate social circles. All of these variables have the potential to influence people's attitude toward climate change. For example, individuals with higher levels of education and Latinos tend to exhibit greater acceptance of climate change and recognize its significance.[43]

My main goal is to evaluate the likelihood of participants attributing climate change or global warming to human activity. To accomplish this, I examine the interaction between the severity of damage incurred from Hurricane Harvey and individuals' partisanship. I ran a logistic regression to estimate the impact of personal damages in conjunction with partisanship and other control variables on the probability of accepting the belief that human activities are responsible for climate change.

The model I used incorporates an interaction term between the personal damage index and partisanship. Survey data reveals that Democratic respondents are more inclined to attribute climate change or global warming to human activity. Therefore, experiencing the aftermath of Hurricane Harvey may not significantly alter their existing beliefs. Survey data also reveals that Republican respondents are more prone to view climate change as a product of natural climate cycles. However, encountering the devastating impacts of Hurricane Harvey firsthand within their own homes may prompt a shift in their convictions.

The results from the statistical analysis offer interesting insights (see table A.7.1 in the appendix for regression results). First, as expected the main effects of the personal damage index for Democratic participants does not yield significant effects—nearly three-quarters of Democrats already embrace the notion that climate change is anthropogenic. In contrast, the main effect for Republican self-identifiers in the absence of personal property damage or vehicular impact indicates that Republicans are approximately 46 percent less likely than Democrats to attribute climate change to human activities.

The interaction term paints an even more interesting picture. It suggests that Republicans who experienced no property damage during Hurricane Harvey are 34 percent more likely to align with the scientific consensus regarding the causes of climate change. As the magnitude of damage escalates, so does the probability that a Republican respondent would attribute climate change to human activities. For instance, an individual identifying as Republican whose home and vehicle were destroyed is 59 percent more likely to acknowledge human activities as the cause of climate change. Figure 7.1 illustrates the progressive increase in probability as personal damage intensifies.

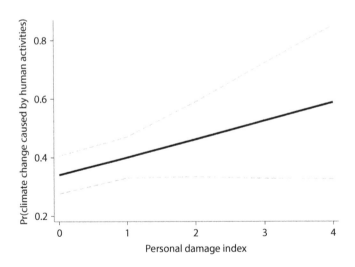

FIGURE 7.1 Probability of Republicans indicating that human activities are the cause of climate change given the level of property damage during Harvey.

Source: Data from the Kinder Area Survey.

THE PERFECT STORM

These findings underscore the intricate relationship between personal experiences and belief systems, especially within the context of political partisanship. The statistical analysis uncovers the nuanced shifts in perspectives that arise when individuals are confronted with the tangible consequences of extreme weather events, serving as a reminder of the profound impact that distance in the form personal encounters can have on shaping attitudes regarding climate change.

In chapter 1, I argued that distance plays a pivotal role in shaping our perceptions of events within our immediate reality, particularly for complex phenomena such as climate change. Our immediate reality can be seen as a bucket of sorts—housing a multitude of social and political processes that intertwine to create a distinct space within which our attitudes are formed. This chapter serves as an important reminder of the significance of distance. As evidenced by Hurricane Harvey's devastation, the impact of spatial proximity can be surprisingly influential, even on attitudes that are typically resistant to change over time. Once we see the lion's fury just steps away, our attitudes change dramatically. The unique characteristics of the space we inhabit, in this case, the degree to which our personal experiences—reflected in the damages we endured—shape our attitudes, hold substantial sway over our perspectives and beliefs.

8

THE GREAT DROUGHT

WITH MARKIE McBRAYER

In chapter 7, I explored the impact of severe storms on individuals' attitudes toward climate change, revealing an increased likelihood of acceptance of climate change when people directly experience extreme weather events. However, modifying attitudes is only one facet of the issue; the true challenge lies in translating these changed perspectives into behavioral shifts in response to extreme weather events.

In this chapter, coauthored with my former student Markie McBrayer, we explore the potential transformation of electoral behaviors arising from the impact of climate change. Our analysis centers on the context of the 2012 congressional election, a critical juncture coinciding with the harrowing Texas drought of 2011. We look at the complex dynamics at play and explain how the repercussions of climate change manifest in the electoral arena.

Between 2010 and 2014, Texas experienced varying degrees of drought and climate change–related events. In October 2010, the state climatologist John Nielsen-Gammon stated that the latest, long-standing drought was one of the most extreme and extensive of this century. Not only did the drought drain water supplies, but it also affected farmers and ranchers, costing them nearly $8 billion in corn, cotton, wheat, hay ($4.4 billion),

THE GREAT DROUGHT

and livestock (3.2 billion), which surpassed the 2006 drought loss of $3.5 billion.[1] Moreover, the human impact was visceral, with wildfires burning 32,000 acres of land and 1,600 houses in Bastrop County alone.[2]

The great drought occurred in Texas in 2011, when more than a third of the state experienced an unyielding "extreme" or "exceptional" drought, as classified by the U.S. Department of Agriculture. By November, approximately 1,000 of the 4,700 public water systems in Texas had taken the necessary step of implementing either voluntary or obligatory water restrictions. Among these, fifty-five systems prohibited any form of outdoor watering, and another twenty-three systems harbored the grim belief that their water supply would be depleted within 180 days.[3]

Regardless of party affiliation, all Texans felt the devastating human and economic impacts of climate change, whether they believe in it or not. The state Republican Party, including prominent Texas representatives and senators, publicly denied the scientific consensus that human activity was affecting the climate. They were highly skeptical of climate change because it challenged their beliefs in the free market and increased the likelihood of government regulations.[4] The 2014 Texas Republican Party platform included this statement about climate change: "While we all strive to be good stewards of the earth, 'climate change' is a political agenda which attempts to control every aspect of our lives. We urge government at all levels to ignore any plea for money to fund global climate change or 'climate justice' initiatives."[5] In contrast, the Texas Democratic Party platform "recognize(s) that climate change is a real and serious threat that is causing drought, crop failure, heat waves, more torrential storms, and extreme climate events."[6] The state of Texas experienced significant impacts resulting from climate change, but the two parties were on opposite sides of an ideological debate, with one party denying and the other acknowledging the existence of climate change.

In this chapter, we investigate the relationship between drought severity in Texas, identified geographically through drought data, and congressional electoral outcomes in 2008 and 2012. By examining the level of support for Democratic and Republican candidates in areas with varying degrees of drought severity, we explore how the severity of drought affects voter preferences and candidate performance. Candidates and political parties signal their policy intentions in electoral speeches, and voters who have viscerally experienced the effects of the drought (i.e., those in the agricultural industry) will have the greatest interest in severe climate events. In places where residents' livelihoods had been affected by the drought, vote margins would probably favor the Democratic Party over the Republican Party. Why? At the very least, the rhetoric of Democratic candidates offers a glimmer of hope going forward because they present potential solutions that align with the Aristotelian notion of alleviating fear (see chapter 1).

Previous research suggests that weather conditions and natural phenomena can have an impact on elections in two distinct ways. First, adverse weather and natural disasters are believed to decrease voter turnout by raising the costs associated with voting. For instance, if there is heavy rainfall on election day, it becomes more challenging for individuals to reach the polling stations. Similarly, when a hurricane hits a town or a region, resulting in damaged infrastructure, it can deter people from voting due to the logistical difficulties it presents. These increased costs of traveling to the voting location contribute to a decline in voter turnout.

Several studies support this idea. Jay Gatrell and Gregory Bierly's examination of Kentucky primary elections from 1990 to 2000 found a statistically significant negative effect of weather conditions on voter turnout.[7] Ron Shachar and Barry Nalebuff included rain as a control variable in their comprehensive analysis of voter turnout and observed that rain dampens voter participation.[8] Brad Gomez, Thomas Hansford, and George Krause analyzed fourteen presidential elections and concluded that rain and snow decrease voter participation in the United States, providing further evidence for the relationship between worsening weather conditions and increased voting costs.[9] However, Steve Knack's research using three years of ANES data found no effect of rain on voter turnout.[10] It is important to note that Knack acknowledges the possibility that the impact may be concentrated among specific populations, such as relatively unengaged voters.

Second, it is believed that poor weather conditions and natural disasters can have a negative impact on the electoral prospects of incumbents or the incumbent party. Voters may hold their elected officials accountable for

THE GREAT DROUGHT

what they perceive as failures in handling the disaster. Christopher Achen and Larry Bartels suggest that voters attribute blame to incumbents for their response to natural disasters, even though the officials may not have direct control over the occurrence of the disaster itself.[11] This claim has been challenged quantitatively by Anthony Fowler and Andrew Hall, but it still hold significant theoretical weight.[12] Elections provide an opportunity for voters to express their dissatisfaction and resentment toward elected officials based on their perceived ability to respond to and mitigate the impacts of the disaster. However, it is not clear why some voters attribute blame while others do not.

Kevin Arceneux and Robert Stein find that attributing blame to the government in the wake of a natural disaster is influenced by citizens' political knowledge and how the disaster has personally affected their life.[13] Voting decisions are then based on voters' assessments of the preparedness and response of local governments in facing natural disasters.

Neil Malhotra and Alexander Kuo demonstrate that voters hold public officials accountable for the deaths that resulted from Hurricane Katrina.[14] Initially, respondents tended to blame officials from the opposing party, but this effect diminished when more information was provided about the roles and responsibilities of the elected officials involved.

John Gasper and Andrew Reeves examined presidential and gubernatorial elections from 1970 to 2006 and found that voters assign responsibility to elected officials for weather-related damage.[15] However, the specific attribution of blame varied depending on the circumstances. For example, if a governor requests federal assistance and the president denies the request, voters may punish the president and support the governor. This punishment has been found in electoral outcomes in Italy after earthquakes.[16]

NO RAIN: DEMOCRAT OR REPUBLICAN?

Voters generally align themselves with the party that reflects their partisan loyalties and policy preferences, and they use retrospective evaluations to reward or penalize incumbent candidates and parties. Political campaigns can influence voters' attitudes and affect electoral turnout by providing information about candidates' policy positions. This reduces some level of uncertainty among voters, enabling them to make choices based on their preferred candidates.[17] However, a tension arises when considering the rhetoric of political campaigns, voters' partisan allegiances, and their lived experiences, particularly regarding politically and ideologically charged issues such as climate change, which may create a filter by which voters' analyze the issue.

Climate change manifests in various ways, including through storms, droughts, wildfires, and hurricanes. How spatially close or distant individuals are to these events influences how they experience them. Initially, individuals may perceive climate change–related events and associated risks as affecting others or as something that will occur in the distant future. However, once people have a direct experience with the effects of climate change events, their attitudes may change, or at the very least differ, from those who have not experienced such effects. Nearby events tend to be analyzed, perceived, and felt more concretely, whereas distant events are often construed more abstractly (see chapter 1).[18]

Voters' attitudes and electoral choices are influenced by a combination of partisan loyalties, policy preferences, campaign rhetoric, media coverage, and personal experiences. The proximity and directness of these experiences can shape individuals' perceptions and attitudes toward climate change and, in turn, influence their electoral decisions. In areas affected by severe drought, voters may find themselves in a state of dissonance when the political discourse and media messages do not align with their lived reality. This dissonance is particularly relevant in the context of climate change.

As voters are exposed to campaign and media messages, they often adopt them as their own.[19] However, in the climate change debate, voters are confronted with uncertainty due to the mismatch between their party's discourse and their personal experiences. The news media's "intent on hearing both sides in a debate [means] that they often are virtually incapable of showing where the majority opinion lies. In the climate debate, the same old skeptics can take up their position and receive equal time against an overwhelming majority of scientists."[20]

Individuals who experience more severe drought will process information differently than those who have no experience or experienced milder drought conditions. People gather information through their daily activities, personal experiences, contacts, news media, and political campaigns.[21] However, the narratives presented by the media and political campaigns often diverge from the lived experiences of voters.

Experiencing the effects of drought shapes voters' emotional disposition (i.e., fear or anxiety), which can outweigh their analytical processes and ideological biases. Direct experience with the here and now of the drought, including its risk dimensions, becomes a significant factor in shaping voters' concerns and beliefs about climate change. "Personal experience of weather and climate change-related events [e.g., experience of a drought] highlights how direct contact with events perceived to be related to climate change can increase concern and action on climate change."[22] Experiencing water shortages attributed to drought can heighten individuals' beliefs in and concerns about climate change.[23] The lived experience of drought and its impacts directly affect individuals' perceptions, prioritizing their immediate concerns over analytical reasoning and ideological biases. The experience of severe drought can create a dissonance between voters' personal experiences and the political and media narratives surrounding climate change. This personal experience becomes a powerful influence on voters' affective dispositions and concerns about climate change, transcending analytical processes and ideological biases.

Voters who experience the dissonance between political rhetoric and their reality are more likely to be motivated to act because the threat of climate change is more tangible and relevant to them. In general, voters tend to punish politicians at the polls during difficult times, even if there is little rational basis to hold the incumbents responsible for their hardships.[24] When a catastrophe occurs, voters seek explanations and attribute responsibility.[25]

Personal experiences may be influenced by preexisting ideological beliefs. Patrick Egan and Megan Mullin found that personal experiences with climate change–related events have a stronger impact among independents or political moderates.[26] And Lawrence Hamilton and Mary Stampone argue that personal experiences are unique to independents.[27] This relationship may not hold as strongly among strong partisans, possibly due to the "relatively innocuous nature of the experiences of climate impacts examined in these studies."[28]

However, when individuals experience extreme manifestations of climate change–related events rather than short-lived changes in local temperatures, their views and behaviors may be influenced, even if they hold ideological opposition to accepting climate change as a significant issue.[29] Those voters who ideologically align with the belief that extreme climate changes are indicative of climate change may shift their support toward the party that does not create a dissonance between political rhetoric and voters' reality.

Voters who experience the dissonance between political rhetoric and their personal experiences of climate change are more likely to act. However, the nature of this action and the extent to which personal experiences influence voters' views and behaviors can be influenced by preexisting ideological beliefs and the severity of the climate change events experienced (see chapter 7). Those who directly experience the effects of droughts are more likely to hold incumbents accountable who deny or downplay the significance of these events. This is particularly true for individuals whose livelihoods are tied to the agricultural sector. These voters are more inclined to believe in and to be concerned about climate change and its consequences even when their perceptions are influenced by polarized political rhetoric.[30]

Samuel Brody and colleagues showed that personal experiences of extreme climate change–related events, such as floods or sea level rise, shape individuals' perceptions of risks associated with their health, personal finances, and local environment.[31] Even less extreme experiences with weather or climate change–related events can influence individuals' attitudes.[32] In essence, those who viscerally experience the direct consequences of climate change events in their personal lives, jobs, and communities are more likely to reward candidates and parties that acknowledge and address their reality.

Individuals who have personal experiences with climate change–related events, particularly those whose livelihoods are affected, may be more likely to support candidates and parties that speak to their lived reality. These individuals are more attuned to the impacts of climate change and are inclined to reward those who acknowledge and propose solutions that address these issues. The Democratic Party began to openly acknowledge the effects of climate change, and it is intuitive that constituents who are most negatively affected by extreme weather events would reward the party that recognizes their reality. In contrast, the drought would have had a positive effect for Republicans in areas where the local labor market was *not* reliant on the agricultural sector. For them the effects of climate are not physically or psychologically proximate.

PLANTING THE SEEDS

The voter tabulation district (VTD), defined by the Texas Legislative Council, serves as the unit of analysis. VTDs are similar to election precincts in other states, but they have the advantage of being more easily linked to census geography. VTDs offer a finer geographic granularity, which allows for a more detailed understanding of the extent to which an area was affected by drought. For example, if the western portion of a county experienced more significant drought than the eastern portion, analyzing VTDs as the primary unit of analysis allows us to capture and depict these variations more accurately.

To evaluate the impact of drought on electoral success, we examine two election years: 2008 and 2012. Choosing these years is deliberate: 2008 predates the onset of the drought, and 2012 represents the most severe drought year (2011) since 2006. Both 2008 and 2012 are presidential election years, which facilitates our comparisons. However, redistricting occurred between these two years, resulting in some constituents being placed into new districts with new incumbent candidates in 2012. To ensure consistency and meaningful analysis, we narrow our focus to VTDs that had the same district and incumbent candidates in both 2008 and 2012.

To examine the differential effects of drought on Democrats and Republicans, the data and analyses are divided into four groups: incumbent

Democratic candidates in 2008, incumbent Republican candidates in 2008, incumbent Democratic candidates in 2012, and incumbent Republican candidates in 2012. The outcome variable is the percentage of total votes received by the incumbent candidate, which allows us to assess the performance of both Democratic and Republican incumbents before and after the drought occurred.

In 2008, the drought had no effect on either Democratic or Republican incumbents. Drought conditions in Texas were minimal, and few constituents had experienced the direct affects of extreme weather events. However, in 2012 Republican incumbents would have faced electoral punishment, and Democrats would be rewarded in areas in which agriculture plays a significant role in employment and the drought conditions were severe.

The main predictor measures the average drought experienced by each voter tabulation district over the year preceding the election. The data comes from the United States Drought Monitor's shapefiles, which provide weekly drought information and maps. The drought impact types were rescaled into five categories ranging from 0 (no drought) to 5 (exceptional drought), and the VTD's average drought value was based on the pixels representing each district's drought level.

The second predictor of interest is the percentage of county residents employed in agriculture. The data comes from the Bureau of Labor Statistics, specifically using the number of private sector employees in agriculture, forestry, and fishing (NAICS category 11) divided by the total number of private sector employees in each county. In cases of missing data, the values were imputed from the closest available year, giving preference to the previous year. If a county had no observations for any year, those cases were dropped from the analysis. We then created an interaction term by combining the agricultural employment indicator with the drought variable.

Several control variables were included at the VTD level, for example, the total population and the percentage of registered voters with a Spanish surname as a proxy for the Hispanic population proportion. VTDs with a higher proportion of Hispanics would in theory show greater support for Democratic candidates and lower support for Republican candidates. At the county level, we included the county unemployment rate for the election year from

THE GREAT DROUGHT

the Bureau of Labor Statistics. The analyses employed ordinary least squares with clustered standard errors at the county level to account for potential spatial dependencies. In simple terms, the clustered standard errors consider the natural grouping or similarity of observations within each county.

THE CROP

The primary focus is on the performance of drought, percentage of agricultural employment, and the interaction between these two variables (see table A.8.1 in the appendix for regression results). It is easier to understand the effects of an interaction through their marginal effects. Figure 8.1 shows the marginal effects of drought on Democrat and Republican vote shares in the 2008 election. As expected, there is no significant conditional effect of drought on either party's incumbents in 2008.

Figure 8.1 confirms these expectations, showing that the conditional effect of drought on both Republican and Democratic incumbents is statistically insignificant, with the 95 percent confidence intervals crossing. There is a minor exception in which Democratic incumbents face some punishment in areas with fewer agricultural employees, but this effect quickly becomes insignificant. We argue that the insignificance of the conditional effect of drought on both parties' vote shares in 2008 can be attributed to the lack of a visceral experience with drought among constituents. Overall, the results indicate an insignificant influence of drought on Democratic and Republican vote shares in 2008. Now let us turn our attention to the conditional effect of drought in 2012.

In 2011, Texas residents endured an extremely severe drought, leading to devastating wildfires and significant agricultural losses. The effects of this drought appear to have influenced the two parties differently in the 2012 election. Figure 8.2 shows the marginal effects of drought on Democrat and Republican vote shares in the 2012 election. The drought had a positive effect on incumbent Democrats in areas in which a larger proportion of the population was employed in the agricultural sector. This aligns

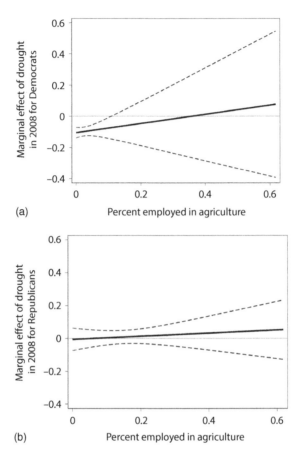

FIGURE 8.1 Marginal effect of drought on Democrat and Republican vote shares in 2008.

Source: Data from the Texas Secretary of State and the National Drought Monitor.

with the discussion in chapter 1 because these communities experienced the brunt of the drought's impacts. The Democratic Party acknowledged the effects of climate change during the 2012 election, so it is reasonable to assume that communities severely affected by extreme weather events would reward the party that recognized their reality and provided some future hope. In contrast, the effect of drought on Republicans is largely

THE GREAT DROUGHT

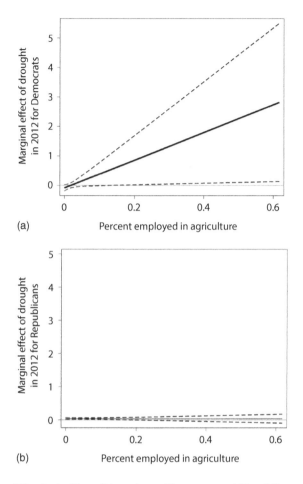

FIGURE 8.2 Marginal effect of drought on Democrat and Republican vote shares in 2012.

Source: Data from the Texas Secretary of State and the National Drought Monitor.

statistically insignificant, similar to the findings from 2008. However, we observe a brief positive effect on Republican incumbents' vote share in areas with a smaller proportion of agricultural employees. This suggests that communities unaffected by the drought rewarded incumbent Republicans. Nevertheless, this effect quickly diminishes, and its positive impact is relatively marginal compared to what Democratic incumbents experience.

The control variables show the expected patterns. The unemployment rate shows a detrimental impact on the vote share for Republican incumbents in both 2008 and 2012, whereas its influence on Democratic incumbents is not statistically significant. The proportion of the VTD population with a Spanish surname also had a negative influence on the vote share of Republican candidates in both election years, suggesting that a growing Hispanic population is linked to a decline in Republican backing. This pattern still holds today, but some shifts have occurred in recent elections. In 2008, a greater percentage of Hispanics benefited Democratic incumbents, but this effect was not observed in 2012. Moreover, the total population tended to disadvantage incumbent Republicans in both years, most likely due to the higher level of Democratic support in densely populated regions such as large urban centers.

Although fallout from the drought includes a range of impacts that can depend on the incumbent's political affiliation, our findings suggest that the immediate experience of extreme weather events significantly shapes people's behavior. The effects of the drought are felt more sharply by voters in rural areas. Many faced the devastating loss of cattle and crops, and their responses may be grounded in the deep-seated fear of losing their entire livelihood.

Democratic incumbents appear to benefit from the fallout of the drought, perhaps by offering a beacon of hope for the future. In stark contrast, the impact of the drought on Republican incumbents in rural areas tends to be neutral. Where there was once a somewhat positive relationship, that seems to have evaporated after the drought. This intriguing dynamic suggests that the direct experience of extreme events such as droughts can shape political landscapes in unexpected ways.

Through many diverse examples I have explored the impact of distance in its various forms on people's attitudes and behaviors. I hope I made a compelling case for the theory I advanced in this book and have piqued your interest regarding the influence of distance. In chapter 9, I summarize the main argument I presented, and I answer one of the most complicated questions in the social sciences: So what?

9

SO WHAT?

Academic research often boils down to a simple "So what?" or more directly to "Who cares?" I hope this book advances our understanding of how spatial, emotional or psychological, temporal, social, and cultural distances influence our attitudes and behaviors. My goal is to illuminate previously unexplored theoretical connections and empirical mechanisms to help us make better sense of the contrasts between our immediate realities and distant imagined realities—that is, between the "here and now" and the "there and later."

Chapter by chapter, I unravel the complex interaction between location and a host of factors: party affiliation, race and ethnicity, immigration status, the flow of information, and direct experiences. I underscore two pivotal ways in which distance may operate: as a catalyst for direct contact and as a filter that shapes our interpretation of events, objects, social groups, and policies. I believe we are guided by our emotions—especially fear and anxiety—and by our previously held beliefs, which may be accentuated even more by distance.

Making a contribution to social science research is a complex and sometimes fruitless task. Progress is born from arguments over terms and definitions and from the perpetual rebuilding of concepts, echoing Weber's belief that understanding the world is a continuous endeavor.[1] By introducing a multidisciplinary perspective on distance, I hope to contribute to this ongoing debate by reimagining something that may seem obvious to many but has long lacked a theoretical and empirical foundation. I do not argue that my theoretical perspective is "the" theoretical perspective. On the contrary, it is "a" theoretical perspective that I hope will be further enhanced and refined by my colleagues in the field.

The theoretical foundation of this book continues the dialogue across disciplines, from the classics to geography, political science, social psychology, and sociology. Although I only scratch the surface of a concept that has been sleepy for several years, particularly since the birth of the internet, in this book I reaffirm the importance of space, distance, emotions, and personal biases and values. These are not isolated factors but interconnected parts of a greater whole. The mechanisms I examine enhance Tobler's First Law, underscoring that proximity makes close objects more relatable than distant ones and detailing a set of plausible mechanisms showing how distance may influence our attitudes and behaviors.

The empirical scaffolding of this book underscores the plausibility of its theoretical foundation. I offer a suite of concepts that are not just familiar and resonant but also parsimonious, coherent, and differentiated, rooted in theory, and encapsulate what John Gerring refers to as "conceptual goodness."[2] The case studies provide important insights regarding distance, enabling us to grasp the nuanced interaction among various factors that affect our attitudes and behaviors. For instance, they shed light on the interaction between distance and health crises and distance and political ideology, presenting a more layered understanding of the factors that mold attitudes and behaviors related to two epidemics and a pandemic. The case studies also probe the association between distance and our emotional reactions, offering insights into the complex dance between fear and anxiety and how cultural differences may be emphasized by distance. Moreover, they illuminate how distance can inform our attitudes and behaviors in the face of environmental challenges. Collectively, these studies serve as valuable lenses through which we can understand the nuanced interplay these

SO WHAT?

factors have on our daily lives and on the decisions we make regarding our attitudes and behaviors.

Chapter 2 provides insight into the complex relationship between public opinion, fear, political dynamics, and distance. First, the case of Zika emphasizes the importance of temporal distance, highlighting the fact that our concerns were relatively low when Zika was not present in the United States. However, as infection rates grew in specific areas, our concerns increased and were influenced by a false sense of spatial closeness created by the passage of time. Second, the case of Ebola highlights the crucial role of the media in shaping how the public perceives a virus when it first appears, emphasizing Aquinas's unexpected factor that causes public opinion to become irrational in the face of a viral threat. Third, the impact of political polarization was evident in our responses to the COVID-19 pandemic, with differences observed across various regions. By analyzing mobility patterns in counties that favored Trump compared to those that supported Biden, the results underscore that places are not merely physical spaces but are also profoundly influenced by social and ideological factors.

Chapter 3 brings attention to the influential role that space and time play in shaping our attitudes and behaviors. I describe the profound impact that specific locations and the timing of events can have on our psychological responses. The case studies presented in this chapter reveal that significant shocks, such as terrorist attacks or mass shootings, can act as catalysts that set off a series of cognitive evaluations. Cognitive evaluations affect our attitudes and behaviors as we wrestle with the anticipation of potential future harm, demonstrating the authentic connections between space, time, and our emotional states. I demonstrate how these connections influence the formation of our attitudes and create a real or imagined hope—in the Aristotelian sense—that molds our behaviors.

The results presented in Chapter 4 emphasize the vital significance emotional bonds and physical separation have on people's perspectives about social movements, particularly the Black Lives Matter movement. The complex interaction between distance and empathy establishes a unique structure for social phenomena, encompassing both concrete and abstract elements that interact with place and its demographic characteristics. Both distance and emotion shape our interactions with protests, exerting a deep influence on our cognitive and emotional reactions. Empathy or a lack thereof shapes how the public chooses to deal with people's legitimate right to protest and how they assess the police response.

Chapters 5 and 6 focus on immigration issues. Chapter 5 examines the link between distance, viewed through the lens of ethnoracial and cultural perspectives, and attitudes toward immigrants from different regions of the world. I describe the diverse elements that mold perceptions and sentiments regarding immigrant communities, confirming that migrants who do not fit neatly within the American ethos—that is, those closer to "us"— tend to receive more negative appraisals. Chapter 6 shows that polarization surpasses divisions based on political parties or ideologies. The presence of both real and perceived geographic distance intensifies perceptions toward construction of a border wall between the United States and Mexico, and proximity magnifies our perception of its national security implications.

Chapters 7 and 8 explore the pressing threat of climate change and how experiencing extreme weather events shape both our attitudes and our electoral behavior. Describing the effects of monstrous storms in Houston and severe drought conditions throughout Texas, respectively, I explain how our attitudes and behaviors are encapsulated by a multitude of interconnected social and political processes that form a distinct environment in which our attitudes and behaviors develop. The results serve as a significant reminder of the importance of distance. In the devastation of Hurricane Harvey in 2017, the influence of physical proximity had a profound effect even on attitudes typically resistant to change over time. The distinctive qualities of the place we occupy and our personal encounters—reflected in the hardships we endured—shape our attitudes. These attitudes have a substantial impact on our perspective and convictions. The repercussions stemming from the 2011 Texas drought encompass a variety of consequences that depended on the political affiliation of incumbents seeking reelection and their personal experiences with severe weather occurrences. The consequences influencing individuals' voting behavior are obvious when the Augustinian concept of loss is taken into account.

SO WHAT?

In this book I introduce a new layer of complexity between policy, public opinion, and distance. When we are close, we experience the policy or the event's effects firsthand, without perceptual barriers. In contrast, when we are distanced from a policy or an event, we rely on abstract and decontextualized information that may lead to inaccurate associations and meanings, which are influenced by preexisting beliefs, attitudes, and emotions. Distance and our preconceptions work in tandem to create a perceptual screen between us and a policy. This distance amplifies or diminishes our selectivity in interpreting and perceiving something or someone, all to maintain consistency with our perceptions. Our exposure to news, political affiliations, and other influential factors interact with the distance that separates us from the real consequences of a policy. This interaction provides crucial information to individuals who are distant from a policy, event, or group of people and enables them to align their beliefs and values with their previously held beliefs.

Future work holds the promise of unraveling the complex interaction between distance, personal beliefs, political inclinations, emotions, and culture. Researchers can delve deeper into the mechanisms through which different forms of distance shape attitudes and behaviors. This may involve exploring the role of cognitive processes, such as information processing and selective attention, in mediating the impact of distance on attitudes and behaviors. Other studies may examine how individual and contextual factors moderate the effects of distance, such as the role of social networks, identity salience, and cultural values. Comparative analyses across diverse cultural and geographical contexts may offer valuable insights into the universality or context-specific nature of the influence of distance. By continuing to test these dimensions, research can contribute to a more comprehensive understanding of how distance shapes our attitudes and behaviors in an increasingly interconnected world.

APPENDIX

CHAPTER 2. OUTBREAKS, EPIDEMICS, AND PANDEMICS: ZIKA, EBOLA, AND COVID-19

TABLE A.2.1 Linear regression predicting worries of being infected by Zika given infection levels in February and June

VARIABLES	FEBRUARY	JUNE
Zika levels	0.03	0.08**
	(0.04)	(0.04)
Heard of Zika	0.18***	0.18***
	(0.04)	(0.04)
Female	0.11*	0.14**
	(0.06)	(0.07)
Hispanic	0.42***	0.56***
	(0.10)	(0.11)
Education	−0.15***	−0.17***
	(0.04)	(0.04)
Income	−0.04***	−0.02
	(0.01)	(0.02)
Republican	0.01	−0.04
	(0.06)	(0.07)
Constant	1.90***	1.94***
	(0.16)	(0.17)
Observations	921	930
R-squared	0.09	0.09

Note: Standard errors in parentheses.

*** $p < 0.01$; ** $p < 0.05$; * $p < 0.1$

TABLE A.2.2 Logistic regression predicting Ebola fears given number of news articles published

VARIABLES	
Number of articles	0.00353***
	(0.00129)
Age	−0.0406
	(0.0566)
Education	0.377***
	(0.117)
Income	0.0898**
	(0.0406)
Race/ethnicity	−0.400***
	(0.0988)
Constant	−0.275
	(0.428)
Observations	572

Note: Standard errors in parentheses.

*** $p < 0.01$; ** $p < 0.05$; * $p < 0.1$

TABLE A.2.3 Linear regression with state fixed-effects predicting mobility patterns given the Interaction between COVID-19 cumulative deaths and the Biden/Trump margin of victory

VARIABLES	
Cumulative deaths	0.00
	(0.00)
Biden/Trump margin of victory	−20.33***
	(0.09)
Cumulative deaths × Biden/Trump margin of victory	−0.00109***
	(0.000130)
Arkansas	3.70***
	(0.23)
Arizona	1.85***
	(0.29)
California	0.33*
	(0.20)
Colorado	4.33***
	(0.23)

Connecticut	8.13***
	(0.35)
Delaware	14.65***
	(0.54)
Florida	−2.05***
	(0.19)
Georgia	4.51***
	(0.18)
Hawaii	−8.81***
	(0.48)
Iowa	12.59***
	(0.22)
Idaho	8.70***
	(0.27)
Illinois	6.27***
	(0.19)
Indiana	3.33***
	(0.19)
Kansas	5.07***
	(0.23)
Kentucky	−0.71***
	(0.20)
Louisiana	−1.93***
	(0.22)
Massachusetts	5.17***
	(0.31)
Maryland	5.93***
	(0.24)
Maine	18.83***
	(0.28)
Michigan	6.55***
	(0.19)
Minnesota	8.07***
	(0.21)
Missouri	11.45***
	(0.20)
Mississippi	2.47***
	(0.22)
Montana	15.01***
	(0.33)
North Carolina	4.66***
	(0.18)

(*continued*)

TABLE A.2.3 (continued)

VARIABLES	
North Dakota	−6.31***
	(0.34)
Nebraska	6.16***
	(0.28)
New Hampshire	15.00***
	(0.32)
New Jersey	5.07***
	(0.25)
New Mexico	−3.09***
	(0.25)
Nevada	3.50***
	(0.34)
New York	4.44***
	(0.19)
Ohio	3.52***
	(0.18)
Oklahoma	4.98***
	(0.21)
Oregon	9.21***
	(0.23)
Pennsylvania	1.87***
	(0.19)
Rhode Island	9.94***
	(0.43)
South Carolina	7.53***
	(0.22)
South Dakota	10.86***
	(0.32)
Tennessee	4.79***
	(0.19)
Texas	−2.13***
	(0.17)
Utah	4.72***
	(0.28)
Virginia	3.05***
	(0.18)
Vermont	11.47***
	(0.32)
Washington	5.90***
	(0.22)

Wisconsin	7.76***
	(0.20)
West Virginia	-1.50***
	(0.26)
Wyoming	1.52***
	(0.32)
Constant	-9.17***
	(0.15)
Observations	678,057
R-squared	0.13

Note: Standard errors in parentheses. Alabama is the reference state, which serves as the state of comparison for the other states. Alaska is missing from the regression since it is not reported in the *New York Times* 2020 election results.

*** $p < 0.01$; ** $p < 0.05$; * $p < 0.1$

CHAPTER 3. BOMBS AND GUNS: BOSTON, PARIS, AND EL PASO

TABLE A.3.1 Linear regression predicting worries of a potential terrorist attack given news attention

VARIABLES	
News attention	0.09***
	(0.01)
Partisanship	0.01**
	(0.01)
Income	-0.01***
	(0.00)
Education	-0.05***
	(0.01)
Gender	0.17***
	(0.03)
Constant	-0.17***
	(0.05)
Observations	7,045
R-squared	0.03

Note: Standard errors in parentheses.

*** $p < 0.01$; ** $p < 0.05$; * $p < 0.1$

CHAPTER 4. PROTESTS: #BLACKLIVESMATTER

TABLE A.4.1 Linear regression predicting the public's attitudes toward the BLM movement

	FIRST STAGE
VARIABLES	
Diversity	0.05***
	(0.01)
Party	−10.05***
	(0.15)
NH Black	10.49***
	(1.20)
Hispanic	2.67**
	(1.21)
Asian	−1.16
	(1.82)
Native American	0.85
	(2.32)
Multiracial	1.50
	(1.79)
Age	−0.17***
	(0.02)
Income	−0.16***
	(0.05)
News attention	−0.07
	(0.33)
Education	0.68***
	(0.17)
Gender	5.25***
	(0.65)
Constant	93.63***
	(1.76)
Observations	6,329
R-squared	0.50

Note: Standard errors in parentheses.

*** $p < 0.01$; ** $p < 0.05$; * $p < 0.1$

TABLE A.4.2 Linear regression predicting individuals' attitudes toward using all available force to address urban unrest

VARIABLES	SECOND STAGE
Predicted values	−0.06***
	(0.00)
Distance from protest site (km)	0.01***
	(0.00)
Constant	6.61***
	(0.06)
Observations	6,329
R-squared	0.45

Note: Standard errors in parentheses.
*** $p < 0.01$; ** $p < 0.05$; * $p < 0.1$

CHAPTER 5. ONE SIZE DOES NOT FIT ALL: ATTITUDES TOWARD IMMIGRATION

TABLE A.5.1 Ordered logistic regression predicting attitudes toward immigration levels after 9/11 in 2002

RACE NEUTRAL IMMIGRATION

	DEPENDENT VARIABLE: MIGRATION LEVELS		
	NH WHITES (1)	AFRICAN AMERICAN (2)	HISPANICS (3)
Present levels	0.986***	1.360***	0.876***
	(0.097)	(0.192)	(0.179)
Education	0.132	−0.320*	0.159
	(0.081)	(0.167)	(0.156)
Gender	−0.087	−0.184	−0.269
	(0.164)	(0.339)	(0.276)
Income	−0.133*	−0.090	0.037
	(0.074)	(0.138)	(0.115)
Ideology	−0.199**	−0.080	0.003
	(0.101)	(0.159)	(0.143)

(*continued*)

TABLE A.5.1 *(continued)*

RACE NEUTRAL IMMIGRATION

	DEPENDENT VARIABLE: MIGRATION LEVELS		
	NH WHITES (1)	AFRICAN AMERICAN (2)	HISPANICS (3)
Married	-0.023 (0.190)	-0.046 (0.342)	0.240 (0.303)
Child<18	0.023 (0.181)	0.086 (0.322)	-0.363 (0.295)
Life satisfaction	0.611* (0.354)	0.964* (0.500)	-0.066 (0.513)
1st gen.	0.754 (0.481)	0.453 (0.611)	0.431 (0.357)
2nd gen.	0.002 (0.264)	0.638 (0.740)	-0.066 (0.335)
Partisanship	0.207** (0.098)	-0.223 (0.232)	0.095 (0.162)
Employed	0.191 (0.186)	0.125 (0.361)	0.141 (0.289)
U.S. satisfaction	-0.118 (0.177)	-0.211 (0.342)	0.487* (0.288)
Church attendance	-0.126** (0.059)	-0.117 (0.114)	-0.088 (0.096)
Midwest	-0.023 (0.227)	-0.207 (0.489)	-0.456 (0.790)
South	-0.452** (0.229)	0.191 (0.394)	0.182 (0.404)
West	-0.057 (0.237)	-0.864 (0.666)	-0.222 (0.398)
Urban	-0.074 (0.200)	-0.394 (0.323)	0.462 (0.291)
Observations	682	200	215

Note: Standard errors in parentheses.

*** $p < 0.01$; ** $p < 0.05$; * $p < 0.1$

EUROPEAN IMMIGRATION

	DEPENDENT VARIABLE:		
	MIGRATION LEVELS		
	NH WHITES	AFRICAN AMERICAN	HISPANICS
	(1)	(2)	(3)
Present levels	−0.780***	−0.492***	−0.100
	(0.100)	(0.164)	(0.169)
Education	−0.250***	0.114	−0.020
	(0.086)	(0.157)	(0.155)
Gender	0.181	−0.293	0.527*
	(0.169)	(0.336)	(0.290)
Income	0.042	0.048	0.029
	(0.077)	(0.126)	(0.117)
Ideology	0.020	−0.126	0.112
	(0.104)	(0.155)	(0.145)
Married	0.312	0.583*	0.063
	(0.198)	(0.336)	(0.311)
Child<18	−0.213	−0.037	0.066
	(0.190)	(0.302)	(0.301)
Life satisfaction	0.252	−0.165	0.275
	(0.362)	(0.436)	(0.532)
1st gen.	−1.628***	−0.333	−0.871**
	(0.563)	(0.608)	(0.360)
2nd gen.	−0.313	−0.841	−0.070
	(0.282)	(0.709)	(0.332)
Partisanship	0.167*	0.307	0.067
	(0.100)	(0.229)	(0.163)
Employed	−0.180	0.056	−0.074
	(0.189)	(0.338)	(0.291)
U.S. satisfaction	−0.516***	−0.677**	0.147
	(0.187)	(0.328)	(0.288)
Church attendance	0.054	−0.137	0.058
	(0.061)	(0.107)	(0.095)
Midwest	0.105	−0.768*	−0.204
	(0.239)	(0.455)	(0.759)
South	0.244	−0.585	−1.229***
	(0.237)	(0.389)	(0.414)

(continued)

EUROPEAN IMMIGRATION

	DEPENDENT VARIABLE: MIGRATION LEVELS		
	NH WHITES	AFRICAN AMERICAN	HISPANICS
	(1)	(2)	(3)
West	0.064	0.433	-0.526
	(0.250)	(0.640)	(0.404)
Urban	-0.336	0.177	0.057
	(0.210)	(0.304)	(0.293)
Observations	640	194	204

Note: Standard errors in parentheses.

*** $p < 0.01$; ** $p < 0.05$; * $p < 0.1$

LATIN AMERICAN IMMIGRATION

	DEPENDENT VARIABLE: MIGRATION LEVELS		
	NH WHITES	AFRICAN AMERICAN	HISPANICS
	(1)	(2)	(3)
Present levels	-0.816***	-0.931***	-0.477***
	(0.093)	(0.180)	(0.175)
Education	-0.144*	0.058	-0.219
	(0.084)	(0.168)	(0.157)
Gender	-0.122	0.003	-0.143
	(0.168)	(0.344)	(0.282)
Income	0.052	0.093	0.179
	(0.077)	(0.131)	(0.117)
Ideology	0.173*	-0.189	0.256*
	(0.102)	(0.160)	(0.147)
Married	0.218	-0.077	0.651**
	(0.196)	(0.344)	(0.316)
Child<18	-0.074	0.072	-0.095
	(0.186)	(0.320)	(0.303)
Life satisfaction	0.132	-1.189**	-0.487
	(0.348)	(0.492)	(0.560)
1st gen.	-0.422	0.515	-0.195
	(0.546)	(0.650)	(0.351)

2nd gen.	0.025	-0.001	0.390
	(0.276)	(0.746)	(0.336)
Partisanship	-0.147	0.657***	0.390**
	(0.100)	(0.241)	(0.164)
Employed	-0.189	0.109	-0.447
	(0.189)	(0.348)	(0.293)
U.S. satisfaction	-0.033	-0.537	0.257
	(0.182)	(0.335)	(0.292)
Church attendance	0.060	-0.038	0.050
	(0.061)	(0.113)	(0.097)
Midwest	0.124	-0.787*	-0.457
	(0.234)	(0.470)	(0.735)
South	0.454*	-0.570	0.071
	(0.234)	(0.405)	(0.408)
West	0.328	1.561**	-0.067
	(0.247)	(0.779)	(0.414)
Urban	0.183	-0.019	-0.217
	(0.210)	(0.316)	(0.296)
Observations	648	195	217

Note: Standard errors in parentheses.

*** $p < 0.01$; ** $p < 0.05$; * $p < 0.1$

ASIAN IMMIGRATION

	DEPENDENT VARIABLE: MIGRATION LEVELS		
	NH WHITES	AFRICAN AMERICAN	HISPANICS
	(1)	(2)	(3)
Present levels	-0.977***	-0.584***	-0.263
	(0.098)	(0.171)	(0.168)
Education	-0.306***	0.049	-0.332**
	(0.088)	(0.163)	(0.159)
Gender	0.042	-0.053	0.287
	(0.175)	(0.343)	(0.284)
Income	0.101	-0.060	0.200*
	(0.080)	(0.130)	(0.117)

(*continued*)

ASIAN IMMIGRATION

	DEPENDENT VARIABLE: MIGRATION LEVELS		
	NH WHITES	AFRICAN AMERICAN	HISPANICS
	(1)	(2)	(3)
Ideology	0.099	-0.111	0.048
	(0.108)	(0.156)	(0.144)
Married	0.091	-0.092	0.124
	(0.203)	(0.339)	(0.312)
Child<18	-0.359*	-0.070	-0.124
	(0.194)	(0.318)	(0.300)
Life satisfaction	-0.082	-0.939*	-0.222
	(0.366)	(0.486)	(0.546)
1st gen.	-0.431	0.112	-0.597*
	(0.598)	(0.609)	(0.357)
2nd gen.	0.041	-1.106	0.328
	(0.293)	(0.722)	(0.336)
Partisanship	0.006	0.386	0.322*
	(0.104)	(0.235)	(0.165)
Employed	-0.137	0.280	0.067
	(0.195)	(0.349)	(0.291)
U.S. satisfaction	-0.358*	-0.658*	-0.455
	(0.191)	(0.338)	(0.289)
Church attendance	0.018	-0.051	-0.013
	(0.063)	(0.113)	(0.095)
Midwest	0.144	-0.010	0.973
	(0.248)	(0.467)	(0.731)
South	0.391	-0.362	-0.258
	(0.243)	(0.395)	(0.399)
West	0.300	1.172	0.503
	(0.257)	(0.728)	(0.402)
Urban	0.155	0.022	-0.004
	(0.221)	(0.318)	(0.295)
Observations	644	195	209

Note: Standard errors in parentheses.

*** $p < 0.01$; ** $p < 0.05$; * $p < 0.1$

AFRICAN AMERICAN IMMIGRATION

	DEPENDENT VARIABLE: MIGRATION LEVELS		
	NH WHITES (1)	AFRICAN AMERICAN (2)	HISPANICS (3)
Present levels	−0.989*** (0.101)	−0.580*** (0.163)	−0.612*** (0.178)
Education	−0.162* (0.086)	−0.339** (0.158)	−0.353** (0.167)
Gender	0.023 (0.168)	−0.018 (0.321)	0.563* (0.297)
Income	−0.045 (0.077)	−0.144 (0.122)	0.331*** (0.123)
Ideology	0.058 (0.103)	−0.108 (0.145)	0.214 (0.153)
Married	0.318 (0.197)	−0.099 (0.321)	0.258 (0.324)
Child<18	−0.119 (0.187)	0.466 (0.300)	0.081 (0.319)
Life satisfaction	−0.288 (0.358)	0.140 (0.429)	0.202 (0.560)
1st gen.	0.023 (0.558)	−0.347 (0.596)	−0.737** (0.373)
2nd gen.	−0.168 (0.277)	−0.557 (0.708)	0.485 (0.354)
Partisanship	0.025 (0.101)	0.142 (0.220)	0.139 (0.167)
Employed	−0.201 (0.190)	0.358 (0.331)	−0.417 (0.305)
U.S. satisfaction	−0.031 (0.186)	−0.598* (0.327)	0.293 (0.299)
Church attendance	0.097 (0.061)	−0.211** (0.106)	−0.128 (0.101)
Midwest	0.112 (0.240)	−0.132 (0.443)	0.546 (0.788)
South	0.491** (0.236)	−1.105*** (0.384)	−0.272 (0.426)

(continued)

AFRICAN AMERICAN IMMIGRATION

	DEPENDENT VARIABLE: MIGRATION LEVELS		
	NH WHITES	AFRICAN AMERICAN	HISPANICS
	(1)	(2)	(3)
West	-0.242	0.793	-0.743*
	(0.245)	(0.659)	(0.433)
Urban	-0.439**	0.552*	-0.254
	(0.212)	(0.302)	(0.313)
Observations	638	196	201

Note: Standard errors in parentheses.

*** $p < 0.01$; ** $p < 0.05$; * $p < 0.1$

ARAB IMMIGRATION

	DEPENDENT VARIABLE: MIGRATION LEVELS		
	NH WHITES	AFRICAN AMERICAN	HISPANICS
	(1)	(2)	(3)
Present levels	-1.030***	-0.891***	-0.656***
	(0.109)	(0.181)	(0.181)
Education	-0.006	0.052	-0.095
	(0.091)	(0.167)	(0.163)
Gender	-0.341*	0.364	0.338
	(0.182)	(0.361)	(0.297)
Income	-0.046	0.157	0.154
	(0.082)	(0.137)	(0.122)
Ideology	0.496***	0.163	0.127
	(0.115)	(0.162)	(0.146)
Married	0.022	-0.068	-0.167
	(0.212)	(0.355)	(0.325)
Child<18	-0.049	-0.061	0.426
	(0.200)	(0.332)	(0.307)

Life satisfaction	-0.106	-0.476	-0.747
	(0.394)	(0.480)	(0.562)
1st gen.	-0.694	-0.307	-0.906**
	(0.569)	(0.635)	(0.376)
2nd gen.	-0.313	0.637	-0.060
	(0.296)	(0.796)	(0.348)
Partisanship	0.013	0.442*	-0.048
	(0.110)	(0.234)	(0.171)
Employed	-0.063	0.016	0.260
	(0.204)	(0.359)	(0.294)
U.S. satisfaction	-0.410**	-0.203	0.025
	(0.201)	(0.339)	(0.301)
Church attendance	0.066	0.098	-0.017
	(0.067)	(0.115)	(0.099)
Midwest	0.101	0.805*	0.765
	(0.258)	(0.486)	(0.815)
South	0.330	0.631	-0.535
	(0.261)	(0.413)	(0.424)
West	-0.323	1.162	-0.251
	(0.263)	(0.711)	(0.411)
Urban	-0.129	-0.129	-0.032
	(0.222)	(0.325)	(0.304)
Observations	647	195	203

Note: Standard errors in parentheses.

*** $p < 0.01$; ** $p < 0.05$; * $p < 0.1$

TABLE A.5.2 Ordered logistic regression predicting attitudes toward immigration levels after immigrant marches in 2006

RACE NEUTRAL IMMIGRATION

	DEPENDENT VARIABLE: MIGRATION LEVELS		
	NH WHITES (1)	AFRICAN AMERICAN (2)	HISPANICS (3)
Present levels	1.083***	0.753***	0.945***
	(0.103)	(0.114)	(0.135)
Education	0.079	−0.228**	0.094
	(0.074)	(0.111)	(0.113)
Gender	0.082	−0.065	0.238
	(0.145)	(0.201)	(0.189)
Income	−0.017	0.032	0.031
	(0.073)	(0.104)	(0.093)
Ideology	−0.344***	−0.083	−0.115
	(0.094)	(0.102)	(0.107)
Married	0.020	0.344	0.106
	(0.167)	(0.233)	(0.214)
Child<18	0.081	−0.216	0.418**
	(0.168)	(0.214)	(0.203)
Life satisfaction	0.032	−0.644**	−0.140
	(0.279)	(0.303)	(0.312)
1st gen.	0.065	1.861***	−0.248
	(0.333)	(0.426)	(0.238)
2nd gen.	0.387*	0.132	0.024
	(0.232)	(0.417)	(0.245)
Partisanship	0.138	−0.180	0.016
	(0.098)	(0.172)	(0.115)
Employed	0.298*	−0.010	0.055
	(0.161)	(0.221)	(0.213)
U.S. satisfaction	0.035	0.600*	0.153
	(0.178)	(0.342)	(0.218)
Church attendance	−0.076	−0.101	0.117*
	(0.052)	(0.075)	(0.067)

Midwest	0.363	-0.050	-0.104
	(0.284)	(0.308)	(0.465)
South	0.037	0.157	-0.158
	(0.234)	(0.261)	(0.313)
West	-0.110	-0.544	-0.317
	(0.233)	(0.377)	(0.310)
Urban	-0.149	0.300	0.209
	(0.151)	(0.215)	(0.190)
Observations	786	417	435

Note: Standard errors in parentheses.

*** $p < 0.01$; ** $p < 0.05$; * $p < 0.1$

EUROPEAN IMMIGRATION

	DEPENDENT VARIABLE: MIGRATION LEVELS		
	NH WHITES	AFRICAN AMERICAN	HISPANICS
	(1)	(2)	(3)
Present levels	-0.775***	-0.435***	-0.144
	(0.106)	(0.111)	(0.123)
Education	-0.206**	-0.158	-0.084
	(0.085)	(0.113)	(0.110)
Gender	-0.088	0.299	0.003
	(0.164)	(0.207)	(0.196)
Income	-0.122	0.101	0.066
	(0.082)	(0.106)	(0.095)
Ideology	0.164	0.074	0.134
	(0.102)	(0.102)	(0.112)
Married	0.022	-0.063	0.554**
	(0.185)	(0.242)	(0.222)
Child<18	-0.470**	-0.233	-0.182
	(0.193)	(0.219)	(0.209)
Life satisfaction	0.458	-0.438	-0.244
	(0.313)	(0.309)	(0.329)
1st gen.	-0.780**	0.372	-0.373
	(0.371)	(0.450)	(0.246)

(continued)

EUROPEAN IMMIGRATION

	DEPENDENT VARIABLE: MIGRATION LEVELS		
	NH WHITES (1)	AFRICAN AMERICAN (2)	HISPANICS (3)
2nd gen.	0.171 (0.273)	−1.301** (0.508)	−0.078 (0.249)
Partisanship	0.189* (0.107)	0.209 (0.183)	0.215* (0.119)
Employed	0.121 (0.182)	0.157 (0.228)	−0.036 (0.227)
U.S. satisfaction	−0.107 (0.196)	0.277 (0.383)	−0.292 (0.227)
Church attendance	−0.028 (0.057)	0.022 (0.077)	−0.039 (0.070)
Midwest	−0.187 (0.333)	0.098 (0.319)	−0.510 (0.466)
South	−0.238 (0.269)	−0.001 (0.270)	−0.177 (0.321)
West	−0.124 (0.268)	0.214 (0.363)	−0.047 (0.314)
Urban	−0.306* (0.172)	0.109 (0.220)	0.086 (0.197)
Observations	753	403	404

Note: Standard errors in parentheses.

*** $p < 0.01$; ** $p < 0.05$; * $p < 0.1$

LATIN AMERICAN IMMIGRATION

	DEPENDENT VARIABLE: MIGRATION LEVELS		
	NH WHITES (1)	AFRICAN AMERICAN (2)	HISPANICS (3)
Present levels	−0.779*** (0.101)	−0.554*** (0.114)	−0.428*** (0.138)
Education	0.007 (0.078)	0.016 (0.112)	−0.131 (0.115)

Gender	-0.129	0.169	-0.262
	(0.152)	(0.203)	(0.205)
Income	0.056	0.159	-0.062
	(0.075)	(0.104)	(0.099)
Ideology	0.196**	0.016	0.044
	(0.096)	(0.101)	(0.116)
Married	-0.091	-0.288	0.327
	(0.174)	(0.236)	(0.234)
Child<18	0.103	0.082	-0.038
	(0.176)	(0.218)	(0.220)
Life satisfaction	-0.084	0.015	-0.427
	(0.298)	(0.312)	(0.364)
1st gen.	0.272	-0.130	0.746***
	(0.338)	(0.434)	(0.258)
2nd gen.	-0.033	0.140	0.311
	(0.251)	(0.469)	(0.257)
Partisanship	-0.137	0.240	-0.00004
	(0.100)	(0.181)	(0.126)
Employed	0.064	-0.317	-0.011
	(0.169)	(0.226)	(0.235)
U.S. satisfaction	-0.222	0.429	0.243
	(0.183)	(0.365)	(0.243)
Church attendance	0.062	0.140*	-0.003
	(0.054)	(0.076)	(0.073)
Midwest	0.102	-0.323	-0.023
	(0.305)	(0.312)	(0.503)
South	0.419*	-0.147	0.241
	(0.247)	(0.267)	(0.342)
West	0.440*	0.399	0.371
	(0.244)	(0.377)	(0.335)
Urban	-0.066	-0.181	-0.097
	(0.158)	(0.217)	(0.205)
Observations	760	408	433

Note: *p; **p; ***p < 0.01

ASIAN IMMIGRATION

	DEPENDENT VARIABLE: MIGRATION LEVELS		
	NH WHITES (1)	AFRICAN AMERICAN (2)	HISPANICS (3)
Present levels	-0.935***	-0.718***	-0.323***
	(0.100)	(0.113)	(0.124)
Education	-0.286***	-0.121	-0.105
	(0.087)	(0.109)	(0.112)
Gender	0.074	-0.192	0.068
	(0.167)	(0.204)	(0.197)
Income	0.066	0.182*	0.280***
	(0.082)	(0.107)	(0.096)
Ideology	0.166	0.159	0.275**
	(0.105)	(0.099)	(0.112)
Married	0.033	-0.274	-0.193
	(0.189)	(0.241)	(0.223)
Child<18	-0.279	-0.031	-0.008
	(0.196)	(0.215)	(0.212)
Life satisfaction	-0.246	0.289	-0.881***
	(0.316)	(0.313)	(0.334)
1st gen.	-0.014	-0.007	-0.045
	(0.406)	(0.473)	(0.250)
2nd gen.	0.155	0.123	-0.379
	(0.274)	(0.468)	(0.249)
Partisanship	0.163	0.240	0.156
	(0.108)	(0.176)	(0.122)
Employed	0.022	-0.054	-0.162
	(0.186)	(0.227)	(0.228)
U.S. satisfaction	-0.151	-0.355	-0.617***
	(0.199)	(0.356)	(0.233)
Church attendance	0.052	-0.015	-0.060
	(0.058)	(0.077)	(0.070)
Midwest	-0.346	0.373	0.534
	(0.351)	(0.318)	(0.484)
South	0.252	-0.133	0.336
	(0.279)	(0.272)	(0.326)

West	0.292	0.008	0.828**
	(0.279)	(0.357)	(0.321)
Urban	-0.074	0.094	0.321
	(0.175)	(0.217)	(0.199)
Observations	748	403	400

Note: Standard errors in parentheses.
*** $p < 0.01$; ** $p < 0.05$; * $p < 0.1$

AFRICAN IMMIGRATION

	DEPENDENT VARIABLE: MIGRATION LEVELS		
	NH WHITES (1)	AFRICAN AMERICAN (2)	HISPANICS (3)
Present levels	-0.811***	-0.465***	-0.125
	(0.102)	(0.106)	(0.122)
Education	-0.317***	-0.078	-0.045
	(0.082)	(0.107)	(0.112)
Gender	-0.177	-0.235	0.098
	(0.158)	(0.194)	(0.195)
Income	-0.043	-0.056	-0.075
	(0.078)	(0.098)	(0.095)
Ideology	0.225**	0.235**	0.156
	(0.099)	(0.096)	(0.111)
Married	-0.133	-0.321	0.517**
	(0.180)	(0.226)	(0.220)
Child<18	-0.497***	-0.089	-0.056
	(0.186)	(0.206)	(0.210)
Life satisfaction	-0.018	-0.281	0.010
	(0.308)	(0.290)	(0.324)
1st gen.	-0.223	-0.080	-0.052
	(0.363)	(0.440)	(0.250)
2nd gen.	0.016	-0.215	0.125
	(0.258)	(0.427)	(0.245)
Partisanship	-0.206**	0.037	-0.0004
	(0.105)	(0.166)	(0.119)

(*continued*)

AFRICAN IMMIGRATION

	DEPENDENT VARIABLE:		
	MIGRATION LEVELS		
	NH WHITES	**AFRICAN AMERICAN**	**HISPANICS**
	(1)	(2)	(3)
Employed	-0.129	0.176	-0.401*
	(0.176)	(0.215)	(0.225)
U.S. satisfaction	-0.260	0.210	0.132
	(0.191)	(0.348)	(0.225)
Church attendance	0.107*	-0.023	-0.196***
	(0.056)	(0.072)	(0.070)
Midwest	0.001	-0.105	0.016
	(0.319)	(0.296)	(0.489)
South	0.447*	-0.220	-0.185
	(0.259)	(0.253)	(0.330)
West	-0.121	-0.499	0.071
	(0.255)	(0.352)	(0.321)
Urban	-0.254	0.095	-0.021
	(0.166)	(0.207)	(0.196)
Observations	741	411	394

Note: *p; **p; ***p < 0.01

ARAB IMMIGRATION

	DEPENDENT VARIABLE:		
	MIGRATION LEVELS		
	NH WHITES	**AFRICAN AMERICAN**	**HISPANICS**
	(1)	(2)	(3)
Present levels	-0.880***	-0.733***	-0.229*
	(0.102)	(0.116)	(0.123)
Education	-0.429***	0.057	-0.003
	(0.084)	(0.113)	(0.109)
Gender	0.046	-0.148	0.012
	(0.156)	(0.209)	(0.194)

Income	0.031	−0.082	0.001
	(0.078)	(0.105)	(0.095)
Ideology	0.239**	0.121	0.267**
	(0.099)	(0.103)	(0.112)
Married	0.195	−0.038	0.279
	(0.181)	(0.245)	(0.221)
Child<18	−0.404**	0.027	0.018
	(0.182)	(0.224)	(0.208)
Life satisfaction	0.079	−0.313	−0.638*
	(0.305)	(0.313)	(0.339)
1st gen.	1.020***	−0.632	−0.634**
	(0.389)	(0.464)	(0.246)
2nd gen.	0.320	−0.386	−0.423*
	(0.267)	(0.458)	(0.245)
Partisanship	−0.162	−0.199	0.280**
	(0.103)	(0.189)	(0.123)
Employed	−0.191	0.209	−0.278
	(0.176)	(0.232)	(0.226)
U.S. satisfaction	−0.355*	−0.027	0.075
	(0.188)	(0.386)	(0.231)
Church attendance	0.008	−0.117	−0.100
	(0.056)	(0.076)	(0.068)
Midwest	−0.546*	−0.148	0.197
	(0.322)	(0.318)	(0.480)
South	−0.296	−0.061	0.022
	(0.261)	(0.272)	(0.332)
West	−0.576**	−0.667*	−0.172
	(0.258)	(0.363)	(0.322)
Urban	−0.263	0.070	0.105
	(0.164)	(0.224)	(0.197)
Observations	730	398	388

Note: Standard errors in parentheses.

*** $p < 0.01$; ** $p < 0.05$; * $p < 0.1$

CHAPTER 6. FROM A DISTANCE: PARTISANSHIP, PUBLIC ATTITUDES, AND GEOGRAPHIC PROXIMITY TOWARD THE U.S.-MEXICO BORDER WALL

TABLE A.6.1 Logit regression predicting support toward building a fence along the Texas-Mexico border given driving distance (Models 1 and 2) and Euclidean distance (Models 3 and 4)

VARIABLES	MODEL 1	MODEL 2	MODEL 3	MODEL 4
log (driving distance)	-0.104	-0.307	—	—
	(0.242)	(0.248)		
log (distance to border)	—	—	-0.111	-0.286
			(0.227)	(0.228)
Republican	0.433	-2.708*	0.431	-2.487*
	(0.308)	(1.613)	(0.308)	(1.502)
Republican × log (driving distance)	—	0.460**	—	—
		(0.232)		
Republican × log (distance to border)	—	—	—	0.440**
				(.222)
U.S. born Hispanic	-0.489	-0.533	-0.489	-0.525
	(0.497)	(0.493)	(0.497)	(0.492)
Foreign-born Hispanic	-1.657**	-1.850**	-1.669**	-1.892***
	(0.711)	(0.724)	(0.713)	(0.734)
Non-Hispanic Black	-1.204***	-1.218***	-1.202***	-1.216***
	(0.451)	(0.453)	(0.451)	(0.453)
Other racial ID	0.086	0.023	0.086	0.027
	(0.44)	(0.439)	(0.44)	(0.44)
Income	-0.002	0.007	-0.002	0.007
	(0.052)	(0.053)	(0.052)	(0.053)
Education	-0.101	-0.107	-0.101	-0.107
	(0.069)	(0.069)	(0.069)	(0.069)
Female	0.045	0.042	0.043	0.044
	(0.234)	(0.234	(0.234)	(0.234)
Age	0.011*	0.011*	0.011*	0.011*
	(0.007)	(0.007)	(0.007)	(0.007)
% Mexican population	-0.473	-0.395	-0.533	-0.355
	(1.706)	(1.625)	(1.664)	(1.583)
Crime	0.002	0.002	0.002	0.002
	(0.003)	(0.003)	(0.003)	(0.003)
Relig. serv. attendance	-0.101	-0.103	-0.101	-0.102
	(0.074)	(0.074)	(0.074)	(0.074)
Trump's approval	1.280***	1.288***	1.280***	1.290***
	(0.119)	(0.120)	(0.119)	(0.12)
Wall effectiveness	2.054***	2.078***	2.053***	2.074***
	(0.26)	(0.261)	(0.26)	(0.261)
Constant	-3.537*	-2.19	-3.504*	-2.404
	(1.981)	(1.988	(1.839)	-1.811)

Observations	1,164	1,164	1,164	1,164
PseudoR²	0.63	0.633	0.63	0.633
χ^2 test	949.6	953.4	949.7	953.4
prob > χ^2	0	0	0	0

Note: Standard errors in parentheses.

*** $p < 0.01$; ** $p < 0.05$; * $p < 0.1$

TABLE A.6.2 Average treatment on the treated with Level 0 as the basis for comparisons against Level 1, Level 2, and Level 3

	COEF.	STD. ERR.	Z	P>Z	[95% CONF. INTERVAL]
100–500 miles	3.75	0.98	3.83	0	1.83 5.67
500 to 1,000 miles	5.86	0.99	5.92	0	3.92 7.80
More than 1,000 miles	5.40	1.05	5.15	0	3.34 7.45

TABLE A.6.3 Covariate balance summary

TREATMENT	OBSERVATIONS RAW	WEIGHTED
Level 0	801	318.1
Level 1	94	322.5
Level 2	126	316.6
Level 3	242	305.8
Total	1,263	1,263

	STANDARDIZED DIFFERENCES		VARIANCE RATIO	
Level 1	Raw	Weighted	Raw	Weighted
FIPS	-0.05	-0.02	1.58	1.54
Income	0.35	-0.03	0.90	1.00
Education	0.05	-0.06	0.81	0.85
Age	0.35	0.01	0.94	1.02
Level 2				
FIPS	-0.31	-0.02	0.83	0.88
Income	0.01	0.00	0.90	0.96
Education	-0.05	-0.05	0.89	0.90
Age	0.36	-0.06	1.04	1.06
Level 3				
FIPS	0.53	0.14	0.72	0.72
Income	0.18	-0.01	0.91	0.93
Education	-0.11	-0.01	0.94	0.94
Age	0.35	0.02	0.90	0.97

Note: A perfectly balanced covariate has a standardized difference of zero and a variance ratio of one in the weighted data.

TABLE A.6.4 Average treatment effects for the treated using Level 0 as the basis for comparisons and Level 1 for the subset of Republicans who reside within 100 to 500 miles away from the border

	COEF.	ROBUST STD. ERR.	Z	P>Z	[95% CONF. INTERVAL]	
(1 vs 0)	0.57	0.053	10.68	0	0.47	0.68
(2 vs 0)	0.63	0.147	4.25	0	0.34	0.91
(3 vs 0)	0.43	0.208	2.08	0.038	0.02	0.84
POmean						
	0.15	0.03	4.98	0	0.09	0.21

The following table expresses the ATET for Level 1 as a proportion of the average potential-outcome of Level 0.

β(Republican-Level 1) / β(Level 0)

COEF.	STD. ERR.	Z	P>Z	[95% CONF. INTERVAL]	
3.75	0.98	3.83	0	1.83	5.67

TABLE A.6.5 Average treatment effects for the treated using Level 0 as the basis for comparisons and Level 2 for the subset of Republicans who reside within 500 to 1,000 miles away from the border

	COEF.	ROBUST STD. ERR.	Z	P>Z	[95% CONF. INTERVAL]	
(1 vs 0)	0.76	0.057	13.34	0	0.65	0.87
(2 vs 0)	0.68	0.039	17.75	0	0.61	0.76
(3 vs 0)	0.57	0.048	11.78	0	0.47	0.66
POmean						
0	0.12	0.02	7.21	0	0.09	0.15

The following table expresses the ATET for Level 2 as a proportion of the average potential-outcome of Level 0.

β(Republican-Level 2) / β(Level 0)

COEF.	STD. ERR.	Z	P>Z	[95% CONF. INTERVAL]	
5.86	0.99	5.92	0	3.92	7.80

TABLE A.6.6 Average treatment effects for the treated using Level 0 as the basis for comparisons and Level 3 for the subset of Republicans who reside more than 1,000 miles away from the border

	COEF.	ROBUST STD. ERR.	Z	P>Z	[95% CONF. INTERVAL]	
(1 vs 0)	0.75	0.058	13.11	0	0.64	0.87
(2 vs 0)	0.73	0.039	18.99	0	0.66	0.81
(3 vs 0)	0.62	0.033	18.7	0	0.56	0.69
POmean						
	0.12	0.02	6.23	0	0.08	0.15

The following table expresses the ATET for Level 3 as a proportion of the average potential-outcome of Level 0.

β(Republican-Level 3) / β(Level 0)

COEF.	STD. ERR.	Z	P>Z	[95% CONF. INTERVAL]	
5.40	1.05	5.15	0	3.34	7.45

TABLE A.6.7 Logit regression predicting support toward building a fence along the Texas-Mexico border given driving distance (Model A1) and Euclidean distance (Model A2) and their interaction with crime

VARIABLES	(1) MODEL A1	(2) MODEL A2
log (driving distance)	0.123	—
	(0.369)	
log (distance to border)	—	0.118
		(0.349)
Crime	0.019	0.019
	(0.021)	(0.020)
log (driving distance) × crime	-0.003	—
	(0.003)	
log (distance to border) × crime	—	-0.003
		(0.003)
Republican	0.442	0.441
	(0.308)	(0.309)
Non-Hispanic Black	-1.184***	-1.179***
	(0.451)	(0.451)
Other	0.089	0.090
	(0.440)	(0.440)

(*continued*)

TABLE A.6.7 (continued)

VARIABLES	(1) MODEL A1	(2) MODEL A2
U.S. born Hispanic	−0.510	−0.513
	(0.500)	(0.500)
Foreign-born Hispanic	−1.599**	−1.601**
	(0.715)	(0.716)
Income	−0.001	−0.001
	(0.052)	(0.052)
Education	−0.104	−0.104
	(0.069)	(0.069)
Female	0.044	0.041
	(0.234)	(0.234)
Age	0.011*	0.011*
	(0.007)	(0.007)
% Mexican population	−0.518	−0.645
	(1.702)	(1.676)
Relig. serv. attendance	−0.101	−0.101
	(0.074)	(0.074)
Trump's approval	1.279***	1.278***
	(0.119)	(0.119)
Wall effectiveness	2.049***	2.051***
	(0.260)	(0.260)
Constant	−5.044*	−4.960**
	(2.732)	(2.526)
Observations	1,164	1,164
PseudoR^2	0.631	0.631
χ^2 test	950.3	950.5
prob > χ^2	0	0

Note: Standard errors in parentheses.

*** $p < 0.01$; ** $p < 0.05$; * $p < 0.1$

TABLE A.6.8 Logit regression predicting support toward building a fence along the Texas-Mexico border given perceived distance: over and under estimation

VARIABLES	NATIONAL SECURITY	ECONOMY	CONTROL
Over/under estimation	1.44**	0.64	0.22
	(0.67)	(0.53)	(0.42)
Liberal	1.28	1.72	2.00*
	(1.10)	(1.32)	(1.11)
Moderate	2.91***	2.75**	2.91***
	(0.98)	(1.31)	(1.09)
Conservative	4.07***	5.05***	4.06***
	(1.14)	(1.49)	(1.20)
Very conservative	3.10**	—	5.10***
	(1.50)	—	(1.56)
Gender	0.84	−0.69	0.63
	(0.58)	(0.55)	(0.47)
Age	−0.02	−0.03	−0.02
	(0.02)	(0.02)	(0.02)
African American	0.62	0.32	0.66
	(0.86)	(0.83)	(0.65)
Hispanic	−0.26	1.52	−1.48*
	(1.11)	(0.95)	(0.86)
Asian	−2.61	1.37	0.06
	(3.73)	(1.27)	(0.99)
Other	−0.57	0.15	0.10
	(1.67)	(1.35)	(0.92)
Education	−0.55**	−0.27	−0.09
	(0.25)	(0.22)	(0.16)
Income	−0.19*	−0.22**	−0.04
	(0.11)	(0.10)	(0.06)
Registered to vote	4.17**	1.98	−0.51
	(1.62)	(1.29)	(1.13)
Plan to vote for Trump	6.73***	—	4.17***
	(1.84)	—	(1.09)
Employed	0.98	0.42	0.63
	(0.67)	(0.59)	(0.46)
Owns a home	0.60	2.28***	0.04
	(0.74)	(0.72)	(0.46)
Constant	−4.86***	−3.57*	−2.53
	(1.85)	(1.95)	(1.88)
Observations	174	131	225

Note: Standard errors in parentheses.

*** $p < 0.01$; ** $p < 0.05$; * $p < 0.1$

CHAPTER 7. THE PERFECT STORM

TABLE A.7.1 Logistic regression predicting the probability of agreeing that climate change is mainly caused by human activities

VARIABLES	
Personal damage index	−0.11
	(0.10)
Republican	−1.85***
	(0.20)
Republican × personal damage index	0.38**
	(0.19)
Past flood	−0.99***
	(0.32)
Social damage index	0.00
	(0.06)
Cumulative total damage	0.00
	(0.00)
African American	−0.82**
	(0.35)
Hispanic	−0.16
	(0.36)
White	−0.94***
	(0.32)
Income	−0.02
	(0.04)
Education	0.10**
	(0.05)
Age	−0.27***
	(0.09)
Gender	0.20
	(0.16)
Constant	2.08***
	(0.50)
Observations	924

Note: Standard errors in parentheses.

*** $p < 0.01$; ** $p < 0.05$; * $p < 0.1$

CHAPTER 8. THE GREAT DROUGHT

TABLE A.8.1 Linear regression with clustered standard errors predicting incumbent vote given drought levels and percent agriculture for the 2008 and 2012 elections

VARIABLES	DEMOCRAT 2012	REPUBLICAN 2012	DEMOCRAT 2008	REPUBLICAN 2008
Drought	−0.09	0.04***	−0.11***	−0.01
	(0.05)	(0.01)	(0.02)	(0.03)
% agriculture	−17.34**	0.73*	−1.13	0.14
	(6.73)	(0.39)	(0.82)	(0.24)
Drought × % agriculture	4.71*	−0.00	0.29	0.09
	(2.27)	(0.12)	(0.40)	(0.19)
Unemployment rate	0.01	−0.03***	0.02	−0.06***
	(0.01)	(0.01)	(0.02)	(0.01)
% Hispanic	0.18*	−0.52***	0.25**	−0.25***
	(0.10)	(0.05)	(0.11)	(0.06)
Total population	0.00	−0.00***	0.00	−0.00***
	(0.00)	(0.00)	(0.00)	(0.00)
Constant	0.76***	0.96***	0.59***	1.07***
	(0.07)	(0.06)	(0.06)	(0.08)
Observations	906	3,522	1,825	2,839
R-squared	0.26	0.41	0.27	0.17

Note: Robust standard errors in parentheses.

*** $p < 0.01$; ** $p < 0.05$; * $p < 0.1$

NOTES

1. THE FOREST AND THE TREES

1. See Frances Cairncross, *The Death of Distance: How the Communications Revolution Is Changing Our Lives* (Boston: Harvard Business School, 2001); and Daniel K. N. Johnson, Nalyn Siripong, and Amy S. Brown, "The Demise of Distance? The Declining Role of Physical Proximity for Knowledge Transmission," *Growth and Change* 37, no. 1 (2006): 19–33.
2. See Regina P. Branton, Gavin Dillingham, Johanna Dunaway, and Beth Miller, "Anglo Voting on Nativist Ballot Initiatives: The Partisan Impact of Spatial Proximity to the U.S.-Mexico Border," *Social Science Quarterly* 88, no. 3 (2007): 882–97; James G. Gimpel, Kimberly A. Karnes, John McTague, and Shanna Pearson-Merkowitz, "Distance-Decay in the Political Geography of Friends-and-Neighbors Voting," *Political Geography* 27, no. 2 (2008): 231–52; Timothy B. Gravelle, "Politics, Time, Space, and Attitudes Toward US–Mexico Border Security," *Political Geography* 65 (2018): 107–16; Theresa Kuhn, "Europa Ante Portas: Border Residence, Transnational Interaction and Euroscepticism in Germany and France," *European Union Politics* 13, no. 1 (March 2012): 94–117; Katja Mirwaldt, "Contact, Conflict and Geography: What Factors Shape Cross-Border Citizen Relations," *Political Geography* 29, no 8 (2010): 434–43; and Sophia J. Wallace, Chris Zepeda-Millán, and Michael Jones-Correa, "Spatial and Temporal Proximity: Examining the Effects of Protests on Political Attitudes," *American Journal of Political Science* 58, no. 2 (2014): 433–48.
3. See, among others, the work of Jeronimo Cortina, "From a Distance: Geographic Proximity, Partisanship, and Public Attitudes Toward the U.S.–Mexico Border Wall," *Political Research Quarterly* 73, no. 3 (2019): 740–54; Ryan D. Enos, *The Space Between Us*

1. THE FOREST AND THE TREES

(Cambridge: Cambridge University Press, 2017); and Daniel J. Hopkins, *The Increasingly United States: How and Why American Political Behavior Nationalized* (Chicago: Chicago University Press, 2018).
4. Elaine B. Sharp, *The Sometime Connection: Public Opinion and Social Policy* (Albany: State University of New York Press, 1999).
5. John R. Logan, "Making a Place for Space: Spatial Thinking in Social Science," *Annual Review of Sociology* 38, no. 1 (2012): 507–24.
6. Gordon W. Allport, *The Nature of Prejudice* (Cambridge, MA: Addison Wesley, 1954); and Enos, *The Space Between Us*.
7. Thomas F. Gieryn, "A Space for Place in Sociology," *Annual Review of Sociology* 26, no. 1 (2000): 463–96.
8. Gieryn, "A Space for Place in Sociology," 464.
9. Gieryn, "A Space for Place in Sociology," 465.
10. Edward W Soja, *Postmodern Geographies: The Reassertion of Space in Critical Social Theory* (London: Verso, 1989).
11. Peter Blau, *Inequality and Heterogeneity* (New York: Free Press, 1977); Jeronimo Cortina and Narayani Lasala-Blanco, "One Vote or Many Mexicos? Income, Heterogeneity, and the 2006–2012 Presidential Elections," *Social Science Quarterly* 97, no. 2 (2016), https://doi.org/10.1111/ssqu.12216.
12. Gieryn, "A Space for Place in Sociology," 465; Enos, *The Space Between Us*; and Anthony Giddens, *The Constitution of Society* (Berkeley: University of California Press, 1986).
13. Logan, "Making a Place for Space"; and Craig Whitaker, *Architecture and the American Dream* (New York: Three Rivers, 1999).
14. Andrew Abbott, "Of Time and Space: The Contemporary Relevance of the Chicago School," *Social Forces* 75, no. 4 (June 1997): 1149–82, at 1152.
15. Janet L. Abu-Lughod, "The City Is Dead. Long Live the City: Some Thoughts on Urbanity," in *Urbanism in World Perspective: A Reader*, 2nd ed., ed. Sylvia Fleis Fava (New York: Crowell, 1968), 154–65; and Benno Werlen, *Society, Action and Space: An Alternative Human Geography* (London: Routledge, 1993).
16. *Cambridge English Dictionary*, s.v. "distance," accessed September 21, 2021, https://dictionary.cambridge.org/dictionary/english/distance.
17. Yaacov Trope and Nira Liberman, "Temporal Construal," *Psychological Review* 110, no. 3 (2003): 403–21; and Nira Liberman, Yaacov Trope, and Elena Stephan, "Psychological Distance," in *Social Psychology: Handbook of Basic Principles*, ed. Arie W. Kruglanski and E. Tory Higgins (New York: Guilford, 2007), 353–84.
18. Toby Bolsen, James N. Druckman, and Fay Lomax Cook, "The Influence of Partisan Motivated Reasoning on Public Opinion," *Political Behavior* 36, no. 2 (2014): 235–62; Ziva Kunda, "The Case for Motivated Reasoning," *Psychological Bulletin* 108, no. 3 (1990): 480–98; Charles S. Taber and Milton Lodge, "Motivated Skepticism in the Evaluation of Political Beliefs," *American Journal of Political Science* 50, no. 3 (2006): 755–69; and Yaacov Trope and Nira Liberman, "Construal-Level Theory of Psychological Distance," *Psychological Review* 117, no. 2 (2010): 440–63.

1. THE FOREST AND THE TREES

19. Logan, "Making a Place for Space"; and Werlen, *Society, Action and Space.*
20. Gieryn, "A Space for Place in Sociology."
21. Liberman, Trope, and Stephan, "Psychological Distance."
22. Kentaro Fujita, Marlone D. Henderson, Juliana Eng, Yaacov Trope, and Nira Liberman, "Spatial Distance and Mental Construal of Social Events," *Psychological Science* 17, no. 4 (2006): 278–82; Edward E. Jones and Keith E. Davis, "From Acts to Dispositions: The Attribution Process in Person Perception," in *Advances in Experimental Social Psychology*, ed. Leonard Berkowitz, vol. 2 (New York: Academic, 1965), 219–66; and Shiri Nussbaum, Yaacov Trope, and Nira Liberman, "Creeping Dispositionism: The Temporal Dynamics of Behavior Prediction," *Journal of Personality and Social Psychology* 84, no. 3 (2003): 485–97.
23. Fujita et al., "Spatial Distance and Mental Construal of Social Events"; Marlone D. Henderson, Cheryl J. Wakslak, Kentaro Fujita, and John Rohrbach, "Construal Level Theory and Spatial Distance: Implications for Mental Representation, Judgment, and Behavior," *Social Psychology* 42, no. 3 (2011): 165–73; and Susan T. Fiske and Shelley E. Taylor, *Social Cognition*, 4th ed. (Thousand Oaks, CA: Sage, 2021).
24. Bolsen, Druckman, and Cook, "The Influence of Partisan Motivated Reasoning on Public Opinion"; Alan Gerber and Donald P. Green, "Misperceptions About Perceptual Bias," *Annual Review of Political Science* 2, no. 1 (1999): 189–210; Kunda, "The Case for Motivated Reasoning"; Liberman, Trope, and Stephan, "Psychological Distance"; Taber and Lodge, "Motivated Skepticism in the Evaluation of Political Beliefs"; Carmit T. Tadmor and Philip E. Tetlock, "Biculturalism: A Model of the Effects of Second-Culture Exposure on Acculturation and Integrative Complexity," *Journal of Cross-Cultural Psychology* 37, no. 2 (2006): 173–90; and Kathleen M. McGraw, "Political Impressions: Formation and Management," in *Oxford Handbook of Political Psychology*, ed. David O. Sears, Leonie Huddy, and Robert Jervis (New York: Oxford University Press, 2003), 394–432.
25. Stanley Feldman and Pamela Johnston Conover, "Candidates, Issues and Voters: The Role of Inference in Political Perception," *Journal of Politics* 45, no. 4 (1983): 810–39; Ruth Hamill, Milton Lodge, and Frederick Blake, "The Breadth, Depth, and Utility of Class, Partisan, and Ideological Schemata," *American Journal of Political Science* 29, no. 4 (1985): 850–70; and Milton Lodge and Ruth Hamill, "A Partisan Schema for Political Information Processing," *American Political Science Review* 80, no. 2 (1986): 505–20.
26. Susan T. Fiske and Shelley E. Taylor, *Social Cognition: From Brains to Culture*, 4th ed. (Los Angeles: Sage, 2021).
27. Angus Campbell, Philip E. Converse, Warren E. Miller, and Donald E. Stokes, *The American Voter* (Chicago: Chicago University Press, 1960).
28. Kunda, "The Case for Motivated Reasoning"; and Taber and Lodge, "Motivated Skepticism in the Evaluation of Political Beliefs."
29. James N. Druckman, "Using Credible Advice to Overcome Framing Effects," *Journal of Law, Economics, and Organization* 17, no. 1 (April 2001): 62–82; John Zaller, *The Nature and Origins of Mass Opinion* (New York: Cambridge University Press, 1992); James M. Snyder and Michael M. Ting, "An Informational Rationale for Political Parties," *American Journal of Political Science* 46, no. 1 (2002): 90–110; and Wendy M. Rahn, "The Role of Partisan

1. THE FOREST AND THE TREES

Stereotypes in Information Processing About Political Candidates," *American Journal of Political Science* 37, no. 2 (1993): 472–96.

30. Fiske and Taylor, *Social Cognition*; and Henderson et al., "Construal Level Theory and Spatial Distance."
31. Fujita et al., "Spatial Distance and Mental Construal of Social Events."
32. Stephen Ansolabehere and David M. Konisky, "Public Attitudes Toward Construction of New Power Plants," *Public Opinion Quarterly* 73, no. 3 (2009): 566–77; B. H. Bishop, "Drought and Environmental Opinion: A Study of Attitudes Toward Water Policy," *Public Opinion Quarterly* 77, no. 3 (2013): 798–810; and Hugo Priemus and Johan Visser, "Infrastructure Policy in the Randstad Holland: Struggle Between Accessibility and Sustainability," *Political Geography* 14, no. 4 (1995): 363–77.
33. Dan Van-der-Horst, "NIMBY or Not? Exploring the Relevance of Location and the Politics of Voiced Opinions in Renewable Energy Siting Controversies," *Energy Policy* 35, no. 5 (2007): 2705–14; and Jeffrey Swofford and Michael Slattery, "Public Attitudes of Wind Energy in Texas: Local Communities in Close Proximity to Wind Farms and Their Effect on Decision-Making," *Energy Policy* 38, no. 5 (2010): 2508–19.
34. Michael Dear, "Understanding and Overcoming the NIMBY Syndrome," *Journal of the American Planning Association* 58, no. 3 (1992): 288–300.
35. Branton et al., "Anglo Voting on Nativist Ballot Initiatives"; Christopher E. Clarke, Dylan Bugden, P. Sol Hart, Richard C. Stedman, Jeffrey B. Jacquet, Darrick Evensen, and Hilary Boudet, "How Geographic Distance and Political Ideology Interact to Influence Public Perception of Unconventional Oil/Natural Gas Development," *Energy Policy* 97 (October 2016): 301–9; Gimpel, Karnes, McTague, and Pearson-Merkowitz, "Distance-Decay in the Political Geography of Friends-and-Neighbors Voting"; Kuhn, "Europa Ante Portas"; Mirwaldt, "Contact, Conflict and Geography"; Wallace, Zepeda-Millán, and Jones-Correa, "Spatial and Temporal Proximity"; and Gravelle, "Politics, Time, Space, and Attitudes Toward US–Mexico Border Security."
36. W. R. Tobler, "A Computer Movie Simulating Urban Growth in the Detroit Region," *Economic Geography* 46 (June 1970): 236–40, at 236.
37. Miller McPherson, Lynn Smith-Lovin, and James M. Cook, "Birds of a Feather: Homophily in Social Networks," *Annual Review of Sociology* 27, no. 1 (August 2001): 415–44, at 429.
38. Cara J. Wong, *Boundaries of Obligation in American Politics* (New York: Cambridge University Press, 2010).
39. Basile Chaix, "Geographic Life Environments and Coronary Heart Disease: A Literature Review, Theoretical Contributions, Methodological Updates, and a Research Agenda," *Annual Review of Public Health* 30 (2009): 81–105, https://doi.org/10.1146/annurev.publhealth.031308.100158.
40. Donald R. Kinder, "Communication and Politics in the Age of Information," in *Oxford Handbook of Political Psychology* (New York: Oxford University Press, 2003), 357–93.
41. Walter Lippmann, *The Phantom Public* (New York: Harcourt, Brace, 1925), 24; William Gamson, David Croteau, William Hoynes, and Theodore Sasson, "Media Images and the Social Construction of Reality," *Annual Review of Sociology* 18, no. 1 (1992): 373–93; and

1. THE FOREST AND THE TREES

Todd Gitlin, *The Whole World Is Watching: Mass Media in the Making & Unmaking of the New Left* (Berkeley: University of California Press, 2003), 6.
42. Donald R. Kinder and Lynn M. Sanders, *Divided by Color: Racial Politics and Democratic Ideals* (Chicago: Chigago University Press, 1996).
43. Fiske and Taylor, *Social Cognition*.
44. James R. Averill, "Emotions in Relation to Systems of Behavior," in *Psychological and Biological Approaches to Emotion*, ed. Nancy L. Stein, Bennett Leventhal, and Thomas R. Trabasso (New York: Psychology, 1990), 385–404.
45. James A. Russell, "Core Affect and the Psychological Construction of Emotion," *Psychological Review* 110, no. 1 (January 2003): 145–72.
46. Plato, "Allegory of the Cave," in *The Republic*, trans. Desmond Lee (New York: Penguin Classics, 2007), 240–49.
47. George E. Marcus, "The Psychology of Emotion and Politics," in *Oxford Handbook of Political Psychology Handbook* (New York: Oxford University Press, 2003), 182–221.
48. Marcus, "The Psychology of Emotion and Politics," 358.
49. Jonathan D. Cohen, "The Vulcanization of the Human Brain: A Neural Perspective on Interactions Between Cognition and Emotion," *Journal of Economic Perspectives* 19, no. 4 (January 2005): 3–24.
50. Cohen, "The Vulcanization of the Human Brain."
51. Marcus, "The Psychology of Emotion and Politics."
52. Roger Giner-Sorolla, Diane M. Mackie, and Eliot R. Smith, "Special Issue on Intergroup Emotions: Introduction," *Group Processes & Intergroup Relations* 10, no. 1 (2007): 5–136.
53. Thomas A. Fergus and Joseph R. Bardeen, "Anxiety Sensitivity and Intolerance of Uncertainty: Evidence of Incremental Specificity in Relation to Health Anxiety," *Personality and Individual Differences* 55, no. 6 (October 2013): 640–44.
54. Ted Brader, E. W. Groenendyk, and Nicholas A. Valentino, "Fight or Flight? When Political Threats Arouse Public Anger and Fear," paper presented at the Midwest Political Science Association Annual Conference, Chicago, 2010.
55. Walter G. Stephan and C. Lausanne Renfro, "The Role of Threat in Intergroup Relations," in *From Prejudice to Intergroup Emotions: Differentiated Reactions to Social Groups*, ed. Diane M. Mackie and Eliot R. Smith (New York: Taylor & Francis, 2002), 191–207.
56. Arne Öhman, "Fear and Anxiety," in *Handbook of Emotions*, 3rd ed., ed. Michael Lewis, Jeannette M. Haviland-Jones, and Lisa Feldman Barrett (New York: Guildford, 2008), 709–29.
57. Ted Brader and George E. Marcus, "Emotion and Political Psychology," in *Oxford Handbook of Political Psychology*, 2nd ed., ed. Leonie Huddy, David O. Sears, and Jack S. Levy (New York: Oxford University Press, 2013), 165–205.
58. Robert Miner, *Thomas Aquinas on the Passions* (Cambridge: Cambridge University Press, 2009), chapter 10, section 10.2.
59. Brader and Marcus, "Emotion and Political Psychology."
60. Miner, *Thomas Aquinas on the Passions*.
61. Aristotle, *Rhetoric*, 350AD, 2.5 1382a2i.

1. THE FOREST AND THE TREES

62. See Miner, *Thomas Aquinas on the Passions*; and Patrick Boyde, *Perception and Passion in Dante's Comedy* (Cambridge: Cambridge University Press, 2009).
63. St. Augustine, *Eighty-Three Different Questions*, trans. David L. Mosher (Washington, DC: Catholic University of America Press, 1982), 62.
64. Brader and Marcus, "Emotion and Political Psychology."
65. Brader and Marcus, "Emotion and Political Psychology."
66. Boyde, *Perception and Passion in Dante's Comedy*.
67. Ted Brader, Nicholas A. Valentino, and Elizabeth Suhay, "What Triggers Public Opposition to Immigration? Anxiety, Group Cues, and Immigration Threat," *American Journal of Political Science* 52, no. 4 (2008): 959–78; Brader, Groenendyk, and Valentino, "Fight or Flight?"; Shana Kushner Gadarian and Bethany Albertson, "Anxiety, Immigration, and the Search for Information," *Political Psychology* 35, no. 2 (April 2014): 133–64; Jennifer S. Lerner, Roxana M. Gonzalez, and Deborah A. Small, "Effects of Fear and Anger on Perceived Risks of Terrorism: A National Field Experiment," *Psychological Science* 14, no. 2 (April 2003): 144–50; and Jennifer L. Merolla and Elizabeth J. Zechmeister, *Democracy at Risk: How Terrorist Threats Affect the Public* (Chicago: University of Chicago Press, 2009).
68. Roberto Gutierrez, Tulsi Hirani, Leo Curtis, and Amanda K. Ludlow, "Metacognitive Beliefs Mediate the Relationship Between Anxiety Sensitivity and Traits of Obsessive-Compulsive Symptoms," *BMC Psychology* 8, no. 1 (April 2020): article 40.
69. Gutierrez et al. "Metacognitive Beliefs Mediate the Relationship"; Rosa J. Seinsche, Bertram Walter, Susanne Fricke, Marie K. Neudert, Raphaela I. Zehtner, Rudolph Stark, and Andrea Hermann, "Social Phobic Beliefs Mediate the Relationship Between Post-Event Processing Regarding the Worst Socially Aversive Experience and Fear of Negative Evaluation," *Current Psychology* 42, no. 18 (February 2022): 1–10.
70. Mar Yam G. Hamedani and Hazel Rose Markus, "Understanding Culture Clashes and Catalyzing Change: A Culture Cycle Approach," *Frontiers in Psychology* 10 (April 2019): article 700; and Stuart Hall, "The Question of Cultural Identity," in *Modernity and Its Futures: Understanding Modern Societies*, ed. Tony McGrew, Stuart Hall, and David Held (Cambridge: Polity, 1992), 274–316.
71. Hall, "The Question of Cultural Identity."
72. Katja Albada, Nina Hansen, and Sabine Otten, "When Cultures Clash: Links Between Perceived Cultural Distance in Values and Attitudes Towards Migrants," *British Journal of Social Psychology* 60, no. 4 (October 2021): 1350–78; Nick Haslam, Louis Rothschild, and Donald Ernst, "Essentialist Beliefs About Social Categories," *British Journal of Social Psychology* 39, part 1 (March 2000): 113–27; and Deborah A. Prentice and Dale T. Miller, "Psychological Essentialism of Human Categories," *Current Directions in Psychological Science* 16, no. 4 (2007): 202–6.
73. Glenn Adams and Hazel Rose Markus, "Toward a Conception of Culture Suitable for a Social Psychology of Culture," in *The Psychological Foundations of Culture*, ed. Mark Schaller and Christian S. Crandall (Mahwah, NJ: Lawrence Erlbaum, 2003), 335–60.
74. Allport, *The Nature of Prejudice*.

2. OUTBREAKS, EPIDEMICS, AND PANDEMICS

75. Alexander O'Connor, *An Analysis of Gordon W. Allport's The Nature of Prejudice* (New York: Perseus, 2017).
76. Thomas F. Pettigrew, "Intergroup Contact Theory," *Annual Review of Psychology* 49, no. 1 (1998): 65–85.
77. Pettigrew, "Intergroup Contact Theory."
78. Robert M. Stein, Stephanie Shirley Post, and Allison L. Rinden, "Reconciling Context and Contact Effects on Racial Attitudes," *Political Research Quarterly* 53, no. 2 (June 2000): 285–303.
79. Thomas F. Pettigrew, *Racially Separate or Together?* (New York: McGraw-Hill, 1971); Marylee C. Taylor, "How White Attitudes Vary with the Racial Composition of Local Populations: Numbers Count," *American Sociological Review* 63, no. 4 (1998): 512–35; and Robert Huckfeldt and John Sprague, *Citizens, Politics and Social Communication: Information and Influence in an Election Campaign* (New York: Cambridge University Press, 1995).
80. Vernon L. Allen and David A. Wilder, "Categorization, Belief Similarity, and Intergroup Discrimination," *Journal of Personality and Social Psychology* 32, no. 6 (1975): 971–77; David A. Wilder, "Cognitive Factors Affecting the Sucess of Intergroup Contact," in *Psychology of Intergroup Relations*, ed. Stephen Worchel and William G. Austin (Chicago: Nelson-Hall, 1986), 49–66; Marilynn B. Brewer, "In-Group Bias in the Minimal Intergroup Situation: A Cognitive-Motivational Analysis," *Psychological Bulletin* 86, no. 2 (1979): 307–24; and Marilynn B. Brewer and Norman Miller, "Beyond the Contact Hypothesis: Theoretical Perspectives on Desegregation," in *Groups in Contact: The Psychology of Desegregation*, ed. Norman Miller and Marilynn B. Brewer (Orlando, FL: Academic, 1984), 281–302.
81. Francesco Rigoli, Michael P. Ewbank, Tim Dalgleish, and Andrew Calder, "Threat Visibility Modulates the Defensive Brain Circuit Underlying Fear and Anxiety," *Neuroscience Letters* 612 (January 2016): 7–13, https://doi.org/10.1016/j.neulet.2015.11.026.

2. OUTBREAKS, EPIDEMICS, AND PANDEMICS: ZIKA, EBOLA, AND COVID-19

1. David M. Morens, Gregory K. Folkers, and Anthony S. Fauci, "What Is a Pandemic?," *Journal of Infectious Diseases* 200, no. 7 (October 2009): 1018–21.
2. Sharon N. DeWitte, "Archaeological Evidence of Epidemics Can Inform Future Epidemics," *Annual Review of Anthopology* 45 (October 2016): 63–77.
3. Steven Taylor, "The Psychology of Pandemics," *Annual Review of Clinical Psychology*, 18 (May 2022): 581–609, https://doi.org/10.1146/annurev-clinpsy-072720-020131.
4. Morens, Folkers, and Fauci, "What Is a Pandemic?"
5. Taylor, "The Psychology of Pandemics."
6. World Health Organization, "Timeline: WHO's COVID-19 Response," 2022, https://www.who.int/emergencies/diseases/novel-coronavirus-2019/interactive-timeline#event-7.
7. Nancy K. Bristow, *American Pandemic: The Lost World of the 1918 Influenza Epidemic* (New York: Oxford University Press, 2012); Mark Honigsbaum, "'An Inexpressible Dread': Psychoses of Influenza at Fin-de-Siècle," *Lancet* 381, no. 9871 (March 2013): 988–89.

2. OUTBREAKS, EPIDEMICS, AND PANDEMICS

8. Steven Taylor, Caleigh A. Landry, Michelle M. Paluszek, Thomas A. Fergus, Dean McKay, and Gordon J. G. Asmundson, "COVID Stress Syndrome: Concept, Structure, and Correlates," *Depression & Anxiety* 37, no. 8 (August 2020): 706–14.
9. William L. Walker, Nicole P. Lindsey, Jennifer A. Lehman, Elisabeth R. Krow-Lucal, Ingrid B. Rabe, Susan L. Hills, Stacey W. Martin, Marc Fischer, and J. Erin Staples, "Zika Virus Disease Cases—50 States and the District of Columbia January 1–July 31, 2016," *Morbidity and Mortality Weekly Report* 65, no. 36 (September 16, 2016): 983–86.
10. Duane J. Gubler, Nikos Vasilakis, and Didier Musso, "History and Emergence of Zika Virus," *Journal of Infectious Diseases* 216, suppl. 10 (December 2017): S860–67.
11. Walker et al., "Zika Virus Disease Cases."
12. Peter J. Hotez, "Zika Is Coming," *New York Times*, April 8, 2016.
13. Walker et al., "Zika Virus Disease Cases."
14. Sean Gregory, "Zika Fears Cause American Olympians to Scramble," *Time*, April 25, 2016.
15. Grant Whal, "Solo: As of Now, I Wouldn't Go to Olympics Over Zika," *Sports Illustrated*, February 9, 2016.
16. Joanna M. Reinhold, Claudio R. Lazzari, and Chloé Lahondère, "Effects of the Environmental Temperature on Aedes Aegypti and Aedes Albopictus Mosquitoes: A Review," *Insects* 9, no. 4 (November 2018): 158.
17. Bianca DiJulio, Jamie Firth, Ashley Krizinger, and Mollyann Brodie, "Kaiser Health Tracking Poll, February 2016," Kaiser Family Foundation, February 25, 2016; Ashley Krizinger, Elise Sugarman, and Mollyann Brodie, "Kaiser Health Tracking Poll, June 2016," Kaiser Family Foundation, June 30, 2016.
18. This is an example of the questions asked: How worried are you, if at all, that you or someone in your family will be affected by the Zika virus? Are you worried, somewhat worried, not too worried, or not at all?
19. Rob Savillo and Matt Gertz, "Ebola Coverage on TV News Plummeted After Midterms," *MediaMatters.org*, November 18, 2014, https://www.mediamatters.org/msnbc/report-ebola-coverage-tv-news-plummeted-after-midterms.
20. Sheila Mulrooney Eldred, "Hidden Viruses: How Pandemics Really Begin: 9 Diseases That Keep Epidemiologists Up at Night," *National Public Radio*, January 29, 2023, https://www.npr.org/sections/goatsandsoda/2023/01/29/1151039454/9-diseases-virus-epidemiologists-pandemic-potential-who.
21. World Health Organization, "Ebola: West Africa, March 2014–2016," accessed March 7, 2022, https://www.who.int/emergencies/situations/ebola-outbreak-2014-2016-West-Africa.
22. Sharon Abramowitz, "Epidemics (Especially Ebola)," *Annual Review of Anthropology* 46 (October 2017): 421–45.
23. Haider Ghazanfar, Fizza Orooj, Muhammad Ahmed Abdullah, and Ali Ghazanfar, "Ebola, the Killer Virus," *Infectious Diseases of Poverty* 4, no. 1 (April 2015): article 15, https://doi.org/10.1186/s40249-015-0048-y.
24. World Health Organization, "Ebola: West Africa, March 2014–2016."

2. OUTBREAKS, EPIDEMICS, AND PANDEMICS

25. Centers for Disease Control and Prevention, "2014–2016 Ebola Outbreak in West Africa," last updated March 8, 2019, https://www.cdc.gov/vhf/ebola/history/2014-2016-outbreak/index.html#_ftn2.
26. Abramowitz, "Epidemics (Especially Ebola)."
27. Michaeleen Doucleff, "The Ebola Outbreak: What's My Risk of Catching Ebola?," *Goats and Soda*, October 23, 2014; and Danielle K. Kilgo, Joseph Yoo, and Thomas J Johnson, "Spreading Ebola Panic: Newspaper and Social Media Coverage of the 2014 Ebola Health Crisis," *Health Communication* 34, no. 8 (July 2019): 811–17.
28. Centers for Disease Control and Prevention, "2014–2016 Ebola Outbreak in West Africa."
29. Jane Gregory and Steve Miller, *Science in Public: Communication, Culture, and Credibility* (New York: Plenum Trade, 1998).
30. Saeed Ahmed and Dorrine Mendoza, "Ebola Hysteria: An Epic, Epidemic Overreaction," *CNN*, October 20, 2014, https://www.cnn.com/2014/10/20/health/ebola-overreaction/index.html.
31. Liz Hamel, Jamie Firth, Bianca DiJulio, and Mollyann Brodie, "Kaiser Health Tracking Poll, October 2014," Kaiser Family Foundation, October 21, 2014, https://www.kff.org/report-section/kaiser-health-tracking-poll-october-2014-methodology/.
32. James L. True, Bryan D. Jones, and Frank R. Baumgartner, "Punctuated-Equilibrium Theory Explaining Stability and Change in Public Policymaking," in *Theories of the Policy Process*, 2nd ed., ed. Paul A. Sabatier (Boulder, CO: Westview, 2007), 155–88. I am thankful to Reviewer 2 for directing me to this theory.
33. National Safety Council, "Odds of Dying," *Injury Facts*, accessed December 15, 2021, https://injuryfacts.nsc.org/all-injuries/preventable-death-overview/odds-of-dying/.
34. Dean Baker, "Ebola Hysteria Fever: A Real Epidemic," *HuffPost*, October 21, 2014, last updated December 21, 2014, https://www.huffpost.com/entry/ebola-hysteria-fever-a-re_b_6020952.
35. Ahmed and Mendoza, "Ebola Hysteria."
36. Newsbank, search term "Ebola," search conducted 2020.
37. Gary King, *A Solution to the Ecological Inference Problem: Reconstructing Individual Behavior from Aggregate Data* (Princeton, NJ: Princeton University Press, 1997).
38. Chioma Ihekweazu, "Ebola in Prime Time: A Content Analysis of Sensationalism and Efficacy Information in U.S. Nightly News Coverage of the Ebola Outbreaks," *Health Communication* 32, no. 6 (June 2017): 741–48; and Bridget Kelly, Linda Squiers, Carla Bann, Alexander Stine, Heather Hansen, and Molly Lynch, "Perceptions and Plans for Prevention of Ebola: Results from a National Survey," *BMC Public Health* 15 (2015): article 1136, https://doi.org/10.1186/s12889-015-2441-7.
39. Grant Lewison, "The Reporting of the Risks from Severe Acute Respiratory Syndrome (SARS) in the News Media, 2003–2004," *Health, Risk & Society* 10, no. 3 (June 2008): 241–62; Sheldon Ungar, "Hot Crises and Media Reassurance: A Comparison of Emerging Diseases and Ebola Zaire," *British Journal of Sociology* 49, no. 1 (May 1998): 36–56; Sheldon Ungar, "Global Bird Flu Communication: Hot Crisis and Media Reassurance," *Science*

2. OUTBREAKS, EPIDEMICS, AND PANDEMICS

Communication 29, no. 4 (March 2008): 472–97; and Peter Washer, "Representations of Mad Cow Disease," *Social Science & Medicine* 62, no. 2 (2006): 457–66.

40. John C. Finn and Joseph Palis, "Introduction: The Medium, the Message, and Media Geography in the 21st Century," *GeoJournal* 80, no. 6 (2015): 781–90.
41. Stanley Cohen, *Folk Devils and Moral Panics: The Creation of the Mods and Rockers* (New York: Routledge, 2002).
42. Finn and Palis, "Introduction: The Medium, the Message, and Media Geography in the 21st Century," 783.
43. World Health Organization, "Timeline: WHO's COVID-19 Response."
44. World Health Organization, "Timeline: WHO's COVID-19 Response."
45. Alex M. Azar, "Determination That a Public Health Emergency Exists," Department of Health and Human Services, Administration for Strategic Preparedness & Response, 2020, https://aspr.hhs.gov/legal/PHE/Pages/2019-nCoV.aspx.
46. Centers for Disease Control and Prevention, "COVID-19 Timeline," David J. Sencer CDC Museum, 2023, https://www.cdc.gov/museum/timeline/covid19.html#Early-2020.
47. World Health Organization, "Timeline: WHO's COVID-19 Response."
48. Donald J. Trump, "Declaring a National Emergency Concerning the Novel Coronavirus Disease (COVID-19) Outbreak," Pub. L. No. 2020–05794, 2 (2020), https://www.federalregister.gov/documents/2020/03/18/2020-05794/declaring-a-national-emergency-concerning-the-novel-coronavirus-disease-covid-19-outbreak.
49. Centers for Disease Control and Prevention, "COVID-19 Timeline."
50. World Health Organization, "Timeline: WHO's COVID-19 Response"; Centers for Disease Control and Prevention, "COVID-19 Timeline."
51. Centers for Disease Control and Prevention, "COVID-19 Timeline."
52. New York Times, "See Reopening Plans and Mask Mandates for All 50 States," last updated July 1, 2021, https://www.nytimes.com/interactive/2020/us/states-reopen-map-coronavirus.html.
53. Centers for Disease Control and Prevention, "COVID-19 Timeline."
54. Kiva A. Fisher, Mark W. Tenforde, Leora R. Feldstein, Christopher J. Lindsell, Nathan I. Shapiro, D. Clark Files, Kevin W. Gibbs, Heidi L. Erickson, Matthew E. Prekker, Jay S. Stengrub, et al., "Community and Close Contact Exposures Associated with COVID-19 Among Symptomatic Adults ≥18 Years in 11 Outpatient Health Care Facilities—United States, July 2020," *Morbidity and Mortality Weekly Report* 69, no. 36 (September 2020): 1258–64.
55. Shana Kushner Gadarian, Sara Wallace Goodman, and Thomas B. Pepinsky, *Pandemic Politics: The Deadliy Toll of Partisanship in the Age of COVID* (Princeton, NJ: Princeton University Press, 2022).
56. Cary Funk and Alec Tyson, "Partisan Differences Over the Pandemic Response Are Growing," *Scientific American* (blog), May 30, 2020, https://blogs.scientificamerican.com/observations/partisan-differences-over-the-pandemic-response-are-growing/.
57. Erik Peterson and Shanto Iyengar, "Partisan Reasoning in a High Stakes Environment: Assessing Partisan Informational Gaps on COVID-19," *Harvard Kennedy School Misinformation Review* 3, no. 2 (2022): 1–20.

2. OUTBREAKS, EPIDEMICS, AND PANDEMICS

58. Gadarian, Goodman, and Pepinsky, *Pandemic Politics*.
59. Julie VanDusky-Allen and Olga Shvetsova, "How America's Partisan Divide Over Pandemic Responses Played Out in the States," *U.S. News*, May 12, 2021.
60. CBS Sacramento, "Modoc County Defies Gov. Newsom's Coronavirus Shutdown Order," *CBS News*, May 1, 2020.
61. Gadarian, Goodman, and Pepinsky, *Pandemic Politics*.
62. Martin Pengelly and Amanda Holpuch, "Coronavirus: Pence Defends Trump Jr. Claim Democrats Want 'Millions' to Die," *The Guardian*, March 1, 2020; Donald G. McNeil, "When an Epidemic Looms, Gagging Scientists Is a Terrible Idea," *New York Times*, February 28, 2020, https://www.nytimes.com/2020/02/28/health/coronavirus-pence-messaging.html; and Brianna Ehley, "The Glaring Loophole in U.S. Virus Response: Human Error," *Politico*, March 2, 2020, https://www.politico.com/news/2020/03/02/loophole-coronavirus-response-human-error-118491.
63. Gadarian, Goodman, and Pepinsky, *Pandemic Politics*, 10.
64. New York Times, "See Reopening Plans and Mask Mandates for All 50 States."
65. Justin Elarde, Joon-Seok Kim, Hamdi Kavak, Andreas Züfle, and Taylor Anderson, "Change of Human Mobility During COVID-19: A United States Case Study," *PLOS ONE* 16, no. 11 (November 2021): e0259031.
66. Terrence Hill, Kelsey E. Gonzalez, and Andrew Davis, "The Nastiest Question: Does Population Mobility Vary by State Political Ideology During the Novel Coronavirus (COVID-19) Pandemic?," *Sociological Perspectives* 64, no. 5 (December 2020): 786–803; and Hunt Allcott, Levi Boxell, Jacob Conway, Matthew Gentzkow, Michael Thaler, and David Yang, "Polarization and Public Health: Partisan Differences in Social Distancing During the Coronavirus Pandemic," *Journal of Public Economics* 191 (November 2020): article 104254, https://doi.org/https://doi.org/10.1016/j.jpubeco.2020.104254.
67. VanDusky-Allen and Shvetsova, "How America's Partisan Divide Over Pandemic Responses Played Out in the States."
68. Marc J. Hetherington, "Resurgent Mass Partisanship: The Role of Elite Polarization," *American Political Science Review* 95, no. 3 (October 2001): 619–31; and Gadarian, Goodman, and Pepinsky, *Pandemic Politics*.
69. Lilliana Mason, *Uncivil Agreement: How Politics Became Our Identity* (Chicago: Chigago University Press, 2018), 14.
70. Google, "COVID-19 Open Data Repository," last updated September 15, 2022, https://health.google.com/covid-19/open-data/.
71. Alice Park, Charlie Smart, Rumsey Taylor, and Miles Watkins, "An Extremely Detailed Map of the 2020 Election," *New York Times*, accessed June 8, 2021, https://www.nytimes.com/interactive/2021/upshot/2020-election-map.html.
72. Scott Horsley, "Election Shows Stark Partisan Divide on Economy, Coronavirus," *NPR*, November 4, 2020, https://www.npr.org/2020/11/04/931308587/good-or-poor-pandemic-economy-splits-voters-along-partisan-lines.
73. Gadarian, Goodman, and Pepinsky, *Pandemic Politics*, 8.
74. Ryan D. Enos, *The Space Between Us* (Cambridge: Cambridge University Press, 2017).

3. BOMBS AND GUNS: BOSTON, PARIS, AND EL PASO

1. FBI, "Terrorism," n.d., https://www.fbi.gov/investigate/terrorism.
2. Michael Connor, *Terrorism, Its Goals, Its Targets, Its Methods—The Solutions* (Boulder, CO: Paladin, 1987).
3. Susan T. Fiske and Shelley E. Taylor, *Social Cognition: From Brains to Culture*, 4th ed. (Los Angeles: Sage, 2021).
4. Stephen Maren, K. Luan Phan, and Israel Liberzon, "The Contextual Brain: Implications for Fear Conditioning, Extinction and Psychopathology," *Nature Reviews Neuroscience* 14, no. 6 (2013): 417–28.
5. Ava Sasani and Luke Vander Ploeg, "Another Patron Who Subdued Assailant at Club Q Acted to Save 'the Family I Found,'" *New York Times*, November 27, 2022.
6. Jesse Bedayn and Sam Metz, "Colorado Springs: How Patrons Disarmed Club Q Gunman," *PBS*, November 22, 2022, https://www.pbs.org/newshour/nation/army-veteran-helped-disarm-gunman-in-colorado-lgbtq-club-shooting.
7. Marie Edinger, "'He Could've Killed Us All': Man Says He Helped Tackle Suspect During Smiles Nite Club Shooting in Florida," *Fox 35 Orlando*, November 23, 2022, fox35orlando.com/news/he-couldve-killed-us-all-man-says-he-helped-tackle-suspect-during-smiles-nite-club-shooting-in-florida.
8. Yvonne M. Ulrich-Lai and James P. Herman, "Neural Regulation of Endocrine and Autonomic Stress Responses," *Nature Reviews Neuroscience* 10, no. 6 (2009): 397–409.
9. Ulrich-Lai and Herman, "Neural Regulation of Endocrine and Autonomic Stress Responses."
10. Maren, Phan, and Liberzon, "The Contextual Brain," 417.
11. Maren, Phan, and Liberzon, "The Contextual Brain."
12. Carmen Keller, Michael Siegrist, and Heinz Gutscher, "The Role of the Affect and Availability Heuristics in Risk Communication," *Risk Analysis* 26, no. 3 (June 2006): 631–39; and Colin MacLeod and Lynlee Campbell, "Memory Accessibility and Probability Judgments: An Experimental Evaluation of the Availability Heuristic," *Journal of Personality and Social Psychology* 63, no. 6 (1992): 890–902.
13. Donald J. Trump, *Twitter*, February 1, 2017, https://twitter.com/realDonaldTrump/status/826774668245946368.
14. Institute for Economics & Peace, "Overall Terorism Index Score," 2022 Global Terrorism Index, https://www.visionofhumanity.org/maps/global-terrorism-index/#/.
15. William Baldwin, "How to Calculate Odds of Winning $1.3 Billion and the Value of a Mega Millions Ticket," *Forbes*, July 28, 2022, https://www.forbes.com/sites/baldwin/2022/07/28/how-to-calculate-odds-of-winning-11-billion-and-the-value-of-a-mega-millions-ticket/?sh=d11309647673; and Emmanuelle Saliba, "You're More Likely to Die Choking Than Be Killed by Foreign Terrorists, Data Show," *NBC News*, February 1, 2017, https://www.nbcnews.com/news/us-news/you-re-more-likely-die-choking-be-killed-foreign-terrorists-n715141.
16. Pew Research Center, "April 18–21, 2013 Omnibus Poll" (Washington, DC: Pew Research Center, 2013); and Pew Research Center, "January 8–11, 2015 Omnibus Poll" (Washington, DC: Pew Research Center, 2015).

3. BOMBS AND GUNS

17. Bruce Drake, "Many in U.S. Followed Charlie Hebdo Story Closely, but Past Terrorist Incidents Abroad Drew More Attention," *Pew Research Center*, January 12, 2015, https://www.pewresearch.org/short-reads/2015/01/12/many-in-u-s-followed-charlie-hebdo-story-closely-but-past-terrorist-incidents-abroad-drew-more-attention/.
18. Institute for Economics & Peace, "Overall Terrorism Index Score."
19. Brigitte L. Nacos, Yaeli Bloch-Elkon, and Robert Y. Shapiro, *Selling Fear: Counterterrorism, the Media, and Public Opinion* (Chicago: University of Chicago Press, 2011), 58.
20. Nacos, Bloch-Elkon, and Shapiro, *Selling Fear.*
21. Pew Research Center, "April 18–21, 2013 Omnibus Poll."; and Pew Research Center, "January 8–11, 2015 Omnibus Poll."
22. American National Election Studies, "ANES 2020 Time Series Study Full Release," February 10, 2022, https://electionstudies.org/data-center/2020-time-series-study/.
23. Nacos, Bloch-Elkon, and Shapiro, *Selling Fear.*
24. Jennifer S. Lerner, Roxana M. Gonzalez, Deborah A. Small, and Baruch Fischhoff, "Effects of Fear and Anger on Perceived Risks of Terrorism: A National Field Experiment," *Psychological Science* 14, no. 2 (April 2003): 144–50; and Leonie Huddy, Stanley Feldman, Charles S. Taber, and Gallya Lahav, "Threat, Anxiety, and Support of Antiterrorism Politics," *American Journal of Political Science* 49, no. 3 (July 2005): 593–608. For threat alerts, see Department of Homeland Security, "Current Advisories," National Terrorism Advisory System, last updated April 15, 2022, https://www.dhs.gov/national-terrorism-advisory-system.
25. John R. Zaller, *The Nature and Origins of Mass Opinion* (New York: Cambridge University Press, 1992), 8.
26. National Consortium for the Study of Terrorism and Responses to Terrorism, "Ankara Terrorist Attack," Global Terrorism Database, October 10, 2015, https://www.start.umd.edu/gtd/search/IncidentSummary.aspx?gtdid=201510100002.
27. National Consortium for the Study of Terrorism and Responses to Terrorism, "Bataclan Terrorist Attack," Global Terrorism Database, November 13, 2015, https://www.start.umd.edu/gtd/search/IncidentSummary.aspx?gtdid=201511130008.
28. Robert J. Morton and Mark A. Hilts, eds., "Serial Murder: Multi-Disciplinary Perspectives for Investigators," San Antonio, Texas, FBI Symposium, August 29—September 2, 2005, 8, https://www.fbi.gov/stats-services/publications/serial-murder#two.
29. United States Congress, "Public Law 112–265," January 14, 2013, https://www.congress.gov/112/plaws/publ265/PLAW-112publ265.pdf.
30. Mark Follman, Gavin Aronsen, and Deanna Pan, "A Guide to Mass Shootings in America," *Mother Jones*, last updated December 6, 2023, https://www.motherjones.com/politics/2012/07/mass-shootings-map/.
31. Mark Follman, "Yes, Mass Shootings Are Occurring More Often," *Mother Jones*, October 21, 2014, https://www.motherjones.com/politics/2014/10/mass-shootings-rising-harvard/; and Paul Slovic, "'If I Look at the Mass I Will Never Act': Psychic Numbing and Genocide," *Judgment and Decision Making* 2, no. 2 (2007): 79–95.
32. Follman, Aronsen, and Pan, "A Guide to Mass Shootings in America."

3. BOMBS AND GUNS

33. Don Terry, "Portrait of Texas Killer: Impatient and Troubled," *New York Times*, October 18, 1991, 14.
34. Zara Abrams, "Stress of Mass Shootings Causing Cascade of Collective Traumas," *Monitor on Psychology* 53, no. 6 (July 2022): 20, last updated October 27, 2023, https://www.apa.org/monitor/2022/09/news-mass-shootings-collective-traumas.
35. James Alan Fox, Nathan E. Sanders, Emma E. Fridel, Grant Duwe, and Michael Rocque, "The Contagion of Mass Shootings: The Interdependence of Large-Scale Massacres and Mass Media Coverage," *Statistics and Public Policy* 8, no. 1 (January 2021): 53–66.
36. Mary Blankenship and Carl Graham, "Assessing the Social and Emotional Costs of Mass Shootings with Twitter Data," *Brookings Institution* (blog), May 5, 2021, https://www.brookings.edu/blog/up-front/2021/05/05/assessing-the-social-and-emotional-costs-of-mass-shootings-with-twitter-data/.
37. Fox et al., "The Contagion of Mass Shootings."
38. Mandi Cai and Chris Essig, "Texas Has Had Nine Mass Shootings in the Past 14 Years, While Lawmakers Have Steadily Loosened Restrictions on Carrying Firearms," *Texas Tribune*, November 12, 2019, last updated May 8, 2023, https://apps.texastribune.org/features/2019/texas-10-years-of-mass-shootings-timeline/.
39. University of Texas-Austin and Texas Tribune, "June 2022 University of Texas/Texas Politics Project Poll," June 16–24, 2022, https://texaspolitics.utexas.edu/polling-data-archive.
40. Ramon A. Vargas, "Why Did They Wait? Uvalde Anger Grows Over Bungled Police Response," *The Guardian*, June 26, 2022.
41. Emma Tucker, Shimon Prokupecz, Dakin Andone, and Peter Nickeas, "5 Key Takeaways from the Uvalde Shooting Report and Video Revealing Failures in Law Enforcement Response," *CNN*, July 18, 2022, https://www.cnn.com/2022/07/18/us/5-key-takeaways-uvalde-report-and-video/index.html.
42. Jollie McCullough and James Barragan, "Texas Politicians Search for Solutions After Another Mass Shooting. Experts Say We've Already Found Them," *Texas Tribune*, June 6, 2022.
43. Caroline Covington, "Texas' Complex Relationship with Firearms: Leading America in Gun Sales, but with a Declining Gun Ownership Rate," *Texas Tribune*, July 28, 2022.
44. Texas Legislature, "Firearm Carry Act of 2021," Pub. L. No. HB 1927 (2021), https://capitol.texas.gov/tlodocs/87R/billtext/pdf/HB01927F.pdf.
45. Texas Department of Public Safety, "Reports & Statistics," n.d., https://www.dps.texas.gov/section/handgun-licensing/reports-statistics-1.
46. Amnesty International, "Gun Violence," 2023, https://www.amnesty.org/en/what-we-do/arms-control/gun-violence/; Gregory Jackson, "Black Communities Are Most Victimized by Gun Violence. Too Often It's Assumed We Are to Blame," *The Guardian*, February 2, 2022; Daniel Trotta, "U.S. Gun Deaths Surged 35 percent in 2020, Higher for Black People," *Reuters*, May 10, 2022, https://www.reuters.com/world/us/us-gun-deaths-surged-35-2020-higher-black-people-cdc-2022-05-10/; Sandy Hook Promise, "11 Gun Violence Facts About Black, Indigenous and People of Color," 2022, https://www.sandyhookpromise.org/blog/gun-violence/ten-gun-violence-facts-about-black-indigenous-and-people-of-color/; and

4. PROTESTS

Marissa Edmund, "Gun Violence Disproportionately and Overwhelmingly Hurts Communities of Color," Center for American Progress, 2022, https://www.americanprogress.org/article/gun-violence-disproportionately-and-overwhelmingly-hurts-communities-of-color/.

47. Trotta, "U.S. Gun Deaths Surged 35 percent in 2020, Higher for Black People."
48. Ashley Killough and Holly Yan, "Suspect in Texas Walmart Massacre That Left 23 Dead in El Paso Pleads Guilty to 90 Federal Charges," *CNN*, February 8, 2023, https://www.cnn.com/2023/02/08/us/el-paso-shooting-suspect-patrick-crusius-federal-plea/index.html.
49. Adam Nagourney, Ian Lovett, and Richard Pérez-Peña, "San Bernardino Shooting Kills at Least 14; Two Suspects Are Dead," *New York Times*, December 3, 2015.
50. BBC, "San Bernardino Shooting: What We Know So Far," December 11, 2015, https://www.bbc.com/news/world-us-canada-34993344.
51. David M Studdert, Yifan Zhand, Jonathan A. Rodden, Rob J. Hyndman, and Garen J. Wintemute, "Handgun Acquisitions in California After Two Mass Shootings," *Annals of Internal Medicine* 166, no. 10 (May 2017): 698–706.

4. PROTESTS: #BLACKLIVESMATTER

1. Legal Information Institute, "Freedom of Assembly and Petition: Overview," Cornell Law School, accessed March 5, 2020, https://www.law.cornell.edu/constitution-conan/amendment-1/freedom-of-assembly-and-petition-overview.
2. Doug McAdam and Yang Su, "The War at Home: Antiwar Protests and Congressional Voting, 1965 to 1973," *American Sociological Review* 67, no. 5 (February 2002): 696–721.
3. Kenneth T. Andrews, Kraig Beyerlein, and Tuneka Tucker Farnum, "The Legitimacy of Protest: Explaining White Southerners' Attitudes Toward the Civil Rights Movement," *Social Forces* 94, no. 3 (March 2016): 1021–44.
4. Sophia J. Wallace, Chris Zepeda-Millán, and Michael Jones-Correa, "Spatial and Temporal Proximity: Examining the Effects of Protests on Political Attitudes," *American Journal of Political Science* 58, no. 2 (September 2013): 433–48.
5. Regina Branton, Valerie Martinez-Ebers, Tony E. Carey Jr., and Tetsuya Matsubayashi, "Social Protest and Policy Attitudes: The Case of the 2006 Immigrant Rallies," *American Journal of Political Science* 59, no. 2 (February 2015): 390–402.
6. Duoduo Xu and Jiao Guo, "In Sight, in Mind: Spatial Proximity to Protest Sites and Changes in Peoples' Political Attitudes," *British Journal of Sociology* 74, no. 1 (January 2023): 83–104.
7. *Washington Post*, "Fatal Force," December 5, 2023, https://www.washingtonpost.com/graphics/investigations/police-shootings-database/.
8. *Washington Post*, "Fatal Force."
9. Maanvi Singh, "George Floyd Told Officers 'I Can't Breathe' More than 20 Times, Transcripts Show," *The Guardian*, July 8, 2020.
10. Derrick Bryson Taylor, "George Floyd Protests: A Timeline," *New York Times*, November 5, 2021.

4. PROTESTS

11. Jill Colvin and Zeke Miller, "Trump Walks Back His Incendiary Minneapolis 'Thugs' Post," *Associated Press*, May 29, 2020, https://apnews.com/article/virus-outbreak-police-donald-trump-ap-top-news-mn-state-wire-f62ed59014cbf43fc1da21e3fcbfe904.
12. Taylor, "George Floyd Protests: A Timeline."
13. Katherine Levine Einstein, David M. Glick, and Maxwell Palmer, "2020 Menino Survey of Mayors: Policing and Protests," Boston University Initiative on Cities, https://www.surveyofmayors.com/files/2021/04/menino-survey-of-mayors-2020-policing-and-protests-report.pdf.
14. Tom Cotton, "Send in the Troops," *New York Times*, June 3, 2020.
15. Kevin Drakulich and Megan Denver, "The Partisans and the Persuadables: Public Views of Black Lives Matter and the 2020 Protests," *Perspectives on Politics* 20, no. 4 (2022): 1191–1208.
16. Kim Parker, Juliana Menasce Horowitz, and Monica Anderson, "Amid Protests, Majorities Across Racial and Ethnic Groups Express Support for the Black Lives Matter Movement," Pew Research Center, June 12, 2020, https://www.pewresearch.org/social-trends/2020/06/12/amid-protests-majorities-across-racial-and-ethnic-groups-express-support-for-the-black-lives-matter-movement/.
17. Ashley Westerman, Ryan Benk, and David Greene, "In 2020, Protests Spread Across the Globe with a Similar Message: Black Lives Matter," *NPR*, December 30, 2020, https://www.npr.org/2020/12/30/950053607/in-2020-protests-spread-across-the-globe-with-a-similar-message-black-lives-matt.
18. Abigail Haworth, "The Global Fight for Black Lives," *Marie Claire*, November 30, 2020, https://www.marieclaire.com/politics/a34515361/black-lives-matter-international/.
19. Haworth, "The Global Fight for Black Lives."
20. Zackary Okun Dunivin, Harry Yaojun Yan, Jelani Ince, and Fabio Rojas, "Black Lives Matter Protests Shift Public Discourse," *Proceedings of the National Academy of Sciences* 119, no. 10 (March 2022): e2117320119.
21. Stephanie Pagones, "Crime Surged Amid George Floyd Protests in Parts of US," *FOXBusiness*, June 10, 2020, https://www.foxbusiness.com/lifestyle/crime-protests-cities-george-floyd.
22. Jennifer Brannock Cox, "Black Lives Matter to Media (Finally): A Content Analysis of News Coverage During Summer 2020," *Newspaper Research Journal* 43, no. 2 (April 2022): 155–75.
23. Allyson Chiu, "Fox News's Tucker Carlson Says George Floyd Protests Are 'Definitely Not About Black Lives,' Prompting Backlash," *Washington Post*, June 9, 2020.
24. Larry Buchanan, Quoctrung Bui, and Jugal K. Patel, "Black Lives Matter May Be the Largest Movement in U.S. History," *New York Times*, July 3, 2020.
25. Catherine Vitro, D. Angus Clark, Carter Sherman, Mary M. Heitzeg, and Brian M. Hicks, "Attitudes About Police and Race in the United States 2020–2021: Mean-Level Trends and Associations with Political Attitudes, Psychiatric Problems, and COVID-19 Outcomes," *PLOS ONE* 17, no. 7 (July 2022): e0271954.
26. Deja Thomas and Juliana Menasce Horowitz, "Support for Black Lives Matter Has Decreased Since June but Remains Strong Among Black Americans," Pew Research

Center, September 16, 2020, https://www.pewresearch.org/fact-tank/2020/09/16/support-for-black-lives-matter-has-decreased-since-june-but-remains-strong-among-black-americans/.
27. Thomas and Horowitz, "Support for Black Lives Matter Has Decreased."
28. Thomas and Horowitz, "Support for Black Lives Matter Has Decreased."
29. Hema Preya Selvanathan and Brian Lickel, "Empowerment and Threat in Response to Mass Protest Shape Public Support for a Social Movement and Social Change: A Panel Study in the Context of the Bersih Movement in Malaysia," *European Journal of Social Psychology* 49, no. 2 (May 2018): 230–43.
30. Parker, Menasce Horowitz, and Anderson, "Amid Protests, Majorities Across Racial and Ethnic Groups Express Support for the Black Lives Matter Movement."
31. Xu and Guo, "In Sight, in Mind."
32. Parker, Menasce Horowitz, and Anderson, "Amid Protests, Majorities Across Racial and Ethnic Groups Express Support for the Black Lives Matter Movement."
33. Jackie Smith, John D. McCarthy, Clark McPhail, and Boguslaw Augustyn, "From Protest to Agenda Building: Description Bias in Media Coverage of Protest Events in Washington, D.C.," *Social Forces* 79, no. 4 (June 2001): 1397–1423.
34. Summer Harlow, "There's a Double Standard in How News Media Cover Liberal and Conservative Protests," *Washington Post*, January 13, 2021.
35. Roberto S. Mariano, "Two-Stage Least Squares," *International Encyclopedia of Statistical Science*, ed. Miodrag Lovric (New York: Springer, 2011), 1616–18.
36. BLM's feeling thermometer does not necessarily depend on the public attitudes toward dealing with urban unrest; however, they are endogenous because the error terms are correlated between the equations, as such we need to correct for the variance-covariance and apply the correct mean squared error. Badi H. Baltagi, *Econometrics*, 6th ed. (New York: Springer, 2021).

5. ONE SIZE DOES NOT FIT ALL: ATTITUDES TOWARD IMMIGRATION

1. Rita J. Simon and Susan H. Alexander, *The Ambivalent Welcome: Print Media, Public Opinion, and Immigration* (Westport, CT: Praeger, 1993); and Aristide R. Zolberg, *A Nation by Design: Immigration Policy in the Fashioning of America* (Cambridge, MA: Harvard University Press, 2006).
2. Jens Hainmueller and Michael J. Hiscox, "Attitudes Toward Highly Skilled and Low-Skilled Immigration: Evidence from a Survey Experiment," *American Political Science Review* 104, no. 1 (2010): 61–84; Gordon H. Hanson, *Why Does Immigration Divide America? Public Finance and Political Opposition to Open Borders* (Washington, DC: Institute for International Economics, 2005); and Kenneth F. Scheve and Matthew J. Slaughter, "What Determines Individual Trade-Policy Preferences?," *Journal of International Economics* 54, no. 2 (August 2001): 267–92.

5. ONE SIZE DOES NOT FIT ALL

3. Jack Citrin, Donald P. Green, Christopher Muste, and Cara Wong, "Public Opinion Toward Immigration Reform: The Role of Economic Motivations," *Journal of Politics* 59, no. 3 (1997): 858–81; and Thomas J. Espenshade and Katherine Hempstead, "Contemporary American Attitudes Toward U.S. Immigration," *International Migration Review* 30, no. 2 (1996): 535–70.
4. Thomas J. Espenshade and Charles A. Calhoun, "An Analysis of Public Opinion Toward Undocumented Immigration," *Population Research and Policy Review* 12 (1993): 189–224; and Lawrence W. Miller, Jerry L. Polinard, and Robert D. Wrinkle, "Attitudes Toward Undocumented Workers: The Mexican American Perspective," *Social Science Quarterly* 65, no. 2 (1984): 482–94.
5. Rodolfo O. de la Garza, Louis DesSipio, F. Chris Garcia, John Garcia, and Angelo Falcon, *Latino Voices: Mexican, Puerto Rican, and Cuban Perspectives on American Politics* (Boulder, CO: Westview, 1992).
6. Espenshade and Hempstead, "Contemporary American Attitudes Toward U.S. Immigration"; and Thomas J. Espenshade and Gregory A. Huber, "Fiscal Impacts of Immigrants and the Shrinking Welfare State," in *The Handbook of International Migration: The American Experience*, ed. Charles Hirschman, Philip Kasinitz, and Josh DeWind (New York: Russell Sage Foundation, 1999), 360–70.
7. E. P. Hutchinson, *Legislative History of American Immigration Policy, 1798–1965* (Philadelphia: University of Pennsylvania Press, 1981); and Steven G. Koven and Frank Götzke, *American Immigration Policy: Confronting the Nation's Challenges* (New York: Springer-Verlag, 2010).
8. Stephen Castles and Mark J. Miller, *The Age of Migration: International Population Movements in the Modern World*, 2nd ed. (London: Macmillan, 1998).
9. Vernon L. Allen and David A. Wilder, "Categorization, Belief Similarity, and Intergroup Discrimination," *Journal of Personality and Social Psychology* 32, no. 6 (December 1975): 971–77; David A. Wilder, "Cognitive Factors Affecting the Success of Intergroup Contact," in *Psychology of Intergroup Relations*, ed. Stephen Worchel and William G. Austin (Chicago: Nelson-Hall, 1986), 49–66; and Marilynn B. Brewer and Norman Miller, "Beyond the Contact Hypothesis: Theoretical Perspectives on Desegregation," in *Groups in Contact: The Psychology of Desegregation*, ed. Norman Miller and Marilynn B. Brewer (Orlando, FL: Academic, 1984), 281–302.
10. Donald T. Campbell, "Ethnocentric and Other Altruistic Motives," in *Nebraska Symposium on Motivation Bd. 13* (Lincoln: University of Nebraska Press, 1965): 283–311; Victoria M. Esses, John M. Jackson, and Tamara L. Armstrong, "The Immigration Dilemma: The Role of Perceived Group Competition, Ethnic Prejudice, and National Identity," *Journal of Social Issues* 57, no. 3 (2001): 389–412; Charles A. Gallagher, "Miscounting Race: Explaining Whites' Misperceptions of Racial Group Size," *Sociological Perspectives* 46, no. 3 (2003): 381–96; and Muzafer Sherif, *Group Conflict and Cooperation: Their Social Psychology* (London: Routledge and Kegan Paul, 1966).
11. Robert M. Stein, Stephanie Shirley Post, and Allison L. Rinden, "Reconciling Context and Contact Effects on Racial Attitudes," *Political Research Quarterly* 53, no. 2 (June 2000): 285–303.

5. ONE SIZE DOES NOT FIT ALL

12. Frank D. Bean and Gillian Stevens, *America's Newcomers and the Dynamics of Diversity* (New York: Russell Sage Foundation, 2003); Frank D. Bean, Susan K. Brown, and Ruben G. Rumbaut, "Mexican Immigrant Political and Economic Incorporation," *Perspectives on Politics* 4, no. 2 (2006): 309–13; and Michael Fix and Jeffrey S. Passel, *Immgration and Immigrants: Setting the Record Straight* (Washington, DC: Urban Institute, 1994).
13. Richard Nadeau, Richard G. Niemi, and Jeffrey Levine, "Innumeracy About Minority Populations," *Public Opinion Quarterly* 57, no. 3 (1993): 332–47; and Lee Sigelman and Richard G. Niemi, "Innumeracy About Minority Populations: African Americans and Whites Compared," *Public Opinion Quarterly* 65, no. 1 (2001): 86–94.
14. Richard Alba, Ruben G. Rumbaut, and Karen Marotz, "A Distorted Nation: Perceptions of Racial/Ethnic Group Sizes and Attitudes Toward Immigrants and Other Minorities," *Social Forces* 84, no. 2 (2005): 901–19; Hubert M. Blalock, *Toward a Theory of Minority-Group Relations* (New York: Wiley, 1967); Gallagher, "Miscounting Race"; and Lincoln Quillian, "Prejudice as a Response to Perceived Group Threat: Population Composition and Anti-Immigrant and Racial Prejudice in Europe," *American Sociological Review* 60, no. 4 (1995): 586–611.
15. Desmond S. King, *Making Americans: Immigration, Race, and the Origins of the Diverse Democracy* (Cambridge, MA: Harvard University Press, 2000), 229.
16. For a detailed review of immigration policy during that period, see John Higham, *Strangers in the Land: Patterns of American Nativism, 1860–1925* (New Brunswick, NJ: Rutgers University Press, 2002). and King, *Making Americans*.
17. King, *Making Americans*; Daniel J. Tichenor, *Dividing Lines: The Politics of Immigration Control in America* (Princeton, NJ: Princeton University Press, 2002); and Zolberg, *A Nation by Design*.
18. Simon and Alexander, *The Ambivalent Welcome*.
19. Victoria M. Esses, John F. Dovidio, and Gordon Hodson, "Public Attitudes Toward Immigration in the United States and Canada in Response to the September 11, 2001 'Attack on America,'" *Analyses of Social Issues and Public Policy* 2, no. 1 (December 2002): 69–85.
20. Lawrence M. Lebowitz and Ira L. Podheiser, "A Summary of the Changes in Immigration Policies and Practices After the Terrorist Attacks of September 11, 2001: The USA Patriot Act and Other Measures," *University of Pittsburgh Law Review* 63, no. 41 (2002): 873–88.
21. Previous waves of immigration from Southern and Eastern Europe that arrived in the United States in the late 1800s also had a significant impact on the demographic landscape; however, the degree of the ethnoracial differences that distinguished them from those of previous waves was not as distinct as the differences that arose after 1965.
22. Simon and Alexander, *The Ambivalent Welcome*; and Tichenor, *Dividing Lines*.
23. Simon and Alexander, *The Ambivalent Welcome*; and Tichenor, *Dividing Lines*.
24. Shamit Saggar, "Immigration and the Politics of Public Opinion," *Political Quarterly* 74, suppl. 1 (2003): 178–94. Also see John F. Kennedy, *A Nation of Immigrants* (New York: Harper Perennial, 2008).
25. Joseph Carroll, "American Public Opinion About Immigration," *Gallup*, July 26, 2005, https://news.gallup.com/poll/14785/Immigration.aspx.

5. ONE SIZE DOES NOT FIT ALL

26. Lebowitz and Podheiser, "A Summary of the Changes in Immigration Policies and Practices After the Terrorist Attacks of September 11, 2001.'"
27. CNN, "Bush Calls for Changes on Illegal Workers: New System 'More Compassionate'," January 7, 2004, https://www.cnn.com/2004/ALLPOLITICS/01/07/bush.immigration/.
28. CNN, "Bush Calls for Changes on Illegal Workers."
29. Rush Limbaugh, "Rush Limbaugh: 'Immigration Proposal Roils America,'" Freerepublic.com, January 7, 2004, https://freerepublic.com/focus/f-news/1053544/posts.
30. Pew Research Center for the People & the Press, "Pew Research Center Poll: November News Interest Index—Politics," by Princeton Survey Research Associates International, November 3–6, 2005, https://doi.org/10.25940/ROPER-31095854.
31. National Center for State Courts, "National Center for State Courts Poll # 2006-NCSC: Sentencing Attitudes," by Princeton Survey Research Associates International, March 6–April 9, 2006, https://doi.org/10.25940/ROPER-31096871.
32. Gallup Organization, "Gallup Organization Poll: May 2006," May 8–11, 2006, https://doi.org/10.25940/ROPER-31110562.
33. Marilyn B. Brewer, "In-Group Bias in the Minimal Intergroup Situation: A Cognitive-Motivational Analysis," *Psychological Bulletin* 86, no. 2 (1979): 307–24; Wilder, "Cognitive Factors Affecting the Success of Intergroup Contact"; and Stein, Post, and Rinden, "Reconciling Context and Contact Effects on Racial Attitudes."
34. Do you think the number of immigrants now entering the United States from each of the following areas is too many, too few, or about the right amount? How about immigrants from European countries, Latin American countries, African countries, Asian countries, or Arab countries?
35. On the whole, do you think immigration is a good thing or a bad thing for this country today?
36. Gallup, "Minority Rights and Relations Poll" (Princeton, NJ: Gallup, 2002, 2006).
37. René Galindo, "Repartitioning the National Community: Political Visibility and Voice for Undocumented Immigrants in the Spring 2006 Immigration Rights Marches," *Aztlán: A Journal of Chicano Studies* 35 (2010): 37–64, https://api.semanticscholar.org/CorpusID:150791658.
38. Besheer Mohamed and Jeff Diamant, "Black Muslims Account for a Fifth of All U.S. Muslims," Pew Research Center, January 17, 2019, https://www.pewresearch.org/fact-tank/2019/01/17/black-muslims-account-for-a-fifth-of-all-u-s-muslims-and-about-half-are-converts-to-islam/.
39. Costas Panagopoulos, "The Polls-Trends: Arab and Muslim Americans and Islam in the Aftermath of 9/11," *Public Opinion Quarterly* 70, no. 4 (December 2006): 608–24.
40. In 2000, for instance, only 2 percent of the foreign-born population living in the United States was born in an Arab country. Angela Brittingham and C. Patricia de la Cruz, "We the People of Arab Ancestry in the United States: Census 2000 Special Report," U.S. Census Bureau, March 2005.
41. Young-ok Yum and William J. Schenck-Hamlin, "Reactions to 9/11 as a Function of Terror Management and Perspective Taking," *Journal of Social Psychology* 145, no. 3 (2005): 265–86.

6. FROM A DISTANCE

42. Yariv Tsfati, "Hostile Media Perceptions, Presumed Media Influence, and Minority Alienation: The Case of Arabs in Israel," *Journal of Communication* 57, no. 4 (December 2007): 632–51.
43. Galindo, "Repartitioning the National Community."
44. Regina P. Branton, Valeria Martinez-Ebers, T. E. Carey Jr., and Tetsuya Matsubayashi, "Social Protest and Policy Attitudes: The Case of the 2006 Immigrant Rallies," *American Journal of Political Science* 59, no. 2 (April 2015): 390–402.
45. Christian Dustmann and Ian Preston, "Racial and Economic Factors in Attitudes to Immigration," *B.E. Journal of Economic Analysis & Policy* 7, no. 1 (2007): 1–14; Nicholas A. Valentino, Ted Brader, and Ashley Jardina, "Immigration Opposition Among U.S. Whites: General Ethnocentrism or Media Priming of Attitudes About Latinos?," *Political Psychology* 34, no. 2 (2013): 149–66; Ted Brader, Nicholas A. Valentino, and Elizabeth Suhay, "What Triggers Public Opposition to Immigration? Anxiety, Group Cues, and Immigration Threat," *American Journal of Political Science* 52, no. 4 (October 2008): 959–78; and Mara Cecilia Ostfeld, "The Backyard Politics of Attitudes Toward Immigration," *Political Psychology* 38, no. 1 (2017): 21–37.
46. Emily M. Farris and Heather Silber Mohamed, "Picturing Immigration: How the Media Criminalizes Immigrants," *Politics, Groups, and Identities* 6, no. 1 (June 2018): 814–24.
47. David G. Gutiérrez, *Walls and Mirrors: Mexican Americans, Mexican Immigrants, and the Politics of Ethnicity* (Berkeley: University of California Press, 1995).
48. De la Garza et al., *Latino Voices*; and Gutiérrez, *Walls and Mirrors*.

6. FROM A DISTANCE: PARTISANSHIP, PUBLIC ATTITUDES, AND GEOGRAPHIC PROXIMITY TOWARD THE U.S.-MEXICO BORDER WALL

This chapter is a modified and expanded version of Jeronimo Cortina, "From a Distance: Geographic Proximity, Partisanship, and Public Attitudes Toward the U.S.-Mexico Border Wall," *Political Research Quarterly* 73, no. 3 (June 2019): 740–54. It has been reproduced here with the permission of the copyright holder under Sage's Archiving and Sharing Green Open Access Policy.

1. Paul Ganster and David E. Lorey, *The U.S.-Mexican Border Into the Twenty-First Century* (Washington, DC: Rowman & Littlefield, 2008).
2. American Immigration Lawyers Association, "The REAL ID Act of 2005: Summary and Analysis of Provisions," 2005.
3. United States Senate, "Roll Call Vote 113th Congress—1st Session," Legislation and Records, 2005; American Immigration Lawyers Association, "The REAL ID Act of 2005: Summary and Analysis of Provisions. No. 05012772." *American Immigration Lawyers Association*, 2005, accessed May 5, 2022, https://www.aila.org/library/the-real-id-act-of-2005-summary-and-analysis.
4. "Transcript: Donald Trump's Full Immigration Speech, Annotated," *Los Angeles Times*, August 31, 2016, https://www.latimes.com/politics/la-na-pol-donald-trump-immigration-speech-transcript-20160831-snap-htmlstory.html.

6. FROM A DISTANCE

5. Fiona B. Adamson, "Crossing Borders: International Migration and National Security," *International Security* 31, no. 1 (summer 2006): 165–99; Peter Andreas, *Border Games: Policing the U.S.-Mexico Divide*, 2nd ed. (Ithaca, NY: Cornell University Press, 2009); Timothy B. Gravelle, "Politics, Time, Space, and Attitudes Toward US–Mexico Border Security," *Political Geography* 65 (2018): 107–16; Lawrence M. Lebowitz and Ira L. Podheiser, "A Summary of the Changes in Immigration Policies and Practices After the Terrorist Attacks of September 11, 2001: The USA Patriot Act and Other Measures," *University of Pittsburgh Law Review* 63, no. 41 (2002): 873–88; and Alexander Spencer, "Linking Immigrants and Terrorists: The Use of Immigration as an Anti-Terror Policy," *Online Journal of Peace and Conflict Resolution* 8, no. 1 (2008): 1–24.

6. Jens Hainmueller and Daniel J. Hopkins, "Public Attitudes Toward Immigration," *Annual Review of Political Science* 17 (2014): 225–49, at 237. Notable exceptions include Regina P. Branton, Gavin Dillingham, Johanna Dunaway, and Beth Miller, "Anglo Voting on Nativist Ballot Initiatives: The Partisan Impact of Spatial Proximity to the U.S.-Mexico Border," *Social Science Quarterly* 88, no. 3 (2007): 882–97; Timothy B. Gravelle, "Party Identification, Contact, Contexts, and Public Attitudes Toward Illegal Immigration," *Public Opinion Quarterly* 80, no. 1 (January 2016): 1–25; George Hawley, "Political Threat and Immigration: Party Identification, Demographic Context, and Immigration Policy Preference," *Social Science Quarterly* 92, no. 2 (2011): 404–22; and Daniel J. Hopkins, *The Increasingly United States: How and Why American Political Behavior Nationalized* (Chicago: Chicago University Press, 2018).

7. Ryan D. Enos, *The Space Between Us* (Cambridge: Cambridge University Press, 2017); Hopkins, *The Increasingly United States*.

8. Marlone D. Henderson, Kentaro Fujita, Yaacov Trope, and Nira Liberman, "Transcending the 'Here': The Effect of Spatial Distance on Social Judgement," *Journal of Personality and Social Psychology* 91, no. 5 (2006): 845–56.

9. On partisan beliefs, see Daniel Bar-Tal and Leonard Saxe, "Acquisition of Political Knowledge: A Social-Psychological Analysis," in *Political Socialization, Citizenship Education, and Democracy*, ed. Orit Ichilov (New York: Teachers College, 1990), 116–33. For partisan discourse on immigration, see Hopkins, *The Increasingly United States*.

10. C. J. Alvarez, "The United States–Mexico Border," *American History*, March 29, 2017, https://doi.org/10.1093/acrefore/9780199329175.013.384; and C. J. Alvarez, *Border Land, Border Water: A History of Construction on the US-Mexico Divide* (Austin: University of Texas Press, 2019).

11. Gravelle, in "Politics, Time, Space, and Attitudes Toward US–Mexico Border Security," suggests that the U.S.-Mexico border is a war zone.

12. Kristin M. Finklea, "CRS Report for Congress Southwest Border Violence: Issues in Identifying and Measuring Spillover Violence Specialist in Domestic Security," February 28, 2013, https://fas.org/sgp/crs/homesec/R41075.pdf; Jonathan Fox and Gaspar Rivera-Salgado, "Building Civil Society Among Indigenous Migrants," in *Indigenous Mexican Migrants in the United States*, ed. Joanthan Fox and Gaspar Rivera-Salgado (San Diego: University of California, Center for Comparative Immigration Studies, 2005), 1–64.

6. FROM A DISTANCE

13. John A. Adams, *Conflict and Commerce on the Rio Grande: Laredo, 1755–1955* (College Station: Texas A&M University Press, 2008).
14. David Martin, "Texas Mayors Oppose Plan for Border Fence," *NPR*, October 16, 2007, http://www.npr.org/templates/story/story.php?storyId=15315131.
15. James Anderson and Liam O'Dowd, "Borders, Border Regions and Territoriality: Contradictory Meanings, Changing Significance," *Regional Studies* 33, no. 7 (1999): 593–604; Alexander Diener and Joshua Hagen, *Borderlines and Borderlands: Political Oddities at the Edge of the Nation-State* (Washington, DC: Rowman & Littlefield, 2010); Anssi Paasi, "Boundaries as Social Practice and Discourse: The Finnish-Russian Border," *Regional Studies* 33, no. 7 (1999): 669–80; and Harriett Romo and Raquel R. Márquez, "Who's Who Across the U.S.-Mexico Border: Identities in Transition," in *Understanding Life in the Borderlands: Boundaries in Depth and in Motion*, ed. William Zartman (Athens: University of Georgia Press, 2010), 217–34.
16. Brady Baybeck, "Sorting Out the Competing Effects of Racial Context," *Journal of Politics* 68, no. 2 (2006): 386–96; Wendy K. Tam Cho, "Contagion Effects and Ethnic Contribution Networks," *American Journal of Political Science* 47, no. 2 (2003): 368–87; Wendy K. Tam Cho and Erinn P. Nicley, "Geographic Proximity Versus Institutions," *American Politics Research* 36, no. 6 (November 2008): 803–23; and David Thelen, "Rethinking History and the Nation-State: Mexico and the United States," *Journal of American History* 86, no. 2 (1999): 438–52.
17. Robert Alvarez Jr., "The Mexican-US Border: The Making of an Anthropology of Borderlands," *Annual Review of Anthropology* 24, no. 1 (October 1995): 447–70; Akhil Gupta and James Ferguson, "Space, Identity, and the Politics of Difference," *Cultural Anthropology* 7, no. 1 (1992): 6–24; and Michael Kearney, "The Local and the Global: The Anthropology of Globalization and Transnationalism," *Annual Review of Anthropology* 24, no. 1 (November 2003): 547–65.
18. Vernon L. Allen and David A. Wilder, "Categorization, Belief Similarity, and Intergroup Discrimination," *Journal of Personality and Social Psychology* 32, no. 6 (1975): 971–77; and David A. Wilder, "Cognitive Factors Affecting the Success of Intergroup Contact," in *Psychology of Intergroup Relations*, ed. Stephen Worchel and William G. Austin (Chicago: Nelson-Hall, 1986), 49–66.
19. Marilynn B. Brewer and Norman Miller, "Beyond the Contact Hypothesis: Theoretical Perspectives on Desegregation," in *Groups in Contact: The Psychology of Desegregation*, ed. Norman Miller and Marilynn B. Brewer (Orlando, FL: Academic, 1984), 281–302.
20. Maria Vittoria Giuliani, "Theory of Attachment and Place Attachment," in *Psychological Theories for Environmental Issues*, ed. Mirilia Bonnes, Terence Lee, and Mario Bonaiuto (New York: Routledge, 2003), 137–70; Harold M. Proshansky, Abbe K. Fabian, and Robert Kaminoff, "Place-Identity: Physical World Socialization of the Self," *Journal of Environmental Psychology* 3, no. 1 (1983): 57–83.
21. Kathleen M. McGraw, "Political Impressions: Formation and Management," in *Oxford Handbook of Political Psychology*, ed. David O. Sears, Leonie Huddy, and Robert Jervis (New York: Oxford University Press, 2003), 394–432.

6. FROM A DISTANCE

22. Stanley Feldman and Pamela Johnston Conover, "Candidates, Issues and Voters: The Role of Inference in Political Perception," *Journal of Politics* 45, no. 4 (1983): 810–39; Ruth Hamill, Milton Lodge, and Frederick Blake, "The Breadth, Depth, and Utility of Class, Partisan, and Ideological Schemata," *American Journal of Political Science* 29, no. 4 (1985): 850–70; Milton Lodge and Ruth Hamill, "A Partisan Schema for Political Information Processing," *American Political Science Review* 80, no. 2 (1986): 505–20; Ziva Kunda, "The Case for Motivated Reasoning," *Psychological Bulletin* 108, no. 3 (1990): 480–98; and Charles S. Taber and Milton Lodge, "Motivated Skepticism in the Evaluation of Political Beliefs," *American Journal of Political Science* 50, no. 3 (2006): 755–69.
23. Angus Campbell, Philip E. Converse, Warren E. Miller, and Donald E. Stokes, *The American Voter* (Chicago: University of Chicago Press, 1980).
24. James N. Druckman, "On the Limits of Framing Effects: Who Can Frame?," *Journal of Politics* 63, no. 4 (November 2001): 1041–66; Wendy M. Rahn, "The Role of Partisan Stereotypes in Information Processing About Political Candidates," *American Journal of Political Science* 37, no. 2 (1993): 472–96; James M. Snyder and Michael M. Ting, "An Informational Rationale for Political Parties," *American Journal of Political Science* 46, no. 1 (2002): 90–110; and John Zaller, *The Nature and Origins of Mass Opinion* (New York: Cambridge University Press, 1992).
25. Reuters, "From Nuns to Republican Millionaires, These Groups Unite Against Trump's Border Wall in Texas," *NBC News*, October 5, 2020, https://www.nbcnews.com/news/latino/nuns-republican-millionaires-these-groups-unite-against-trump-s-border-n1242128.
26. Trip Gabriel, "A Timeline of Steve King's Racist Remarks and Divisive Actions," *New York Times*, January 15, 2019, https://www.nytimes.com/2019/01/15/us/politics/steve-king-offensive-quotes.html.
27. Enos, *The Space Between Us*.
28. Hopkins, *The Increasingly United States*.
29. The February 2017 Political Survey, sponsored by the Pew Research Center, obtained telephone interviews with a nationally representative sample of 1,503 adults age 18 or older living in the United States. The survey was conducted by Princeton Survey Research Associates International. The interviews were administered in English and Spanish by Princeton Data Source. Numbers for the landline sample were drawn with equal probabilities from active blocks (area code + exchange + two-digit block number) that contained one or more residential directory listing. The cellular sample was not list-assisted but was drawn through a systematic sampling from dedicated wireless 100-blocks and shared service 100-blocks with no directory-listed landline numbers. The margin of sampling error for the complete set of weighted data is ±2.9 percentage points.
30. Given that linearity is not a reasonable assumption due to the nature of the main predictor and that the outcome variable is all-positive, taking the logarithm of the outcome variable could remedy these situations. For a discussion, see Andrew Gelman and Jennifer Hill, *Data Analysis Using Regression and Multilevel/Hierarchical Models* (New York: Cambridge University Press, 2007).

6. FROM A DISTANCE

31. Francis P. Boscoe, Kevin A. Henry, and Michael S. Zdeb, "A Nationwide Comparison of Driving Distance Versus Straight-Line Distance to Hospitals," *Professional Geographer* 64, no. 2 (April 2012).
32. Kai Arzheimer and Jocelyn Evans, "Geolocation and Voting: Candidate-Voter Distance Effects on Party Choice in the 2010 UK General Election in England," *Political Geography* 31, no. 5 (2012): 301–10.
33. Regina P. Branton and Johanna Dunaway, "Spatial Proximity to the U.S.-Mexico Border and Newspaper Coverage of Immigration Issues," *Political Research Quarterly* 62, no. 2 (June 2009): 289–302.
34. Branton and Dunaway, "Spatial Proximity to the U.S.-Mexico Border and Newspaper Coverage of Immigration Issues."
35. Jack Dennis, "Political Independence in America, III: In Search of Closet Partisans," *Political Behavior* 14, no. 3 (1992): 261–96; Steven Greene, "The Psychological Sources of Partisan-Leaning Independence," *American Politics Quarterly* 28, no. 4 (October 2000): 511–37; Bruce E. Keith, David B. Magleby, Candice J. Nelson, Elizabeth A. Orr, Mark C. Westlye, and Raymond E. Wolfinger, *The Myth of the Independent Voter* (Berkeley: University of California Press, 1992); and John R. Petrocik, "An Analysis of Intransitivities in the Index of Party Identification," *Political Methodology* 1, no. 3 (1974): 31–47.
36. Thomas J. Espenshade and Katherine Hempstead, "Contemporary American Attitudes Toward U.S. Immigration," *International Migration Review* 30, no. 2 (1996): 535–70; Thomas J. Espenshade and Gregory A. Huber, "Fiscal Impacts of Immigrants and the Shrinking Welfare State," in *The Handbook of International Migration: The American Experience*, ed. Charles Hirschman, Philip Kasinitz, and Josh DeWind (New York: Russell Sage Foundation, 1999), 360–70; Gravelle, "Party Identification, Contact, Contexts, and Public Attitudes Toward Illegal Immigration"; Hainmueller and Hopkins, "Public Attitudes Toward Immigration"; and Benjamin R. Knoll, David P. Redlawsk, and Howard Sanborn, "Framing Labels and Immigration Policy Attitudes in the Iowa Caucuses: 'Trying to Out-Tancredo Tancredo,'" *Political Behavior* 33, no. 3 (2011): 433–54.
37. Hainmueller and Hopkins, "Public Attitudes Toward Immigration"; Gordon H. Hanson, *Why Does Immigration Divide America? Public Finance and Political Opposition to Open Borders* (Washington, DC: Institute for International Economics, 2005); and Kenneth F. Scheve and Matthew J. Slaughter, "What Determines Individual Trade-Policy Preferences?," *Journal of International Economics* 54, no. 2 (August 2001): 267–92.
38. Michael Fix and Jeffrey S. Passel, *Immigration and Immigrants: Setting the Record Straight* (Washington, DC: Urban Institute, 1994); Barry Edmonston and Ronald Lee, eds., *Local Fiscal Effects of Illegal Immigration* (Washington, DC: National Academy Press, 1996); and Gordon H. Hanson, *Why Does Immigration Divide America? Public Finance and Political Opposition to Open Borders* (Washington, DC: Institute for International Economics, 2005).
39. Jack Citrin, Donald P. Green, Christopher Muste, and Cara Wong, "Public Opinion Toward Immigration Reform: The Role of Economic Motivations," *Journal of Politics* 59, no. 3 (August 1997): 858–81.

40. Brewer and Miller, "Beyond the Contact Hypothesis"; Thomas J. Espenshade and Charles A. Calhoun, "An Analysis of Public Opinion Toward Undocumented Immigration," *Population Research and Policy Review* 12 (1993): 189–224; and David G. Gutiérrez, *Walls and Mirrors: Mexican Americans, Mexican Immigrants, and the Politics of Ethnicity* (Berkeley: University of California Press, 1995).
41. Robert M. Stein, Stephanie Shirley Post, and Allison L. Rinden, "Reconciling Context and Contact Effects on Racial Attitudes," *Political Research Quarterly* 53, no. 2 (June 2000): 285–303.
42. Easy Analytic Software, "EASI Crime Index," 2017, https://www.easidemographics.com/.
43. Hopkins, *The Increasingly United States*.
44. The main effects of geographic distance or partisanship must not be interpreted as the mean effects of a change in these variables based on the probability of supporting building a fence along the U.S.-Mexico border. The effect of partisanship on the probability of supporting the construction of the wall depends on individuals' proximity to the border. The coefficient on partisanship captures only the effect of party identification on the probability of supporting the fence when proximity to the border is zero, and the coefficient of geographic distance captures the effect on the outcome variable when partisanship is zero. See Brambor et al. for a discussion on how to interpret interaction models: Thomas Brambor, William R. Clark, and Matt Golder, "Understanding Interaction Models: Improving Empirical Analyses," *Political Analysis* 14 (2005): 63–82.
45. To further parse the results, it is necessary to estimate the change in the support of building a fence along the border due to a change in geographic distance from the border. In a logistic regression that incorporates a transformed predictor (i.e., $log(x)$), the odds-ratio associated with a relative change in the predictor (i.e., multiplying X by a factor q) is given by $e^{\hat{\beta} \log(q)}$ or equivalently to $q^{\hat{\beta}}$ in contrast to a logistic regression with an untransformed predictor in which the change of the outcome variable associated with a one-unit increase in the predictor is given by $e^{\hat{\beta}}$. See Jose Barrera-Gómez and Xavier Basagaña, "Models with Transformed Variables: Interpretation and Software," *Epidemiology* 26, no. 2 (March 2015): e16–17.
46. James J. Heckman, "The Scientific Model of Causality," *Sociological Methodology* 35 (2005): 1–97; Paul W. Holland, "Statistics and Causal Inference," *Journal of the American Statistical Association* 81, no. 396 (1986): 945–60; Judea Pearl, *Causality: Models, Reasoning, and Inference* (New York: Cambridge University Press, 2000); Donald B. Rubin, "Estimating Causal Effects of Treatments in Randomized and Nonrandomized Studies," *Journal of Educational Psychology* 66, no. 5 (1974): 688–701; Donald B. Rubin, "Causal Inference Using Potential Outcomes," *Journal of the American Statistical Association* 100, no. 469 (2005): 322–31; and Jerzy Splawa-Neyman, D. M. Dabrowska, and T. P. Speed, "On the Application of Probability Theory to Agricultural Experiments. Essay on Principles. Section 9," *Statistical Science* 5, no. 4 (1990): 465–72.
47. For an introduction, see Stephen L. Morgan and Christopher Winship, *Counterfactuals and Causal Inference: Methods and Principles for Social Research* (New York: Cambridge University Press, 2015).

6. FROM A DISTANCE

48. For a review, see Andrew Gelman and Jeronimo Cortina, eds., *A Quantitative Tour of the Social Sciences* (Princeton, NJ: Princeton University Press, 2012).
49. Matias D. Cattaneo, "Efficient Semiparametric Estimation of Multi-Valued Treatment Effects Under Ignorability," *Journal of Econometrics* 155, no. 2 (April 2010): 138–54.
50. Two important assumptions need to be made. First, the outcome for a particular individual depends only on its assignment to a particular treatment (i.e., Level 0, Level 1, Level 2, or Level 3), not on the assignment of other individuals to another particular treatment. (This assumption is known as the Stable Unit Treatment Value Assumption [SUTVA].) The second assumption is that each treatment level is independent of the potential outcomes after conditioning a series of covariates. In other words, the probability of being assigned to a particular treatment is a function of certain observable characteristics (income, education, county of residence, and age) and is conditionally independent of the potential outcomes (i.e., the ignorability assumption). For the SUTVA assumption, there is no reason to believe that it does not hold; that is, there is no reason to believe that the attitudes of a Republican living in Wichita, Kansas, who is "assigned" to a Level 2 treatment depend on the attitudes of a Republican living in Houston, Texas, who is "assigned" to a Level 1 treatment. For the ignorability assumption, given the covariates it seems reasonable to assume that the treatments and potential outcomes are independent (see table A7.1 in the appendix for balance and overlap).
51. Gordon W. Allport, *The Nature of Prejudice* (Cambridge, MA: Addison Wesley, 1954); and Stein, Post, and Rinden, "Reconciling Context and Contact Effects on Racial Attitudes."
52. See Steven W. Webster and Bethany Albertson, "Emotion and Politics: Noncognitive Psychological Biases in Public Opinion," *Annual Review of Political Science* 25, no. 1 (May 2022): 401–18; and Dennis Chong and James N. Druckman, "Framing Theory," *Annual Review of Political Science* 10, no. 1 (May 2007): 103–26.
53. Brian Reed and Zoe Chace, "Fear and Loathing in Homer and Rockville," *This American Life*, July 21, 2017.
54. U.S. Census Bureau, "Selected Social Characteristics in the United States: Homer, Alaska," American Community Survey, 2019, https://data.census.gov/cedsci/table?q=homer, alaska&t=Native and Foreign Born.
55. Reed and Chace, "Fear and Loathing in Homer and Rockville."
56. Reed and Chace, "Fear and Loathing in Homer and Rockville."
57. In the 2016 Cooperative Election Study, the first vignette provided this summary. "The Federation for American Immigration Reform found that Illegal immigration costs U.S. taxpayers about $113 billion a year at the Federal, State and local level . . . the annual outlay that illegal aliens cost U.S. taxpayers is an average amount per native-headed household of $1,117." Thinking now about the border wall, do you favor or oppose building a fence or physical barrier along the U.S.-Mexico border?
58. In the 2016 Cooperative Election Study, the second vignette provided this summary. "The Federation for American Immigration Reform found that terrorists can and will take advantage of the same unenforced immigration policies that have flooded this country with illegal immigrants—there is irrefutable proof that the terrorists understand where

6. FROM A DISTANCE

we are vulnerable. We can be certain that there are many more terrorists who entered the country illegally or overstayed visas." Thinking now about the border wall, do you favor or oppose building a fence or physical barrier along the U.S.-Mexico border?

59. In the 2016 Cooperative Election Study, this vignette was also presented. The Federation for American Immigration Reform found that illegal immigrants have a significant presence in the United States. Thinking now about the border wall, do you favor or oppose building a fence or physical barrier along the U.S.-Mexico border? Eronimo Cortina, "Framing Immigration: An Experimental Design," Congressional Cooperative Election Study, 2016.
60. Gelman and Hill, *Data Analysis Using Regression and Multilevel/Hierarchical Models.*

7. THE PERFECT STORM

1. Irene Lorenzoni and Nick F. Pidgeon, "Public Views on Climate Change: European and USA Perspectives," *Climatic Change* 77, no. 1 (2006): 73–95.
2. Christopher P. Borick and Barry G. Rabe, *Personal Experience, Extreme Weather Events, and Perceptions of Climate Change*, vol. 1 (New York: Oxford University Press, 2017).
3. A. Spence, W. Poortinga, C. Butler, and N. F Pidgeon, "Perceptions of Climate Change and Willingness to Save Energy Related to Flood Experience," *Nature Climate Change* 1 (March 2011): 46–49, https://doi.org/10.1038/nclimate1059; Stuart B. Capstick, Christina C. Demski, Robert G Sposato, Alexa Spence, and Adam Corner, "Public Perceptions of Climate Change in Britain Following the Winter 2013/2014 Flooding," 2015, https://orca.cardiff.ac.uk/id/eprint/74368/1/URG%2015-01%20Flood%20Climate%20report%201%20May%202015%20final.pdf; Lisa Zaval, Elizabeth A. Keenan, Eric J. Johnson, and Elke U. Weber, "How Warm Days Increase Belief in Global Warming," *Nature Climate Change* 4, no. 2 (2014): 143–47; Christina Demski, Stuart Capstick, Nick Pidgeon, Robert Gennaro Sposato, and Alexa Spence, "Experience of Extreme Weather Affects Climate Change Mitigation and Adaptation Responses," *Climatic Change* 140, no. 2 (2017): 149–64.
4. Rachel I. McDonald, Hui Yi Chai, and Ben R. Newell, "Personal Experience and the 'Psychological Distance' of Climate Change: An Integrative Review," *Journal of Environmental Psychology* 44 (December 2015): 109–18, https://doi.org/10.1016/j.jenvp.2015.10.003; Kate Sambrook, Emmanouil Konstantinidis, Sally Russell, and Yasmina Okan, "The Role of Personal Experience and Prior Beliefs in Shaping Climate Change Perceptions: A Narrative Review," *Frontiers in Psychology* 12 (July 2021): 669911, https://www.frontiersin.org/articles/10.3389/fpsyg.2021.669911; Lorenzoni and Pidgeon, "Public Views on Climate Change: European and USA Perspectives"; and Elke U. Weber, "What Shapes Perceptions of Climate Change?," *WIREs Climate Change* 1, no. 3 (May 2010): 332–42.
5. Spence et al., "Perceptions of Climate Change and Willingness to Save Energy Related to Flood Experience"; Andrea Taylor, Wändi Bruine de Bruin, and Suraje Dessai, "Climate Change Beliefs and Perceptions of Weather-Related Changes in the United Kingdom," *Risk Analysis* 34, no. 11 (November 2014): 1995–2004; Päivi Lujala, Haakon Lein, and Jan

7. THE PERFECT STORM

Ketil Rød, "Climate Change, Natural Hazards, and Risk Perception: The Role of Proximity and Personal Experience," *Local Environment* 20, no. 4 (April 2015): 489–509; and Magnus Bergquist, Andreas Nilsson, and P. Wesley Schultz, "Experiencing a Severe Weather Event Increases Concern About Climate Change," *Frontiers in Psychology* 10 (February 2019), https://www.frontiersin.org/articles/10.3389/fpsyg.2019.00220.

6. Sambrook et al., "The Role of Personal Experience and Prior Beliefs in Shaping Climate Change Perceptions."
7. Gabrielle Wong-Parodi and Dana Rose Garfin, "Hurricane Adaptation Behaviors in Texas and Florida: Exploring the Roles of Negative Personal Experience and Subjective Attribution to Climate Change," *Environmental Research Letters* 17, no. 3 (2022): 034033.
8. Matthew Ryan Sisco, "The Effects of Weather Experiences on Climate Change Attitudes and Behaviors," *Opinion in Environmental Sustainability* 52 (2021): 111–17.
9. Elke U. Weber, "What Shapes Perceptions of Climate Change? New Research Since 2010," *WIREs Climate Change* 7 (2016): 125–34.
10. Craig Hlavaty, "Remembering Memorial Day 2015's Costly, Deadly Flooding," *Houston Chronicle*, May 26, 2018.
11. Water Resources Mission Area, "Water in the United States," United States Geological Survey, 2019, https://www.usgs.gov/mission-areas/water-resources/science/water-use-united-states.
12. Water Smart, "What Does 2 Billion Gallons of Water Look Like?," accessed January 4, 2023, https://www.watersmart.com/what-does-2-billion-gallons-of-water-look-like/.
13. Mike Morris, "See the Scope of the Damage from Houston's Memorial Day Flood," *Houston Chronicle*, June 10, 2015.
14. Morris, "See the Scope of the Damage from Houston's Memorial Day Flood."
15. Hlavaty, "Remembering Memorial Day 2015's Costly, Deadly Flooding."
16. Morris, "See the Scope of the Damage from Houston's Memorial Day Flood."
17. Hlavaty, "Remembering Memorial Day 2015's Costly, Deadly Flooding."
18. Stephen Klinberg, "Kinder Houston Area Survey," Kinder Institute for Urban Research, accessed January 4, 2023, https://kinder.rice.edu/initiative/kinder-houston-area-survey.
19. Matt Lanza, "Houston's Tax Day Flooding Put Into Historical Perspective," Space City Weather, April 16, 2016, https://spacecityweather.com/houstons-flooding-review/.
20. Mike Morris and Mihir Zaveri, "As Rescues Continue, Officials Eye Recovery from Flood," *Houston Chronicle*, April 20, 2016.
21. Lanza, "Houston's Tax Day Flooding Put Into Historical Perspective."
22. Neena Satija, Kiah Collier, and Al Shaw, "Boomtown, Flood Town," *Propublica* and *Texas Tribune*, December 7, 2016, https://projects.propublica.org/houston-cypress/.
23. Harris County Flood Control District, "Hurricane Ike 2008," accessed January 4, 2024, https://www.hcfcd.org/About/Harris-Countys-Flooding-History/Hurricane-Ike-2008.
24. Harris County Flood Control District, "Hurricane Harvey," accessed January 4, 2024, https://www.hcfcd.org/About/Harris-Countys-Flooding-History/Hurricane-Harvey.
25. Mathilde Carlier, "Automobile Registrations in the United States in 2021, by State," *Statista*, August 24, 2023, https://www.statista.com/statistics/196010/total-number-of-registered-automobiles-in-the-us-by-state/.

7. THE PERFECT STORM

26. Monique Welch, "Hurricane Harvey by the Numbers: 5 Years Later, See the Storm's Lasting Toll on Houston," *Houston Chronicle*, August 23, 2022.
27. Welch, "Hurricane Harvey by the Numbers."
28. World Bank, "GDP in Current USD," accessed January 4, 2024, https://data.worldbank.org/indicator/NY.GDP.MKTP.CD?most_recent_value_desc=false.
29. Anthony Leiserowitz, Edward Maibach, Seth Rosenthal, John Kotcher, Parrish Berquist, Matthew Ballew, Matthew Goldberg, and Abel Gustafson, "Climate Change in the American Mind: November 2019," Yale Program on Climate Change Communication, 2019, https://climatecommunication.yale.edu/publications/climate-change-in-the-american-mind-november-2019/toc/2/.
30. Muhammad Mehedi Masud, Rulia Akhatr, Shamima Nasrin, and Ibrahim Mohammed Adamu, "Impact of Socio-Demographic Factors on the Mitigating Actions for Climate Change: A Path Analysis with Mediating Effects of Attitudinal Variables," *Environmental Science and Pollution Research* 24, no. 34 (December 2017): 26462–77.
31. Alec Tyson, Cary Funk, and Brian Kennedy, "What the Data Says About Americans' Views of Climate Change," Pew Research Center, August 9, 2023, https://www.pewresearch.org/short-reads/2023/04/18/for-earth-day-key-facts-about-americans-views-of-climate-change-and-renewable-energy/.
32. Tyson, Funk, and Kennedy, "What the Data Says About Americans' Views of Climate Change."
33. Cary Funk, "How Americans' Attitudes About Climate Change Differ by Generation, Party and Other Factors," Pew Research Center, May 26, 2021, https://www.pewresearch.org/short-reads/2021/05/26/key-findings-how-americans-attitudes-about-climate-change-differ-by-generation-party-and-other-factors/.
34. Tyson, Funk, and Kennedy, "What the Data Says about Americans' Views of Climate Change."
35. Klinberg, "Kinder Houston Area Survey."
36. Global Climate Change, "The Causes of Climate Change," National Aeronautics and Space Administration, accessed December 20, 2023, https://climate.nasa.gov/causes/.
37. United Nations, "What Is Climate Change?," Climate Action, accessed January 4, 2023, https://www.un.org/en/climatechange/what-is-climate-change.
38. Jeff Turrentine, "What Are the Causes of Climate Change?," Natural Resources Defense Council, September 13, 2022, https://www.nrdc.org/stories/what-are-causes-climate-change.
39. National Geographic, "Causes of Global Warming," accessed December 20, 2022, https://www.nationalgeographic.com/environment/article/global-warming-causes.
40. Lacy M. Johnson, "Introduction: More City Than Water," in *More City Than Water: A Houston Flood Atlas*, ed. Lacy M. Johnson and Cheryl Beckett (Austin: University of Texas Press, 2022), 7.
41. Klinberg, "Kinder Houston Area Survey."
42. Bennet B. Murdock Jr., "The Serial Position Effect of Free Recall," *Journal of Experimental Psychology* 64, no. 5 (1962): 482–88; and Shirley Dex, *The Reliability of Recall Data: A Literature Review* (Colchester, UK: University of Essex, 1991).

8. THE GREAT DROUGHT

43. Beatrice I. Crona, Amber Wutich, Alexandra Brewis, and Meredith Gartin, "Perceptions of Climate Change: Linking Local and Global Perceptions Through a Cultural Knowledge Approach," *Climatic Change* 119, no. 2 (July 2013): 519–31; and Samantha Harrington, "Why Climate Change Matters to Latinos," Yale Climate Connections, May 19, 2022, https://yaleclimateconnections.org/2022/05/why-climate-change-matters-to-latinos/.

8. THE GREAT DROUGHT

1. Blair Fannin, "Updated 2011 Texas Agricultural Drought Losses Total $7.62 Billion," *AgriLife Today*, March 21, 2012, https://agrilifetoday.tamu.edu/2012/03/21/updated-2011-texas-agricultural-drought-losses-total-7-62-billion/.
2. Texas Parks & Wildlife, "Life After Wildfire: The Future of Bastrop State Park," accessed December 5, 2023, https://tpwd.texas.gov/spdest/findadest/parks/bastrop/fire/.
3. Susan Combs, "The Impact of the 2011 Drought and Beyond," Texas Comptroller of Public Accounts, February 6, 2012, https://texashistory.unt.edu/ark:/67531/metapth542095/m2/1/high_res_d/txcs-0790.pdf.
4. Aaron M. McCright and Riley E. Dunlap, "The Politicization of Climate Change and Polarization in the American Public's Views of Global Warming, 2001–2010," *Sociological Quarterly* 52, no. 2 (May 2011): 155–94.
5. Republican Party of Texas, "Report of Permanent Committee on Platform and Resolutions as Amended and Adopted by the 2014 State Convention of the Republican Party of Texas," 2014 Platform, 8, https://www.texasgop.org/wp-content/uploads/2014/06/2014-Platform-Final.pdf.
6. Texas Democratic Party, "2014 Texas Democratic Party Platform," *Texas Tribune*, 2014, 33, accessed August 5, 2023, https://s3.amazonaws.com/static.texastribune.org/media/documents/2014-TDP-Platform.pdf.
7. Jay D. Gatrell and Gregory D. Bierly, "Weather and Voter Turnout: Kentucky Primary and General Elections, 1990–2000," *Southeastern Geographer* 42, no. 1 (2002): 114–34.
8. Ron Shachar and Barry Nalebuff, "Follow the Leader: Theory and Evidence on Political Participation," *American Economic Review* 89, no. 3 (June 1999): 525–47.
9. Brad T. Gomez, Thomas G. Hansford, and George A. Krause, "The Republicans Should Pray for Rain: Weather, Turnout, and Voting in US Presidential Elections," *Journal of Politics* 69, no. 3 (2007): 649–63.
10. Steve Knack, "Does Rain Help the Republicans? Theory and Evidence on Turnout and the Vote," *Public Choice* 79, no. 1–2 (1994): 187–209.
11. Christopher H. Achen and Larry M. Bartels, *Democracy for Realists: Why Elections Do Not Produce Responsive Government* (Princeton, NJ: Princeton University Press, 2016).
12. Anthony Fowler and Andrew B. Hall, "Do Shark Attacks Influence Presidential Elections? Reassessing a Prominent Finding on Voter Competence," *Journal of Politics* 80, no. 4 (August 2018): 1423–37.

8. THE GREAT DROUGHT

13. Kevin Arceneaux and Robert M. Stein, "Who Is Held Responsible When Disaster Strikes? The Attribution of Responsibility for a Natural Disaster in an Urban Election," *Journal of Urban Affairs* 28, no. 1 (2006): 43–53.
14. Neil Malhotra and Alexander G. Kuo, "Attributing Blame: The Public's Response to Hurricane Katrina," *Journal of Politics* 70, no. 1 (2008): 120–35.
15. John T. Gasper and Andrew Reeves, "Make It Rain? Retrospection and the Attentive Electorate in the Context of Natural Disasters," *American Journal of Political Science* 55, no. 2 (2011): 340–55.
16. Giuliano Masiero and Michael Santarossa, "Natural Disasters and Electoral Outcomes," *European Journal of Political Economy* 67 (2021): 101983, https://doi.org/https://doi.org/10.1016/j.ejpoleco.2020.101983.
17. R. Michael Alvarez, *Information and Elections* (Ann Arbor: University of Michigan Press, 1998); Larry M. Bartels, "Messages Received: The Political Impact of Media Exposure," *American Political Science Review* 87, no. 2 (1993): 267–85; Scott J. Basinger and Howard Lavine, "B," *American Political Science Review* 99, no. 2 (2005): 169–84; Shanto Iyengar and Donald R Kinder, *News That Matters* (Chicago: University of Chicago Press, 1987); and Samuel L. Popkin, *The Reasoning Voter*, 2nd ed. (Chicago: University of Chicago Press, 1991).
18. Yaacov Trope and Nira Liberman, "Construal-Level Theory of Psychological Distance," *Psychological Review* 117, no. 2 (2010): 440–63.
19. Gabriel S. Lenz, "Learning and Opinion Change, Not Priming: Reconsidering the Priming Hypothesis," *American Journal of Political Science* 53, no. 4 (2009): 821–37.
20. Markus Becker, "Accepting Global Warming as Fact," *Nieman Reports, Cambridge* 59, no. 4 (Winter 2005): 97–98, at 98.
21. John H. Aldrich, Christopher Gelpi, Peter Feaver, Jason Reifler, and Kristin Thompson Sharp, "Foreign Policy and the Electoral Connection," *Annual Review of Political Science* 9 (June 2006): 477–502.
22. Rachel I. McDonald, Hui Yi Chai, and Ben R. Newell, "Personal Experience and the 'Psychological Distance' of Climate Change: An Integrative Review," *Journal of Environmental Psychology* 44 (December 2015): 109–18, at 110, https://doi.org/10.1016/j.jenvp.2015.10.003.
23. James Hansen, Makiko Sato, and Reto Ruedy, "Perception of Climate Change," *Proceedings of the National Academy of Sciences* 109, no. 37 (2012): E2415–23.
24. Christopher H. Achen and Larry M. Bartels, *Blind Retrospection: Electoral Responses to Drought, Flu, and Shark Attacks9* (Madrid: Instituto Juan March de Estudios e Investigaciones, 2004).
25. Arceneaux and Stein, "Who Is Held Responsible When Disaster Strikes?"
26. Patrick J. Egan and Megan Mullin, "Turning Personal Experience Into Political Attitudes: The Effect of Local Weather on American's Perceptions About Global Warming," *Journal of Politics* 74, no. 3 (2012): 796–809.
27. Lawrence C. Hamilton and Mary D. Stampone, "Blowin' in the Wind: Short-Term Weather and Belief in Anthropogenic Climate Change," *Weather, Climate, and Society* 5 (2013): 112–19.

9. SO WHAT?

28. McDonald, Chai, and Newell, "Personal Experience and the 'Psychological Distance' of Climate Change," 111.
29. McCright and Dunlap, "The Politicization of Climate Change."
30. Var R. Haden, Meredith T. Niles, Mark Lubell, Joshua Perlman, and Louise E. Jackson, "Global and Local Concerns: What Attitudes and Beliefs Motivate Farmers to Mitigate and Adapt to Climate Change?," *PLOS ONE* 7, no. 12 (2012): E52882.
31. Samuel D. Brody, Sammy Zahran, Arnold Vedlitz, and Himanshu Grover, "Examining the Relationship Between Physical Vulnerability and Public Perceptions of Global Climate Change in the United States," *Environment and Behavior* 40, no. 1 (August 2008): 72–95.
32. Jeff Joireman, Heather Barnes Truelove, and Blythe Duell, "Effect of Outdoor Temperature, Heat Primes and Anchoring on Belief in Global Warming," *Journal of Environmental Psychology* 30, no. 4 (2010): 358–67; Stephan Lewandowsky, Gilles E. Gignac, and Samuel Vaughan, "The Pivotal Role of Perceived Scientific Consensus in Acceptance of Science," *Nature Climate Change* 3, no. 4 (2013): 399–404; Ye Li, Eric J. Johnson, and Lisa Zaval, "Local Warming: Daily Temperature Change Influences Belief in Global Warming," *Psychological Science* 22, no. 4 (March 3, 2011): 454–59; and Jane L. Risen and Clayton R. Critcher, "Visceral Fit: While in a Visceral State, Associated States of the World Seem More Likely," *Journal of Personality and Social Psychology* 100, no. 5 (2011): 777–93.

9. SO WHAT?

1. Max Weber, *The Methodology of the Social Sciences* (Glencoe, IL: Free Press, 1949).
2. John Gerring, "What Makes a Concept Good? A Criterial Framework for Understanding Concept Formation in the Social Sciences," *Polity* 31, no. 3 (July 1999): 357–93.

INDEX

Italicized page numbers refer to figures or tables.

Achen, Christopher, 153
advertisements, political campaign, 18
African Americans: adults supporting BLM movement, 85; border wall and, 122–23; with gun licenses, 73; immigration, *181–82, 189–90*; on immigration, 109; police shootings of, 78–80, 84. *See also* Black Lives Matter movement
Africans, immigration, 22, 105, *189, 190*, 220n34
agriculture: drought, elections and, 23, 157–59, *160–61*, 161, *199*; practices and greenhouse gas emissions, 144; U.S. Department of Agriculture, 151. *See also* drought in Texas
Alabama, 50, *50*, 52
Alaska, 127–28
Allegory of the Cave, 15
Allport, Gordon, 19–20
American National Election Studies (ANES), 62–63, 78, 152
American Psychological Association, 68

amygdala, fear and, 56, *57*
ANES (American National Election Studies), 62–63, 78, 152
animosity, intergroup, 20
Ankara, Turkey, 64
anxiety: fear and, 16–20, 22, 26, 39, 56, 59, 68, 163–64; after mass shootings, 68
Aquinas, Thomas, 18, 43, 54, 57–58, 127, 165
Arabs, immigration, 109–10, 113, 122, *182–83, 190–91*, 220n34, 220n40
Arbery, Ahmaud, 79
Arceneux, Kevin, 153
Aristotle, 17–18, 22, 43, 57, 127–28, 152, 165
Arizona, 44, 115, 123, 125
Arkansas, 45, 82
Asian-Pacific Islanders, with gun licenses, 73
Asians, 94, 98–99, 101, 122, *179–80, 188–89*, 220n34
as-the-crow-flies (Euclidean) distance, 119–20, 123, *124, 192–93, 195–96*, 225n31

INDEX

Atlanta, 69
Augustine (Saint), 18, 20, 54, 61, 127, 166
authority confirmation, 20
Azar, Alex, 44

background checks, guns, 70
Bartels, Larry, 153
behaviors, 3, 20, 49; distance and, 21, 23–24, 164–65, 167; electoral, 23, 150, 166; emotions and, 15–16; extreme weather events and shifts in, 135, 150, 156; geographic distance, public attitudes and, 4, 11
beliefs: biases and, 9; homophily and, 13; metacognitive, 18–19; personal experiences, partisanship and, 149, 155–56; personal experience with climate change and shifts in, 141, 143; political, 21, 54; values aligned with, 10
biases, 6, 9, 21, 52, 119, 128; cognitive, 19; from endogeneity, 89; partisan, 50, 126; racial, 98; recency, 60, 144–45
Biden, Joseph, 46, 50, 52–54, *53*, 56, 165, *170–73*
Bierly, Gregory, 152
"birds of a feather flock together," 13
"Black Lives Matter May be the Largest Movement in U.S. History" (Buchanan, Bui and Patel), 83–84
Black Lives Matter (BLM) movement: emotional attachment to, 90, *91*, *92*, 165; Floyd and, 79–81, 83; geographic distance and, 22, 90; marchers and demonstrations May to July 2020, *84*; media and, 85, 86, 87; with number of protesters, 81–84, *84*, 86; police brutality and, 77; protests and police, 82, 87, 166; proximity, urban unrest and, 85–86; public attitudes toward, 86, 89–90, *174*; racism versus law and order, 83–87; social justice and, 78–80; supporters, 82, 84, 85, 87, *88*
Black Muslims, 109
Blake, Jacob, 84

blame, on politicians with natural disasters, 152–53
BLM movement. *See* Black Lives Matter movement
Bloch-Elkon, Yaeli, 63–64
Blount County, Alabama, 50, *50*, 52
border, U.S.-Mexico: border patrol officers, 114, 125; crime and, 126, 127, *195–96*; crossing points, 119, 120, *121*, 129–30, *130*; levels of distance, 125, *193–95*, 227n51; militarization of, 116–17
Border Protection, Antiterrorism, and Illegal Immigration Control Act (2005), 105
Border Security, Economic Opportunity, and Immigration Modernization Act (2013), 115
border wall, U.S.-Mexico: geographic distance and, 23, 113, 115–16, 118–23, 126–30, 132, 166, 226nn45–46; illegal immigration and, 115, 127, 129, 227nn58–59, 228n60; immigration and, 115, 116, 118, 120–22, 125, 127–29, 132–33, 227nn58–59, 228n60; partisanship and, 23, 114–15, 117–23, *124*, 131–32, *194–95*, 226n45; public attitudes on, 115–22, 126–31; public opinion on, 23, 116–18; support for, 122–29, *124*, 131, 132, *192–93*, *195–97*; terrorists and immigration policies, 228n59. *See also* immigration
Boston, BLM movement and, 87
Boston Marathon bombing (2013), 60, 61
Boston Tea Party (1773), 77
Boulder, Colorado, 69
brain, 15, 16, 56, 57
Branton, Regina, 120
Brazil, 29, 30, 32, 82
Brody, Samuel, 156
Brown, Michael, 78, 79
Brunswick, Georgia, 79
Buchanan, Larry, 83–84
Bui, Quoctrung, 83–84
Bureau of Labor Statistics, U.S., 158, 159
Bush, George W., 102, 103, 104, 114–15

INDEX

"cada quien habla de la feria según como le fue en ella" (everyone speaks about what's fair according to how it goes for them), 145

California, 36, 105; BLM movement and, 87; border wall and, 114, 125; COVID-19 and, 44, 45, 47; terrorist attack in, 75–76

Cambridge Dictionary, 8

Canada, 28

Carlson, Tucker, 83

CDC (Centers for Disease Control and Prevention), 44–46

Census, U.S., 97, 122

Centers for Disease Control and Prevention (CDC), 44–46

Charlie Hebdo shootings (2015), 60

Chicago, Illinois: BLM movement and, 87; Houston versus, 5–6, 8, 9

children, 39, 56, 68, 107. *See also* schools

China, 27, *28*, 43–44

Chow, Edwin, 84

civil rights movement, 78, 81

climate change (global warming): acceptance of, 23, 147, 150, 166; denial of, 134, 151, 152, 155; distance and, 143, 149, 154; extreme weather events, 23, 135, 137–39, 141, 145, 147, 149–50, 155–57, 166; here and now of, 133, 134, 141, 155; human activities as main cause of, 134, 136, 141, 143–44, 147–48, *148*, 151, *198*; media and, 135; natural phenomena impacting, 144; partisanship and, 23, 134, 142–43, 146–49, *148*, 151–52, 156–57, 160–62; political campaigns and, 154, 155; public opinion on, 136, 140–41, *141*; storms and, 140–49; as threat, 142–43; threat of, 155; voters with personal experience of, 23, 154–57, 160, 161, 166; wildfires, 151, 154, 159. *See also* drought in Texas

Clinton, Bill, 114

Cloud Gate, 8

Club Q, mass shooting, 56–57

cognitive biases, 19

cognitive evaluations, 16, 17, 165

cognitive responses, emotional and, 1, 8, 16

Colorado, 56–57, 69

comorbidities, COVID-19 and, 46

concealed carry applications, 22, 72–73, 76

conceptual connections, 12

conceptual framework, potential-outcomes model, 123

"conceptual goodness," 164

conceptualizing destinations, 120

Congress, U.S., 78, 115

congressional elections: Texas drought and 2008, 151–52, 157–59, *160*, 161–62, 166, *199*; Texas drought and 2012, 23, 150–52, 157–62, *161*, 166, *199*

Connecticut, 68

connections: conceptual, 12; emotional, 4, 12, 13, 15, 20, 90, 117; homophily and, 12–13; interconnection and degree of, 12; spatial, 12, 13, 90

conscious awareness, 15, 16

Constitution, U.S., 77

"constitutional carry bill" (HB-1927), 71

Consulate, U.S., 82

contextual information (context), 4, 9, 56–58, 85–86, 118

Cooperative Election Study (2016), 129, 227nn58–59, 228n60

coronavirus. *See* COVID-19 pandemic

Cortina, Jeronimo, 221n1

Costa Rica, GDP, 140

Cotton, Tom, 82

covariate balance summary, *193*

COVID-19 pandemic, 25, 39, 72; deaths, 21, 29, 45–46, 49–50, 52–54, *53*, 56, *170–73*; Google Open Data Repository, 49; Google trends in China and U.S., 27, *28*; mobility and, 21, 29, 48–50, *50–51*, 52–54, 165, *170*; outbreaks, 26–27, 29, 43–44; partisanship and, 29, 46–49, 53–54

Covington, Caroline, 70

INDEX

crime, 1; EASI index, 122; U.S.-Mexico border and, 126, 127, *195–96*
crossing points, U.S.-Mexico border, 119, 120, *121*, 129–30, *130*
Crowd Counting Consortium, 83–84
culture: closeness, 66–67; distance, 60, 61, *62*, 92, 104, 109–10, 112–13, 163; with distance and information processing, 2; emotions and, 2, 20, 21; frames, emotion and, 2, 21; place, distance and, 19–20; place and, 5; role of, 4; values, 60, 66

Dallas, Texas, 32, 36, 38, 39, 68, 73, 87
Dave (bartender), 57
deaths: children, 56, 68; COVID-19, 21, 29, 45–46, 49–50, 52–54, *53*, 56, *170–73*; deadly force by police, 78–81, 83; extreme weather events, 139; floods, 136, 137; of Floyd, 79–81, 83; hurricanes, 139, 140, 153; mass shootings, 56, 64, 67–68, 73, 76; odds of being killed by undocumented migrant, 59; in terrorist attacks, 64
Democratic Party: BLM movement and, 82, 85; border wall and, 114, 115, 123, 132; with climate change, 142, 143, 147–48, 151, 152, 157, 160, 161; COVID-19 pandemic and, 47–49; with Hispanic support, 162; immigration and, 103; with incumbents and drought in 2008 and 2012, 157–58; marginal effect of drought on vote shares in 2008 for, *160*; marginal effect of drought on vote shares in 2012 for, *161*; voters, 23, 120
democratic principles, 60, 77
Democratic Republic of Congo, 37
Department of Agriculture, U.S., 151
Department of Health and Human Services (HHS), U.S., 44
Department of Homeland Security (DHS), U.S., 44, 101, 117
Department of Public Safety (DPS), Texas, 71–72

destinations, conceptualizing, 120
DHS (Department of Homeland Security), U.S., 44, 101, 117
discrimination, 39, 98
distance: as-the-crow-flies, 119–20, 123, *124*, *192–93*, *195–96*, 225n31; attitudes toward border wall impacted by, 126–31; attitudes toward immigration influenced by, 104–13, 166; behaviors and, 21, 23–24, 164–65, 167; climate change and, 143, 149, 154; context and, 57, 85–86; cultural, 60, 61, *62*, 92, 104, 109–10, 112–13, 163; defined, 8–11; emotional response and, 15, 149, 164; empathy and, 165–66; frames and, 12–14, 21; "From a Distance," 221n1; individual attitudes influenced by, 9, 23; pandemics and, 26, 27; place, culture and, 19–20; place, emotions and, 14–19; with prejudice reduced, 8, 126; public opinion, policy and, 167; role and influence of, 1–4, 21, 163; social, 10, 47; spatial, 10–11, 22, 60, 76, 78, 90, 105, 132; spatial proximity, 10, 43, 54, 67, 69, 105, 149; support for border wall given perceived, *197*; temporal, 10, 21, 22, 29, 34, 165; urban unrest, emotions and, 22; U.S.-Mexico border and levels of, 125, *193–95*, 227n51; from U.S.-Mexico border by zip code, 120, 129, *130*. *See also* geographic distance
"divide by 4 rule," 131
domestic terrorism, 55, 59
DPS (Department of Public Safety), Texas, 71–72
driving: logit regression predicting support for border wall construction given crime with Euclidean and driving distance, *195–96*; logit regression predicting support for border wall with Euclidean distance and, *192–93*; route to nearest border crossing point, 119–20, 129–30, *130*
drought in Texas (2011): with congressional elections in 2008, 151–52, 157–59, *160*, 161–62, 166, *199*; with congressional

INDEX

elections in 2012, 23, 150–52, 157–62, *161*, 166, *199*; economy and, 150–51; loss, 151, 159, 162; marginal effect on Democrat and Republican vote shares in 2008, *160*; marginal effect on Democrat and Republican vote shares in 2012, *161*; voters with personal experience of climate change, 154–57, 160, 161, 166; VTD and, 157–59, 162

due process, 60

Dunaway, Johanna, 120

earthquakes, 153

EASI crime index, 122

Ebola virus disease (EVD): fear of epidemic in U.S., 21, 36–40, *40*, 42–43; impacts of, 25; media and, 36, 37–43, *40*, 43, 54, 56, 165, *170*; outbreaks, 28, 37, 39, 43; public opinion and, 28

Economic Freedom Fighters, South Africa, 82

economy, 60, 82; border wall costs, 115; drought impacting, 150–51; flood damage and, 136; hurricane damage and, 137–40; illegal immigration costs, 129, 227n58; with Mexico and U.S., 126

education, 39, 90, 106, 120, 131. *See also* schools

Egan, Patrick, 155–56

elections: ANES, 62–63, 78, 152; Cooperative Election Study, 129, 227nn58–59, 228n60; gubernatorial, 153; Kentucky primaries from 1990 to 2000, 152. *See also* congressional elections; presidential elections

electoral behavior, 23, 150, 166

elevator pitch, 21

El Paso, Texas, 22, 69–70, 73–76, *75*, 117

Emergency Operations Center, CDC, 44

emotional distress symptoms, COVID-19 and, 27–28

emotional response: anxiety and fear, 16–18, 56; cognitive and, 1, 8, 16; lion example with distance and, 15, 149, 164; mechanisms, 56–57; of New Yorkers to 9/11, 109–10; with time and space, 56, 58, 76, 165

emotions: anxiety and fear, 16–20, 22, 26, 39, 56, 59, 68, 163–64; attachment to BLM movement, 90, *91*, 92, 165; closeness, 90; connections, 4, 12, 13, 15, 20, 90, 117; culture and, 2, 20, 21; empathy, 8, 12, 165–66; frames, culture and, 2, 21; mass shootings impacting, 68–69; place, distance and, 14–19; sentiment text analysis and, *65*, 65–66; sorrow, 18; urban unrest, distance and, 22. *See also* fear

empathy, 8, 12, 165–66

employment, 98, 102, 107, 158–59, 162

endogeneity, 89, 217n36

Enos, Ryan D., 54

epidemics, 25–26, 164; EVD in U.S. and fear of, 21, 36–40, *40*, 42–43; West Africa EVD, 39; Zika, 21, 32, 37

Erdoğan, Tayyip, 64, *65*, 66

ethnicity, race and, 2, 94–96, 98, 116, 121, 131, 147, 163. *See also specific ethnicities*

Euclidean (as-the-crow-flies) distance, 119–20, 123, *124*, *192–93*, *195–96*, 225n31

Europe, immigration, 22, 96–99, 101, 105, *177–78*, *185–86*, 219n21, 220n34

EVD. *See* Ebola virus disease

everyone speaks about what's fair according to how it goes for them ("cada quien habla de la feria según como le fue en ella"), 145

face masks, 36, 45

FBI (Federal Bureau of Investigation), 55, 67, 80

fear, 64, 166, *170*; amygdala and, 56, 57; anxiety and, 16–20, 22, 26, 39, 56, 59, 68, 163–64; of EVD epidemic in U.S., 21, 36–40, *40*, 42–43; hope to alleviate, 18, 45–46, 128, 132, 152, 160, 162. *See also* terrorism

239

INDEX

February 2017 Political Survey (Pew Research Center), 119, 224n30
Federal Bureau of Investigation (FBI), 55, 67, 80
Federal Emergency Management Agency (FEMA), 136, 146–47
Federation for American Immigration Reform, 227nn58–59, 228n60
FEMA (Federal Emergency Management Agency), 136, 146–47
Ferguson, Missouri, 78–79
Fierro, Richard, 56–57
fight-or-flight response, 15, 16, 57
Finn, John, 43
First Amendment, 77
First Baptist Church of Sutherland Springs, Texas, 68
floods: catastrophic, 144; deaths, 136, 137; 500-year event, 134–35; Houston-area survey, 145, 146; Hurricane Harvey, 139–40, 146; Memorial Day, 135–36, 137, 140; with sea level rise, 156; Tax Day, 137, 140, 141
Florida, 29, 44, 57, 79, 87, 135
Floyd, George, 79–81, 83
foreign-born population, 97, 97–99, 99, 101, 122, 220n40
fossil fuels, 143, 144
Fowler, Anthony, 153
Fox News, 83
frames: of border wall issues impacting public attitudes, 126–28; distance and, 12–14, 21; emotion, culture and, 2, 21
France, 55, 60, 64–66, 65
freedom of the press, 60
"From a Distance" (Cortina), 221n1

Gadsden Purchase (1853), 114
Gallup Minority Rights and Relations poll, 105, 106
Gallup Today poll, 102–3
Galveston, Texas, 137, 138
gaps, knowledge, 47

Garfin, Dana Rose, 135
Garza, Rodolfo O. de la, 94
Gasper, John, 153
Gatrell, Jay, 152
Gelman, Andrew, 131
gender, 34, 63, 79, 90, 107, 120, 131; concealed carry applications and, 72; equality, 77
geographic distance: BLM movement and, 22, 90; border wall and, 23, 113, 115–16, 118–23, 126–30, 132, 166, 226nn45–46; with emotional and cognitive responses, 1; with outbreaks and pandemics, 26, 27; partisanship and, 113, 115–16, 118–20, 123, 126, 132, 226n45; public attitudes, behaviors and, 4, 11; terrorist attacks and, 62
geographic location, 2, 5, 6, 129
geographic proximity, 3, 11, 27, 90, 119, 221n1
geography, climate change and, 142
Georgia, 45, 79
Germany, 97
Gerring, John, 164
Gieryn, Thomas, 6
global warming. *See* climate change
goals, shared, 20
Gomez, Brad, 152
Google: COVID-19 Open Data Repository, 49; mobility index for retail and recreation places, 50, *50–51*
Google Trends, 27, *28*, 30, *31*
greenhouse gas emissions, 134, 143–44
gubernatorial elections, 153
guest worker program, 102
Guinea, 37
guns, police shootings, 78–80, 84
guns, Texas with: background checks, 70; concealed carry applications, 22, 72–73, 76; laws, 69–70, 71; licenses, 22, 71–76, *72*, *74*, *75*; openly carry, 69, 71–72; sales, 70, 71, 76; violence, 68, 70, 73. *See also* mass shootings

H1N1 (swine) flu (2009), 27, 36
Hadwick, Heather, 47

240

INDEX

Hall, Andrew, 153
Hamilton, Lawrence, 156
Hansford, Thomas, 152
Harlow, Summer, 86
Harris County, Texas, 137, 139–40
Hart-Celler (Immigration and Nationality) Act (1965), 96–99, 102, 125
HB-1927 ("constitutional carry bill"), 71
Headley, Walter, 81
here and now, 6, 8, 10, 21, 23, 163; border wall and, 116–18; of climate change, 133, 134, 141, 155
HHS (Department of Health and Human Services), U.S., 44
Hill, Jennifer, 131
Hispanics, 84, 158, 162; border wall and, 117, 122; on immigration, 106–7, 109, 111, 113, 121–22
Hollande, Francois, 65, 65–66
Homer, Alaska, 127–28
homophily, 12–13
Hopkins, Dan, 123
Hotez, Peter, 29
Houston, Texas: Chicago versus, 5–6, 8, 9; floods in, 135–37, 139–41, 145, 146; Hurricane Harvey and, 137–40, 141, 143, 145–47, 166; KHAS, 136, 140–41, 144, 146; Zika and, 29, 32
Houston Chronicle (newspaper), 137
human activities, climate change and, 134, 136, 141, 143–44, 147–48, *148*, 151, *198*
Hurricane Andrew (1992), 138
Hurricane Harvey (2017): floods, 139–40, 146; module, 144–49; personal damage index, 147–48, *148*; storm, 137–40, 141, 143, 145–47, 166
Hurricane Ike (2008), 137–38, 140
Hurricane Katrina (2005), 138, 139, 153
Hurricane Rita (2005), 138
hurricanes, 135, 152

Ibelli, Paul, 57
ignorability assumption, 227n51

Illinois, 5–6, 8, 9, 45, 87
immigrants, 59, 73, 112, 113; external shocks and, 22–23, 92, 96, 105, 106, 110; foreign-born population, *97*, 97–99, *99*, 101, 122, 220n40; *A Nation of Immigrants*, 102; as threats, 18, 101, 103–4, 228n59
immigration, 58, 93; African Americans, *181–82*, *189–90*; Africans, 22, 105, *189*, *190*, 220n34; Arabs, 109–10, 113, 122, *182–83*, *190–91*, 220n34, 220n40; Asians, 98–99, 101, 122, *179–80*, *188–89*, 220n34; Border Security, Economic Opportunity, and Immigration Modernization Act, 115; border wall and, 115, 116, 118, 120–22, 125, 127–29, 132–33, 227nn58–59, 228n60; distance influencing attitudes toward, 104–13, 166; European, 22, 96–99, 101, 105, *177–78*, *185–86*, 219n21, 220n34; Federation for American Immigration Reform, 227nn58–59, 228n60; Hart-Celler Act and, 96–99, 102, 125; illegal, 59, 103, 105, 112–13, 115, 127, 129, 227nn58–59, 228n60; in-groups, 95–96, 98, 101–2, 105, 109, 112–13; Latin Americans, 22, 94, 98–99, 101, 105, 111–12, 122, *178–79*, *186–87*, 220n34; 9/11 and attitudes toward, 23, 101, 102–3, 105, 107–10, 113, *175–83*; out-groups, 95–96, 105, 112, 113; policies, 94, 96–99, 102–3, 105, 116, 125, 228n59; public opinion on, *100*, 100–104, 220nn34–35; race neutral, *175–76*, *184–85*; results of 2002 ordered logistic regression model, 107–8, *108*; results of 2006 ordered logistic regression model, 110–11, *111*; terrorism and, 103, 105, 228n59; 2006 marches and attitudes toward, 23, 105–6, 110–13, *184–91*
Immigration and Nationality Act. *See* Hart-Celler Act
Independents, 120, 156
independents, with climate change, 156
Indigenous people, 116, 118

241

INDEX

information, 19, 26, 47; contextual, 4, 9, 56–58, 85–86, 118; decontextualized, 2, 11, 21, 118, 167
information processing, 2, 167
infrastructure, 11, 136, 140, 152
in-groups, 4, 20, 95–96, 98, 101–2, 105, 109, 112–13
Inland Regional Center, mass shooting, 76
intangible realm, place as, 6
intergroups, optimal interaction, 20
international terrorism, 55, 59
Iowa, 45, 118
Ireland, 97
ISIL (Islamic State of Iraq and Levant), 64
Islamic State, 76
Islamic terrorism, 58
Italy, 44, 153

James, Thomas, 56
January 6 Capitol attack (2021), 55
Japan, 44
Johnson, Lacy M., 144

Kaiser Family Foundation (KFF) Health Tracking Polls, 32, 38, 39
Kapoor, Anish, 8
Kennedy, John F., 102
Kennedy, Ted, 103
Kentucky, 79, 152
KFF (Kaiser Family Foundation) Health Tracking Polls, 32, 38, 39
KHAS (Kinder Houston Area Survey), 136, 140–41, 144, 146
Killeen massacre (1991), 68
Kinder Houston Area Survey (KHAS), 136, 140–41, 144, 146
King, Desmond, 96
King, Steve, 118
Knack, Steve, 152
Krause, George, 152
Kuo, Alexander, 153

Las Vegas, Nevada, 69
Latin Americans, immigration, 22, 94, 98–99, 101, 105, 111–12, 122, *178–79*, *186–87*, 220n34
Latinos, 73, 80, 94, 110, 112–13, 147
law and order, 78, 83–87, 89, 90
Liberia, 37
licenses, gun, 22, 72–73, 76
License to Carry (LTC), in Texas, 22, 71–76, *72, 74, 75*
Likert scale, 63
Limbaugh, Rush, 103–4
Lindsay, Sandra, 45
lion example, emotions and distance, 15, 17, 149
location, 2, 5–6, 56, 58, 76, 129, 165. *See also* place
London, England, 60
Los Angeles, California, 44, 105
loss, 18, 20, 25, 166; drought, 151, 159, 162; in extreme weather events, 135, 137–39, 145. *See also* deaths
lottery odds, 59
Louisville, Kentucky, 79
LTC (License to Carry), in Texas, 22, 71–76, *72, 74, 75*
Luby's cafeteria, mass shooting, 68

Maine, 123
majority opinion, media with, 154
Malhotra, Neil, 153
Marie Claire (magazine), 82
market economy, 60
Marriott hotel bombing, Pakistan, 61
Maryland, 50, *50–51*, 52
Massachusetts, 45, 103
mass murder, 67
mass shootings: at Charlie Hebdo offices, 60; at clubs, 56–57; cognitive evaluations and, 165; deaths, 56, 64, 67–68, 73, 76; emotional impact of, 68–69; in Norway, 61; police response, 70; in schools, 56, 68, 70; in Texas, 22, 56, 67–68, 70, 73
McDade, Tony, 79

242

INDEX

McPherson, Miller, 13
mechanisms: amygdala, 56–57; context, 4, 9, 56–58, 85–86; distance and frames, 12–14, 21; place, distance and culture, 19–20; place, distance and emotions, 14–19
media, 18, 19, 47, 83, 112, 135, 154; BLM movement and, 85, 86, 87; epidemics and, 42, 43; EVD and, 36, 37–43, *40*, 43, 54, 56, 165, *170*; NewsBank and, 29, 38, 41, 209n36; news consumption, 38, 41, 60, 62–64; social, 1, 7, 58, 68–69, 76; Space City Weather, 138–39; terrorism and, *62*, 64, *173*; *This American Life*, 127; threats and, 42–43; Zika in, 29–30
Mega Millions jackpot, 59
Memorial Day flood (2015), 135–36, 137, 140
mental health, 69, 71
metacognitive beliefs, 18–19
Mexican Americans, 112
Mexico, 115, 116, 122, 126. *See also* border, U.S.-Mexico; border wall, U.S.-Mexico
militarization, 81, 116–17
military force, 81, 82
Millennium Park, Chicago, 8
Miner, Robert, 17–18
Minneapolis, Minnesota, 79, 81
Minnesota, 46, 79, 81
minorities, 72–73, 78–81, 83, 105, 106
Missouri, 78–79
mobility, COVID-19 pandemic and, 21, 29, 48–50, *50–51*, 52–54, 165, *170*
mosquitoes, 29, 32
Mother Jones (magazine), 68
Mullin, Megan, 155–56
murder, 67, 79, 83, 122, 127. *See also* mass shootings; terrorism
music, dissonant, 18
Muslims, 58, 101, 109

Nacos, Brigitte, 63–64
Nalebuff, Barry, 152
Nashville, Tennessee, 87

National Guard, 81, 117
National Rifle Association, 69
National Terrorism Advisory System, 64
Nation of Immigrants, A (Kennedy, J. F.), 102
Native Americans, 118
nativism, 102
natural disasters, 139, 144, 152–53
Nature of Prejudice, The (Allport), 19–20
Navarro College, Texas, 39
Nebraska, 45
Nevada, 69
New Hampshire, 45
NewsBank, 29, 38, 41, 209n36
news consumption, 38, 41, 60, 62–64
Newsom, Gavin, 47
New York City, 41, 44, 45, 64, 82, 87, 109–10. *See also* 9/11
New York State, 45
New York Times (newspaper), 29, 68, 82, 83–84
Nielsen-Gammon, John, 150
NIMBY (Not In My Backyard) framework, 11
9/11, 60, 64; attitudes toward immigration after, 23, 101, 102–3, 105, 107–10, 113, *175–83*; terrorism attacks after, 55
North Carolina, 87
North Dakota, 45
Norway, 61
Not In My Backyard (NIMBY) framework, 11

Obama, Barack, 64–65, *65*
Ohio, 45, 87
Olympic Games, Rio de Janeiro, 30, 32
openly carrying, guns, 69, 71–72
ordinal regression, 106
Oregon, 45, 125
Outbreak (film), 36
outbreaks, 18, 21, 25; COVID-19, 26–27, 29, 43–44; EVD, 28, 37, 39, 43; SARS, 27; Zika, 28, 37
out-groups, 4, 20, 95–96, 105, 112, 113

INDEX

Pakistan, 61
Palis, Joseph, 43
Palm Coast, Florida, 57
Panama, GDP, 140
pandemics, 21, 25–27, 29, 36, 164. *See also* COVID-19 pandemic
Paris, France, 55, 60, 64, *65*
partisanship: with BLM movement, 82, 85; border wall and, 23, 114–15, 117–22, 123, *124*, 131–32, *194–95*, 226n45; climate change and, 23, 134, 142–43, 146–49, *148*, 151–52, 156–57, 160–62; COVID-19 pandemic and, 29, 46–49, 53–54; geographic distance and, 113, 115–16, 118–20, 123, 126, 132, 226n45; January 6 Capitol attack and, 55; mobility and, 50; personal experiences, belief systems and, 149, 155–56; as social identity marker, 49; voters with, 23, 120, *194*, *195*
party identification, 90, 115, 118, 146, 226n45
Patel, Jugal K., 83–84
Patriot Act, 101
Peña Nieto, Enrique, 115
personal damage index, Hurricane Harvey, 147–48, *148*
personal experiences: belief systems, partisanship and, 149, 155–56; with climate change and shifts in attitude and beliefs, 141, 143; dissonance between party discourse and, 154, 155, 156; with extreme weather events, 135, 145, 149, 155–57; of voters with climate change, 23, 154–57, 160, 161, 166; voters with electoral choices and, 154
Pew Omnibus surveys, 59–60, 61
Pew Research Center: on BLM movement, 84; on climate change, 142; on COVID-19 pandemic, 47; February 2017 Political Survey, 119, 224n30; on immigration, 104; on terrorism, 59–60, 61
Philadelphia, 41, 82
physicality, place and, 6

place: context and, 118; defined, 4–8; distance, culture and, 19–20; distance, emotions and, 14–19; Google mobility index for retail and recreation, 50, *50–51*; workplace, 44, 45, 47, 98, 102, 105, 107, 158–59, 162
Plato, 15–16, 43
police: BLM movement protests and, 82, 87, 166; with deadly force, 78–81, 83; law and order, 78, 83–87, 89, 90; mass shootings and response of, 70; militarization of, 116; as 9/11 first responders, 109; racism and violence, 78, 87, 89, 92; reform, 81, 83, 85; shootings, 78–80, 84; with urban unrest, 81, 82; violence, 77–80, 82–83, 87, 89, 92
police chiefs, 81
political campaigns: advertisements, 18; border wall and 2016 presidential, 115; climate change and, 154, 155; COVID-19 and, 53–54
politicians: blamed with natural disasters, 152–53; voters punishing, 153, 154, 155, 158, 159
populations: of BLM protesters, 84; foreign-born, 97, 97–99, *99*, 101, 122, 220n40; growth, 25, 97, 98, 143; Muslims, 109; VTD, 162
potential-outcomes model, 123
prejudice: distance and reducing, 8, 126; immigration and, 98, 110, 112, 118; *The Nature of Prejudice*, 19–20
presidential elections: border wall and 2016, 115, 132; COVID-19, partisanship and 2020, 48; COVID-19 deaths and 2020, 21, 29, 45, 49–50, 53–54; January 6 Capitol attack and 2020, 55; from 1970 to 2006, 153; Texas drought with 2008 and 2012, 157; voter participation decreased with rain and snow, 152
primates, nonhuman, 37
Prince George's County, Maryland, 50, *50–51*, 52

INDEX

Princeton Survey Research Associates International, 224n30

protesters: BLM movement, 81–84, *84*, 86; on immigration, 112

protests: BLM movement and total number of, *84*; conservative, 86–87; immigration marches of 2006, 23, 105–6, 110–13, *184–91*; media and, 86; police and BLM movement, 82, 87, 166. *See also* urban unrest

proximity: cultural closeness, 66–67; fear and, 64; spatial, 10, 43, 54, 67, 69, 105, 149; temporal, 10; urban unrest, BLM movement and, 85–86. *See also* distance; geographic proximity

public attitudes: toward BLM movement, 86, 89–90, *174*; on border wall, 115–22, 126–31; climate change and, 141, 142, 143, 147; distance influencing, 9, 23; with framing of border wall issues, 126–28; geographic distance, behaviors and, 4, 11; NIMBY framework and, 11; social damage scale and, 147; toward urban unrest, 217n36; toward using all available force with urban unrest, 22, 87, *88*, 89–90, *91*, 92, *175*

Public Law 112-265, 67

public opinion: behaviors and, 3; BLM movement and, 82–83; on border wall, 23, 116–18; on climate change, 136, 140–41, *141*; distance, policy and, 167; EVD and, 28; on immigration, *100*, 100–104, 220nn34–35; irrationality of, 54; on mass shootings, 70; media on urban unrest influencing, 86; outbreaks, epidemics, pandemics and, 21; policy outcomes and, 4; Zika and, 28

Puerto Rico, 127

punishment, of politicians, 153, 154, 155, 158, 159

Qaeda, al-, 55

race, 90; bias, 98; concealed carry applications and, 72; ethnicity and, 2, 94–96, 98, 116, 121, 131, 147, 163; gun licenses in Texas by, 72–73, *74*; gun-related fatalities and, 73; gun violence and, 73; income and, 106. *See also* immigration

race neutral immigration, *175–76*, *184–85*

racism, 80, 81, 82; law and order versus, 83–87; police violence and, 78, 87, 89, 92

rain, voter turnout and, 152. *See also* floods; hurricanes

rape, 122, 127

Real ID Act (2005), 115

recency bias, 60, 144–45

Reed, Brian, 127, 128

Reeves, Andrew, 153

regression: 2SLS, 89, 90; ordinal, 106

regression analysis, 32, 34, 42; attitudes toward immigration after 9/11 in 2002, *175–83*; climate change mainly caused by human activities, 136, *198*; Ebola fears and news articles published, *170*; immigration and 2002 ordered logistic model, 107–8, *108*; immigration and 2006 ordered logistic model, 110–11, *111*; incumbent vote with drought and agriculture for 2008 and 2012 elections, 159, *199*; individual attitudes with using all available force with urban unrest, 22, 90, *175*; mobility patterns, COVID-19 deaths and Biden/Trump margin of victory, *170–73*; news consumption and worries about terrorism, 63; predicting support for border wall construction given crime with Euclidean and driving distance, *195–96*; predicting support for border wall given perceived distance, *197*; predicting support for border wall with Euclidean and driving distance, *192–93*; public attitudes toward BLM movement, 89–90, *174*; relationship between cumulative deaths and Biden/Trump margin of victory, 52, 53; worries about terrorist attack with media attention, *173*; worries about Zika infection, *169*

245

INDEX

Republican Party: BLM movement and, 82, 85; border wall and, 114–15, 118, 122, 123, *124*, 132; climate change and, 142–43, 147–48, *148*, 151–52, 160–62; COVID-19 pandemic and, 47–49; with denial of climate change, 151, 152; with extreme weather events, 157; with Hispanic support, 162; immigration and, 102; with incumbents and drought in 2008 and 2012, 157–58; marginal effect of drought on vote shares in 2008 for, *160*; marginal effect of drought on vote shares in 2012 for, *161*; voters, 23, 120, *194*, *195*
Rhetoric (Aristotle), 17–18
rhetoric, political, 82, 117, 155–56
Rhode Island, 45
Rio de Janeiro, Brazil, 82
Robb Elementary School, Texas, 56, 68, 70
Robbins, Mel, 38
Rousseau, Jean-Jacques, 66
Ruiz, Ruben, 70
Russian flu (1889), 27

San Bernardino, California, 75–76
San Diego, California, 114, 125
Sandy Hook Elementary School, Connecticut, 68
San Francisco, California, 44, 87
SARS outbreak (2002), 27
schools: closures during COVID-19 pandemic, 39, 44, 45; with gun laws in Texas, 71; mass shootings, 56, 68, 70
sea level rise, 156
Seattle, Washington, 87
Secure Fence Act (2006), 115
sentiment text analysis, *65*, 65–66
September 11, 2001. *See* 9/11
Shachar, Ron, 152
Shapiro, Robert Y., 63–64
shocks, external: concealed firearms licenses and, 76; immigrants and, 22–23, 92, 96, 105, 106, 110; out-groups and, 20

shootings, police, 78–80, 84. *See also* mass shootings
Sierra Leone, 37
Smiles Nite Club, mass shooting, 57
snow, voter turnout and, 152
social damage scale, 147
social distances, 10
social distancing, with COVID-19, 47
social identity, partisanship and, 49
social justice: BLM movement and, 78–80; opposition to, 83; police reform and, 81
social media, 1, 7, 58, 68–69, 76
social phenomena, 8, 9, 165
Solo, Hope, 30
South Africa, 82
South Carolina, 46
South Dakota, 45
South Korea, 44
Space City Weather, Houston, 138–39
Spanish flu (1918), 27
spatial connections, 12, 13, 90
spatial distance, 10–11, 22, 60, 76, 78, 90, 105, 132
spatial proximity, 10, 43, 54, 67, 69, 105, 149
Sports Illustrated (magazine), 30
Stable Unit Treatment Value Assumption (SUTVA), 227n51
Stampone, Mary, 156
stay-at-home orders, COVID-19 and, 45–47
Stein, Robert, 153
Stockholm, Sweden, 82
storms: climate change and, 140–49; extreme weather events, 23, 135, 137–39, 141, 145, 147, 149–50, 155–57, 166; floods, 134–37, 139–41, 144–46, 156. *See also* hurricanes
suicide bombers, 60, 64
Sutherland Springs, Texas, 68, 70
SUTVA (Stable Unit Treatment Value Assumption), 227n51
Sweden, 82
swine (H1N1) flu (2009), 27, 36

INDEX

Taft, William, 117
Tallahassee, Florida, 79
Tarrant County, Texas, 50, *50–51*, 52
Tax Day flood (2016), 137, 140, 141
Taylor, Breonna, 79
temporal distance, 10, 21, 22, 29, 34, 165
temporal proximity, 10
terrorism, 18, 58, 59, 63, 115; Boston Marathon bombing, 60, 61; cognitive evaluations and, 165; cultural closeness and, 66–67; in France, 60, 64–65, *65*; immigration and, 103, 105, 228n59; January 6 Capitol attack, 55; London transit system bombing, 60; in media, 62, 64, *173*; National Terrorism Advisory System, 64; 9/11, 23, 55, 60, 64, 101, 102–3, 105, 107–10, 113, *175–83*; in San Bernardino, 75–76; in Turkey, 64–66, *65*; World Trade Center bombing, 64. *See also* mass shootings
Texas: on climate change, 151–52; with crossing points along Mexican border, *121*, *130*; Dallas, 32, 36, 38, 39, 68, 73, 87; DPS, 71–72; El Paso, 22, 69–70, 73–76, *75*, 117; EVD and, 36, 38, 39; Galveston, 137, 138; with guns, 22, 68–76, *72*, *74*, *75*, with hurricane survey, 135; mass shootings in, 22, 56, 67–68, 70, 73; Tarrant County, 50, *50–51*, 52; Zika and, 29, 32. *See also* drought in Texas; Houston, Texas
Texas Tribune (newspaper), 69, 70
Thailand, 44
there and later, 6, 163
This American Life (radio program), 127
time, emotional response with space and, 56, 58, 76, 165
Time magazine, 30
Tobler, Waldo R., 12, 164
Tobler's First Law, 12, 164
Trace, The (non-profit news agency), 70
transgender people, 79
Trump, Donald J., 58, 81, 86, 165; border wall and, 115, 117, 123, 131–32; COVID-19 pandemic and, 45, 47, 50, 52–54, *53*, *170–73*; with January 6 Capitol attack, 55
Turkey, 64–66, *65*
Twitter, 58, 69
2SLS (two-stage least squares) regression, 89, 90

unemployment, 158–59, 162
uniqueness, place and, 6
United Kingdom, 97
United States (U.S.): Bureau of Labor Statistics, 158, 159; Census, 97, 122; Congress, 78, 115; Constitution, 77; Consulate in South Africa, 82; coronavirus Google trends in, 27, *28*; cultural values in, 60, 66; Department of Agriculture, 151; Department of HHS, 44; DHS, 44, 101, 117; economy with Mexico and, 126; emotional distress symptoms and COVID-19, 28; fear of EVD epidemic in, 21, 36–40, *40*, 42–43; National Guard, 81, 117; U.S.-Mexican War, 116; worries about terrorism attacks in, 63. *See also* border, U.S.-Mexico; border wall, U.S.-Mexico; congressional elections; presidential elections
United States Drought Monitor, 158
University of Texas *Texas Tribune* (UT/TT) polls, 69–70
urban unrest: emotions, distance and, 22; law and order during, 78, 89, 90; police response to, 81, 82; proximity, BLM movement and, 85–86; public attitudes toward, 217n36; riots, 87; supporters of using all available force with, 22, 87, *88*, 89–90, *91*, 92, *175*; violence and, 81–83, 86–87. *See also* Black Lives Matter movement
U.S. *See* United States
U.S.-Mexican War (1849–1855), 116
us versus them, 20, 94, 95, 104, 105, 166

247

INDEX

UT/TT (University of Texas *Texas Tribune*) polls, 69–70
Uvalde, Texas, 56, 68, 70

vaccines, COVID-19, 45–47
values: beliefs aligned with, 10; cultural, 60, 66; SUTVA, 227n51
violence: gun, 68, 70, 73; police, 77–80, 82–83, 87, 89, 92; political campaigns and images of, 18; urban unrest and, 81–83, 86–87; U.S.-Mexico border and, 116. *See also* terrorism
Voltaire, 66
voters: electoral choices and personal experiences, 154; Hispanics in Texas, 158, 162; with partisanship, 23, 120, *194*, *195*; with personal experience of climate change, 23, 154–57, 160–61, 166; politicians punished by, 153, 154, 155, 158, 159; turnout and natural disasters, 152–53
voter tabulation district (VTD), 157–59, 162

Walmart mass shooting, El Paso, 22, 70, 73
Walz, Tim, 81
Washington, D.C., 41, 87, 116
Washington Post (newspaper), 80
Washington State, 45, 87
water, 151, 152, 155, *195–96*. *See also* drought in Texas; floods
weather events, extreme, 141, 149, 155, 157; behavior shifts with, 135, 150, 156; climate change acceptance with, 23, 147, 150, 166; loss in, 135, 137–39, 145. *See also* climate change; drought in Texas; storms
Weber, Max, 164
West Africa, EVD outbreak, 37, 39
whites, 72, 73, 80, 84, 101; on immigration, 94, 109, 112, 113; police officers, 78, 79, 81
white supremacists, 73
WHO (World Health Organization), 26–27, 37, 43–44, 45
wildfires, 151, 154, 159
winds, 137–38. *See also* hurricanes
wind turbines, 11
Wisconsin, 45
Wong-Parodi, Gabrielle, 135
workplace: COVID-19 pandemic and, 44, 45, 47; employment, 98, 102, 107, 158–59, 162; undocumented workers, 105
World Health Organization (WHO), 26–27, 37, 43–44, 45
World Trade Center bombing (1993), 64
Wuhan province, China, 27, 43–44

Zaller, John, 64
Zika, 28, *31*, *33*, 34–35, *35*, *169*, 208n18; epidemic, 21, 32, 37; in media, 29–30; threat of, 25, 54, 56, 165
"Zika Is Coming" (Hotez), 29
zip codes, 72, 122, 147; distance from U.S.-Mexico border by, 120, 129, *130*; of LTCs granted in El Paso, 74–76, *75*